BETRAYAL OF POLAND

FOR MARIA

BETRAYAL OF POLAND

FIRST-HAND ACCOUNTS FROM THE SECOND WORLD WAR

SIMON REES

Pen & Sword
MILITARY
AN IMPRINT OF PEN & SWORD BOOKS LTD.
YORKSHIRE – PHILADELPHIA

First published in Great Britain in 2024 by
PEN AND SWORD MILITARY
An imprint of
Pen & Sword Books Limited
Yorkshire – Philadelphia

ISBN 978 1 03611 209 7

A CIP catalogue record for this book is available from the British Library.

Typeset in Times New Roman 11.5/14.5 by
SJmagic DESIGN SERVICES, India.
Printed and bound in the UK by CPI Group (UK) Ltd.

Pen & Sword Books Limited incorporates the imprints of Atlas, Archaeology, Aviation, Discovery, Family History, Fiction, History, Maritime, Military, Military Classics, Politics, Select, Transport, True Crime, Air World, Frontline Publishing, Leo Cooper, Remember When, Seaforth Publishing, The Praetorian Press, Wharncliffe Local History, Wharncliffe Transport, Wharncliffe True Crime and White Owl.

For a complete list of Pen & Sword titles please contact
PEN & SWORD BOOKS LIMITED
George House, Units 12 & 13, Beevor Street, Off Pontefract Road,
Barnsley, South Yorkshire, S71 1HN, England
E-mail: enquiries@pen-and-sword.co.uk
Website: www.pen-and-sword.co.uk

or

PEN AND SWORD BOOKS
1950 Lawrence Rd, Havertown, PA 19083, USA
E-mail: uspen-and-sword@casematepublishers.com
Website: www.penandswordbooks.com

MIX
Paper | Supporting responsible forestry
FSC® C013604

CONTENTS

GLOSSARY

AK: Poland's clandestine Home Army. Formed in February 1942, it was loyal to the Underground State and the Polish government based in London.

General Government: A German-created fiefdom that included Warsaw, although its 'capital' was Krakow.

IPB: The Polish 1st Independent Parachute Brigade. Commanded by General Stanisław Sosabowski until late 1944.

Katyn massacres: The execution of more than 25,000 Poles, including thousands of Polish Army officers, by the NKVD from April-May 1940. The horrors of the Katyn burial site near Smolensk were revealed to the world by the Germans in April 1943.

MP: Military Police.

NCO: Non-commissioned officer.

NKVD: People's Commissariat for Internal Affairs. The Soviet security service headed by Lavrentiy Beria.

PAF: Polish Air Force.

Polish 1st Armoured Division: Vanguard formation of the Polish I Corps and part of the Canadian II Corps' order of battle during the Northwest Europe campaign 1944-1945. Commanded by General Stanisław Maczek.

Polish II Corps: Seconded to the British Eighth Army during its Italian campaign from 1944-1945. Commanded by General Władysław Anders.

RAF: Royal Air Force.

September 1939: Germany invaded Poland on 1 September 1939, with its Soviet ally attacking on 17 September. The campaign ended on 6 October while a new Polish government had already formed in France.

SS: Answerable to Heinrich Himmler, the SS operated the German concentration system and the Reich Security Main Office. The latter was responsible for intelligence, counter-intelligence, surveillance and investigative policing. This included the Gestapo. Born out of earlier combat formations, the Waffen SS was its military arm.

Underground State: Governing coalition of Poland's largest democratic parties and loyal to the Polish government based in France and then Britain. It ran a series of shadow ministries, including clandestine education and legal systems.

USAAF: US Army Air Forces.

VE Day: Victory in Europe Day. Effective 8 May 1945 for the Western Allies and 9 May for the Soviet Union and its satellite states.

WAAF: Women's Auxiliary Air Force (WAAF), its personnel were nicknamed Waafs.

Wehrmacht: Armed forces of the Third Reich, comprising the Heer (Army), Kriegsmarine (Navy) and Luftwaffe (Air Force).

ZWZ: Union of Armed Struggle. The AK's main precursor, it was formed in November 1939 by amalgamating early clandestine organisations. Loyal to the Polish government based in France and then Britain.

INTRODUCTION

Exploring memory is rather like advancing through a form of mental marshland; clear accounts create firm pathways, while vague recollections promise faint or obstructed trails. Efforts to recall complex events only amplify the difficulties and – layered onto this – is a person's innate desire to be seen positively. The distorting lens of the present plays upon the past as well, while perspective matters too. There is also the brain's dislike for excess baggage; important memories are retained but the finer points are often jettisoned, including names and dates or who said what to whom. Sometimes the essential details remain but are jumbled and require sorting.

But what about recollections described as crystal clear? These memories usually relate to key moments in a person's life but no memory can ever be described as truly transparent. Discussing Polish women and the Second World War, the work *Forgotten Force* noted: 'Memory is not like a crystal-clear window allowing an unrestricted view of the past. It is rather like a gauze veil shrouding the bygone experience with a subtle layer of feelings.'[1] So, how does the historian highlight Polish voices and feel confident he or she has presented the reader with firmer pathways? Fortunately, an extensive English-language historiography can assist. This includes works specific to Poland at war by historians like Norman Davies, Józef Garliński, Roger Moorhouse and Adam Zamoyski. At a broader level, volumes by Martin Gilbert, Richard Overy, Timothy Snyder and many others contain important analysis of the country and its people during the conflict. Finding primary sources is a tricker prospect as it can take time to unearth materials from the era. Nonetheless, they are available if one looks hard enough and come backed with plenty of post-war memoirs.

Concerning methodology, oral history is often presented via specific themes or chronologies. This has the merit of comparing or contrasting voices within a set framework and ensures a degree of brevity, although the nuances found in complete accounts are often lost. In addition, the personality and motivations of an interviewee can become a secondary concern. This work presents accounts in their entirety to ensure the witnesses take centre stage, although readers will note there are plenty of shared elements within the testimonies presented.

All interviewees used 'Russia' and 'Russians' as synonyms for the USSR and the Soviets, which was a common shorthand for the period. Of course, the Soviet Union was a vast multi-ethnic empire born out of what had once been Imperial Russia and most readers will have a fair knowledge of this and the Second World War in general. However, some of the events, personalities and battles specific to the Polish experience of the Second World War might be unfamiliar and so endnotes and appendices have been included to assist. For example, many of the placenames mentioned have long since changed and modern versions are given as endnotes on first mention. The appendices can be used in tandem with the testimony or consulted after reading the relevant text.

English-language equivalents of well-known places or topographic features are also used. Thus, Warsaw not Warszawa and River Vistula not River Wisła, although elements like street names or abbreviations are presented in their Polish form. For example, Nowy Świat not New World Street and AK for the clandestine Home Army. Interviewee photos were kindly lent to the author for reproduction, while other images were sourced from various archives, the Józef Piłsudski Institute of London or the author's own collection. Quality varies because of the source material's age and original condition.

The legwork for this project started many years ago at the Piłsudski Institute of London, where I discussed the Second World War with several of its senior members. Its support since has been especially welcome. I also received assistance from the Sikorski Institute and Museum during the early phases of this project and help from the Antokol Care Home, Copernicus Lodge, the Polish Underground Movement Study Trust and SPK Toronto. In addition, I would like to thank all those who responded to independent requests for interviews; those who organised meetings with family members or close friends; and those who assisted the author in follow-up correspondence.

The interviewees freely discussed their experiences of the war and were very generous with their time. Most were teenagers or in their early 20s at the start of the conflict and they were also members of a broad and diverse society: the world of the Second Polish Republic. Almost all major European countries suffered sociopolitical problems and economic woes during the interwar years and Poland was no exception. Despite this, it was their home and seeing it overrun by tyrannical regimes, both fascist and communist, can only be described as utterly devastating.

Churchill and Roosevelt appeased Stalin concerning post-war Poland's fate, with its borders and political future manipulated almost entirely to the Soviet Union's satisfaction. In acquiescing to nearly all of Stalin's demands, the principals for which the Western Allies fought were blotted and the hopes and dreams of the long-suffering Polish people, including the interviewees in this book, were swept aside. In this sense, the testimonies presented here act as a warning: appeasing tyrants invariably leads to further suffering, often for many decades afterwards.

Simon Rees, 2024

STANISŁAW ADAM

I was born in Lwów. My father was a policeman who'd served in the Austro-Hungarian Army during the First World War. He deserted in 1918, leaving Hungary and returning to Poland to join the new Polish Army being organised by Józef Piłsudski. This was just after the country won independence.[1] We had a good life before the Second World War and my family comprised my father, mother, sister and me. My sister had completed the equivalent of high school and I'd completed middle school just before the war started in September 1939. My next step was meant to have been a military college. I'd have then qualified as an officer cadet, with my commission awarded once I'd spent time with the other ranks and built up enough practical experience. The armed forces had always appealed to me as youngster and I was keen to join the Polish Air Force (PAF), although my father insisted I become an army officer. This didn't come as a surprise because he and many of his relatives had already served in the Polish Army, including three of my uncles. One of them had been killed on the approach to Kiev[2] in spring 1920, while the other two had retired respectively in 1936 and 1938.

Most Poles believed the Germans would fail to overrun us and I suppose our thinking was rooted in government propaganda, which convinced us the country could defend itself. In truth, our army wasn't large enough and lacked the necessary armaments. We were also over-reliant on cavalry, which – to be frank – was a ridiculous situation by 1939. Our air force was completely outnumbered against the enemy but it did quite well in one-on-one combat. My father had been called up and was taken prisoner during the campaign and we had no idea about his fate until he suddenly arrived home. He'd been wounded by a German bayonet while escaping. Meanwhile, I'd seen how the Germans mistreated the Jews. Many of them ran small shops in Lwów[3] and the surrounding area, with German soldiers entering their premises and dragging them out and beating them on the streets. I saw this with my own eyes.[4] The Germans then withdrew and the Russians took over. Later, we discovered the city had been included in Russian-occupied Poland under the Molotov-Ribbentrop Pact, which used the Curzon Line as a rough guide.[5]

The Russians claimed to be protecting us from the bourgeoise, the people supposedly taking advantage of us, and they really believed they were our saviours. It became dangerous soon afterwards and we started hearing about Poles being taken away. This was eventually followed by a big deportation of Poles to Russia and we prayed it wouldn't happen to us.[6] Unfortunately, they came for my family around March or April 1940. We'd moved to my uncle's house in a little village and my father was hiding in the woods, knowing the Russians would probably come for him. A unit arrived one night, telling us to pack some belongings and get ready for transportation into the Soviet Union. My mother was shocked and crying, while my father had been alerted and came running into the house:

> 'I give myself up, please leave my family alone,' he pleaded.
>
> 'Well, all of you have to go,' their leader said. 'There's a better life waiting for everyone in the Soviet Union.'

My uncle was a retired officer but they weren't bothered with him; it was just my father and his immediate family they wanted.

Our captors took us to a railway station and put us on a train composed of cattle wagons. We waited and waited. The NKVD suddenly arrived one day and took my father off the train and it was the last time we ever saw him. They didn't say why they wanted him and we never discovered his fate.[7] Ultimately, all of this was Stalin's doing and it wasn't just the Poles who suffered: people in Lithuania, Latvia, Estonia and many other countries experienced similar miseries.

My mother, sister and I were deported to Kazakhstan and they sent us to a little village located around 185 miles (300km) from the nearest train station. We were given some accommodation but it was very primitive and nothing like back in home – there was no kitchen or anything like that. We were given jobs on a collective farm, called a kolkhoz, and only those who worked received food. We were in a part of Kazakhstan that didn't see much rain, although the collective was growing a lot of vegetables and these needed irrigation channels. One of our first tasks was to help cut these out but we didn't have much machinery. I also helped look after the horses, getting up early and riding onto the steppe to gather them up and bring them in. We'd let them roam off again at the end of the day's work. I had no experience with horses before any of this but I learnt to ride pretty quickly and actually enjoyed this part of it. We stole food whenever possible and one way of doing this was to tie our trouser legs with string and put grain down them. We'd use grindstones to make flour and my mother would then bake some extra bread.

Our education ceased on being deported, although there were efforts by the collective's management to convince us Stalin was a great leader and the Soviet Union was a superb place. They also pretended people in the USA and Western Europe were starving and we didn't believe a word of it. The irrigation work was finished by early summer 1940 and we were relocated to a barrack block out on the steppe, which is where we spent the rest of summer. It was divided into two: men on one side and women on the other. We returned to the village when autumn arrived and our first winter in Kazakhstan was something else; the snow piled up outside and you'd open the door and just see a wall of it. The only way out was through the roof, although you needed to be careful because snowstorms came in quickly and it didn't take much to get lost, which is when people risked freezing to death.

This was no firewood because there were no forests. However, quite a lot of the summer had been spent collecting dry cow dung out on the steppe and putting this into sacks for use as winter fuel. In fact, it burned rather well and gave off quite a bit of heat. There wasn't much work during the winter, except for helping the animals – the cows or sheep etc. – and keeping their stalls clean. Dinner was the main meal of the day and this was almost always soup and maybe some beans. There would be meat every so often and it was usually lamb served by a person announcing who got which cut. That was so nobody could complain about someone taking too much.

We had no idea the Germans would declare war on Russia but my mother sensed something was about to happen, having us pack up and leave for a nearby train station in spring 1941. We simply walked off and people from the collective came on horseback to find us and convince us to return. They didn't punish us but said we shouldn't do it again and insisted we had a good life. Anyway, things got a little bit easier after the Germans invaded Russia in June and we were now free to leave and we travelled to a place called Emba,[8] which had a relatively large train station. We soon saw lots of wounded Red Army soldiers coming through and were amazed to find some Poles waiting on the platform one day. 'We're going to Tashkent in Uzbekistan,' someone said. 'A Polish army is being organised there.' We knew nothing about this and they told us about the Sikorski–Maisky Agreement and the formation of a Polish army in the USSR.[9]

Other Poles came through the train station during this period and I thought it might represent an opportunity. 'I'm going to jump on a train and go to Uzbekistan,' I told my mother one day. She didn't want me to leave but I really believed it was our best chance. I didn't have much food for the journey – just some dried bread – and it took me about three days to reach Tashkent. I tried joining the Polish Army immediately on arrival but they wouldn't take me because I was too young. Well, that certainly put a dampener on things!

I returned to Emba and discovered my mother had contracted typhoid fever. She'd been taken to a hospital and died… It was a terrible time for my sister and I. The hospital gave my mother a wooden casket and I was told to take her away, without them offering any assistance. Thankfully, a friend helped me and we gave her a proper burial. I decided to try again at Tashkent and discovered the situation had changed a quite a bit since my first visit. For example, a military school had been established for boys and I managed to secure a place. My sister soon followed me from Emba to Tashkent and was accepted for training as a nurse in a Polish field hospital. The situation was tough because many of the boys were suffering serious diseases, like malaria and typhoid, and some of them died as a result. We had no proper facilities like showers and our 'toilets' were just holes in the ground, with some of the sicker kids falling into them because they were so weak from malnutrition and illness. The soldiers tried to help, setting aside some of their wages for our benefit – even though they weren't being paid much to begin with.

There was an agreement between the USSR and Poland in March 1942 that Polish forces could be sent to Persia and we were taken to a port on the Caspian Sea called Krasnovodsk.[10] It was terrible; there were people everywhere on our ship and there was no fresh water nor any toilets. Many people were very ill and you'd even see a dead body being slung overboard every now and then. Reaching Persia was like arriving in heaven and local traders soon approached us, accepting Russian money. I bought a dozen eggs and scrambled them into a huge portion, although I got sick from this and had severe diarrhoea as a result.

We were staying in a sort of temporary transit area at this stage and I recovered pretty quickly, joining the others as the British soon transferred us into another camp. We were told to remove all our clothes and throw them into a big pile, which they promptly burnt. They also shaved our heads, armpits and all other hair and then disinfected us. They finished the process by giving us brand-new uniforms and sending us to a camp where everyone was put on a special diet; they were watching us carefully because – and as I'd already discovered – you can't just start eating large portions of rich food when you're starving.

I stayed in Persia for about two or three months, until our group was taken to a Polish military school established in British-controlled Palestine, located roughly 40 miles (65km) from Tel Aviv. We had schooling and military training and lived in tents, playing football in our spare time. In fact, things were looking good for us during this period and I was 17 when my schooling came to an end. The Polish II Corps was in Egypt by then, finishing its training and being transported to the Italian theatre in late 1943 and early 1944. It was still early days but General Anders and his senior officers were already thinking about the inevitable losses that lay ahead, which meant they started selecting people from the military school and forwarded them for basic training in Egypt. I was among the first group chosen and our basic training was tough, although we expected this. It was the sand that really annoyed us most; we'd leave our tents in the morning and return in the afternoon to find it had been blown inside. It meant we were constantly having to shake everything out. We were moved to Alexandria after basic training and then boarded a transport ship to Taranto as part of a convoy shadowed by British frigates.

We were given a choice not long after arriving: what branch of the Polish Army would you like to join? That might be a cavalry/reconnaissance unit, a tank regiment or artillery etc. An older chap came up to me: 'Listen son, choose the infantry because you'll be much better off and don't go anywhere else.' I took his advice and was assigned to the 5th Kresowa Division. We were also starting to get familiar with Italy around this time, meeting quite a few locals and learning a little Italian as well. My group was then forwarded to a town called Campobasso, which is where they assigned us to specific units.

Our next destination was Monte Cassino and we arrived at night, following a Greek transport unit of mules that was taking up ammunition and rations.[11] Unfortunately, there was an artillery strike before we neared the frontlines and a lot of mules and some of the Greeks were killed as a result. It was the first time I'd experienced any real fighting and I didn't think it was too bad when I first saw the artillery flashes and heard things flying about. Then shells hit close to us... well, let's just say we were grateful nobody in our unit was hit.

I was in 3rd Company, 14th Battalion[12] and we reached the spot where I was assigned to a platoon. The commanding officer came over and welcomed me:

> 'You'll be on point with a Bren gun and you'll be helping the gunner and his mate,' he explained. 'Are you scared?'
>
> 'No Sir!' I said, trying not to sound scared – even though I was and he could see it.
>
> 'Look,' he replied. 'Don't tell anyone but I'm rather scared too.'

He was killed the next day.

We took some incoming artillery fire on our position that night and I saw a sergeant hit by a shell. All that was left of him was a leg. There was a medical station down the hill and a place where you took bodies for collection and four of us put the leg in a blanket and took it there, along with his identification tag. It was a terrible shock for me to see someone killed like that and, while I sort of knew what to expect before arriving, how could basic training prepare me for something like Monte Cassino? My unit was facing Monte Cairo and holding a defence line, just in case the Germans used this sector to launch a counter-attack. That was lucky for me because we weren't used in the major assaults, although we took casualties just by manning our positions. Some people kept their morale up by joking around a little bit, while others played cards to try and forget the danger. Still, we weren't down in the dumps and most of us were young and energetic.

I remember one night particularly well. We were in a sort of bunker built from rocks, with its roof covered with wood and sand.[13] You couldn't go out during the day because the Germans held the high ground and had us covered and you couldn't smoke at night because snipers and artillery spotters were always looking for the glow of cigarette ends. Anyway, we got hit by an artillery shell and it took out a corner of our position. I was hit in the leg by a chunk of rock and, thinking I'd been wounded, I felt around for blood. Luckily, I was okay and I ran into a nearby bunker that belonged to another unit and there was a guy in there who looked at me in a funny sort of way:

> 'Who are you?' he asked.
>
> 'I'm in the 14th Battalion,' I said.
>
> 'Well, we don't know you… you might be a German spy!'

He looked like he might kill me or something. I quickly told them who my commanding officer was and added he'd recently been killed, which is when this fellow believed me. I later started to understand his way of thinking; you'd cover an area and get extremely suspicious if things weren't right. For example, there were occasions when Germans dressed in Allied uniforms approached us and tried to inspect our lines.

I remember the victory at Monte Cassino. It was quiet on our line and I got out of my bunker, seeing the Polish flag on the monastery ruins in the distance. I thought this was it – that we had won. I'd only left our bunker because my socks were in bad shape and I needed replacements. I'd spotted a dead guy and was taking some spare socks out of his kit when a German aircraft roared over and shot-up our position. I scrambled back barefooted and, thinking about it now, it was a weird experience. Incidentally, the Germans almost always used single-seat aircraft – it was never bombers.

There was a major reorganisation of the Polish II Corps after Monte Cassino and a lot of people were moved around or reassigned. This included my company, which had a lot of new arrivals who I didn't recognise. We were sent to Bari, allowing us to rest and recuperate and there were all kinds of Allied troops there: British, Gurkhas, Indians, New Zealanders and even some Yugoslavs, although I don't recall any Americans. We were there for about a fortnight and it's where I got drunk for the first time in my life; I had an excellent time with some Australians but I couldn't make it back to the camp and they had to carry me!

The Polish II Corps was now advancing north along the Adriatic coast and I was given a choice just beforehand: I could either go to Rome for a holiday or put myself forward for an officer's course. I chose the break and it was great fun but I regret it now because I was never again given the opportunity to earn a commission. All of this was before Ancona, which some people might remember for the hard fighting that occurred there. There were plenty of other places where things got difficult as well, including Predappio, which was where Benito Mussolini was born and where his family had lived. It contained a big memorial to him and his brother and we met quite a lot of resistance from the Germans because of this.[14] The advance went on until the onset of winter 1944/45, after which there wasn't much fighting until spring 1945, when the focus was around Bologna. Thankfully, the enemy had pretty much evacuated the city by the time we approached.

I got into a bit of trouble in Bologna. We weren't too far away when we heard the Germans had left and two buddies and I got into a jeep and headed into the city without permission. We came across a building with a giant door that had metal studs and assumed it was a place where someone in authority might be found. A woman came to the entrance after we knocked and we were able to speak some basic Italian by then:

> 'Who are you?' she asked. 'You're not Germans?'
>
> 'No, we're Polish.'
>
> 'Come on in,' she said.

It turned out we had stumbled onto a brothel! After a speedy exit, we returned to our unit and discovered our absence had been noted. They almost court martialled us because of this.

I remember the war's last day,[15] although I'm not sure of the exact location – it was at a hillside farm overlooking a field. We spotted a lot of movement, with several German units shooting at us and we were firing back when news of the ceasefire arrived, which is when we stopped. How did I feel? Well, I thought it was something to take in our stride and some of us were already thinking about returning to Poland. I wasn't too concerned about the precise details, although we knew about Yalta and what had happened during the Warsaw Uprising.

My sister had worked in a Polish hospital based in Iran, Iraq and then Egypt and she only reached Italy after the war. She was stationed in Bari and I was studying at a nearby military school. I used to visit her every weekend and she was married to a Polish officer by then. He was in a unit based next to the hospital and they eventually resettled in Wales, while I was posted to Coventry and then demobilised at York. We were given a choice of employment but the British didn't seem to like us much by then. I guess we were the first foreign group to arrive in large numbers in modern times and they certainly didn't like Poles who couldn't speak English. You'd go on the bus and everyone was talking in Polish and other passengers would tell us to speak English.

Then I met my wife. She came from Scotland and her family all worked in the car industry in the British Midlands. Incidentally, she lived in Coventry when it got bombed during the Blitz. My sister and brother-in-law then emigrated to Argentina and were doing quite well. My wife and I decided to join them and had everything arranged when I received letter from them telling us not to come because there were big problems with President Juan Perón. I suggested we try the USA but the Americans sent me lots of forms to fill in and one of the questions was ridiculous, going along the lines of: 'Was your father a member of a communist party?' I couldn't believe it!

We applied for Canada instead and were accepted. The first time I returned to Poland was in 1967 and it was difficult because we had to report to the police all the time, telling them how long we'd be staying and who we'd be seeing etc. We went back in 1975 and then visited not too long before the communists collapsed. I returned in 1992 – after Poland had become a democracy – and this was as part of a Polish veterans' reunion. In addition, I was involved in organising the donation of an ambulance to a Polish children's hospital. I was also in Poland recently and the changes have been amazing.

STANISŁAW BERKIETA

I was born in November 1919. My mother went up north to give birth to me in a holiday town called Pilica, although I've no idea why she went there. We returned to Warsaw and my father died of tuberculosis soon afterwards, so I never knew him. My mother started working at a school and remarried several years later, while my paternal uncle was still around, working on the railways. My school had been established by a Lutheran denomination and was called Mikołaja Reja, with most of my classmates either German or Poles of German origin. However, there were quite a few Polish Catholics like me.

I studied there until aged 14 and the German language was frequently used, so I became quite familiar with it. I was also a Scout, with the Polish version of this organisation teaching boys and teenagers about outdoor activities and how to use guns etc. It was all very patriotic stuff but this was probably intentional as the government sought to develop a sense of national identity among young Poles. After all, Poland was still newly independent and had only just thrown off the Russians, Germans and Austrians.

My next step was to attend the Henryk Sienkiewicz Gymnasium, where I studied engineering. I got a job in 1937 with the Cegielski engineering and manufacturing company at its works in Rzeszów, southern Poland.[1] Getting this position involved quite a bit of back scratching and a lot of fretting. People today forget Poland wasn't fully industrialised before the war and there were only a limited number of technical and engineering jobs available, which meant the competition to win a place was always fierce. Theoretically, the section I worked in produced Swiss-designed machine tools and other components under licence. I say theoretically because it's unlikely we made any of that stuff; our role was to covertly produce 37mm and 40mm guns.[2] However, I was just a junior designer at this stage and only performed simple tasks.

The threat of war wasn't really on my mind in the late 1930s, even after Hitler annexed the Sudetenland in 1938. Like many others, I didn't realise most of Europe – Poland included – was busy preparing for conflict and that my factory's output was just one small part of this. However, it was obvious war was on the horizon by mid-1939, with tensions nearing boiling point. Not many people openly talked about the dangers but, deep down, I think most Poles knew our country lacked the financial and industrial strength to defeat Germany and there was absolutely no way we'd win on our own.

I'd saved enough money to take a little holiday on the Baltic Coast in August 1939 and, returning by train, the topic of conversation in the compartment was about the possibility of war. Being naïve and enthusiastic, I was busy pronouncing judgement and saying things like 'Poland will never give way' or 'we'll fight until the end.' I was back at work in Rzeszów when the invasion started, with the Germans already advancing quite far into Poland when we were told our factory was relocating to the southeast. The plan was to operate a facility just beyond the River Bug, where we'd repair and recycle equipment used on the frontlines, including tanks. That was the theory because, in practise, things were a complete mess. To begin with, our company had to organise its own transport, which was almost impossible because there were very few vehicles available and hardly any petrol left.

I remember travelling with some colleagues in an old Fiat, sitting on the floor with my legs up to my chest. The other engineers were using a lorry in which we'd placed some bicycles, including my own. I'd built that bicycle myself and it introduced me to the English language because several components were made in Britain and came with English instructions. Anyway, we struggled southeast and it wasn't long before we heard reports the Russians had also invaded. We'd entered a large forest and the vehicles started running out of fuel, or – to be more precise – a form of industrial alcohol because petrol was now impossible to obtain. Several of our managers went on ahead and we were waiting for them to send word back if they found anything but nothing happened.

The head engineer eventually called me over and ordered me to get on my bike and go find them. So, I cycled off and finally came across a car by the roadside. It belonged to the missing party and a company secretary was inside, sitting on a trunk that contained the factory's cash. I couldn't see any managers or other employees and it seemed like a strange situation; maybe they'd told her to guard the money and promised to return? Anyway, I explained the engineers were still waiting and wanted instructions. 'You'd all better head back west,' she said, opening the trunk and handing me wads of cash to help us. I stuffed this money into my cycling socks – the knee-high type – taking thousands-upon-thousands of crisp, brand-new bank notes. She also gave me a personal sum of around 20,000 zloty, a stunning amount of money for a youngster to have all at once, especially as I only earnt around 400 zloty per month.[3]

Returning to the engineers, I handed over the cash and kept quiet about my cut. I also told them what the secretary had said about heading west and they stood around debating, which is when I decided to head home to Warsaw. I'd had enough and one of my colleagues, who also had a bicycle, felt the same way. He joined me and the going was quite easy at first, although we had no idea the forest was rapidly filling-up with Ukrainian gangs and militia units.[4] They'd entered the area claiming it for Ukraine, setting up roadblocks and taking guns off any straggling Polish soldiers or stealing valuables from anyone else. It was our bad luck to stumble into one of these groups.

They waved us down and, on closer inspection, we saw they were nervous youngsters. They asked us who we were and why we were riding through the forest:

> 'We're coming back from a holiday,' I said.
>
> It was a ridiculous lie but the best I could come up with.
>
> 'Put all your stuff over there, including your bikes,' their leader said.
>
> Losing my bike appalled me because it was my pride and joy.
>
> 'You're not getting the bicycle,' I replied.

> 'Leave it over there!' he shouted, approaching me with a carbine pointed at my belly. I wasn't going to argue with this and did as I was told.
>
> 'Okay, now get lost,' he said.

The theft of our bicycles was a great blow but the argument had one important advantage: the gang members were so unsettled they'd forgotten to pat us down for valuables, which meant I'd kept my money.

We reached the town of Kowel[5] after a difficult journey and it wasn't pretty a sight. People from across the region had fled there, trying to avoid the Russians and Ukrainians. The treatment of Polish citizens in this region was terrible, with lots of people being murdered, and one of the worst sights I've ever witnessed occurred at this time. We'd reached the town's railway station and tried to board one of the last trains heading west. This proved impossible because there wasn't an inch of space left, although thank God we didn't succeed because Russian guns located in the vicinity opened fire on the train as it pulled away. I remember trying to help in the aftermath, with the dead and injured everywhere. It was the first time I saw the horrors of war.

Shaken, my friend and I decided train travel was too risky and we left for Warsaw on foot. The journey took almost a month because we were always on our guard and careful not to attract unwanted attention. Getting food wasn't a problem because farms and cafes along the way still had supplies and there were no shortages in the countryside. It was a different story when we finally approached the capital and discovered almost nothing was available. One of the first things my mother asked me on my return was whether I had any bread and that was a shock because bakery goods had always been available in Warsaw. Thankfully, things slowly improved regarding the food supply but we queued in long lines to obtain rations and it was usually one loaf per family. My stash of money also helped us a great deal, allowing us to buy essentials on the black market for a few months. However, finding work at this stage was impossible and most of us took odd jobs fixing the damage from the city's siege in September. Even doctors and other professionals were involved in this.[6]

Several of my friends eventually contacted me, including a few from my factory. They told me some colleagues had returned to Rzeszów and were working in relatively good conditions, although I later discovered things were far from rosy and these people were treated harshly. Still, my priority was to find a job and I went to my company's Warsaw offices to ask if a position was available. Knocking on the main door, I was surprised to be met by a German officer and instantly realised I shouldn't have been there – and the expression on his face reflected this. It's difficult to explain to those who never experienced the Occupation just how dangerous situations like this could be: one word out of place and the repercussions could be terrible for you and your family. I started speaking in German and this put him on the back foot. In fact, he responded by treating me almost as a human being and I quickly explained the offices had previously belonged to my company and I must have made a mistake. I made a profuse apology and then hurried off.

I attended secret evening classes to keep busy and it wasn't long before I'd been accepted into the Union of Armed Struggle (ZWZ), a resistance organisation that later developed into the Home Army (AK). I was put in charge of five students and had no idea about other parts of the organisation. For example, I only knew my direct superior by his code name. These were standard security measures in case someone was pulled in and tortured or the unit was infiltrated by an enemy stooge. It's harder to betray people if you don't know their real names. However, these were still early days and there was little my group could do other than learn about guns or secure diagrams of weaponry and one of my jobs was to translate some these documents, which was trickier than it sounds.

I left Warsaw in April 1940, having decided to try and reach France and join the Polish Army there.[7] I was travelling with Stanisław Srodowski, a school friend of mine, and our departure was swift and we only took what we thought was essential. We decided to cross at Przemyśl from German-occupied Poland into Russian-occupied Poland and then make a dash for the Hungarian border.[8] We assumed it was going to be an easier part of the journey, naively thinking there was less surveillance and danger in the Russian partition of Poland. Another part of our reasoning stemmed from my having camped in the region when I'd been a Scout, which meant I had a fair idea of the geography.

Stanisław and I started our journey by taking the train to Rzeszów, where we met some friends and got a little extra help.

Back on a train and heading for Przemyśl, I noticed a lady travelling with a little girl in our carriage. She was teaching the child English, which was most unusual when one considers the time and place. The lady saw us, scribbled a message on a piece of paper and passed it to me. It read 'via Hungary?' and I shook my head because you simply didn't know who you were talking to and who was listening:

> 'I'm an American and this is my daughter,' she said.
>
> Apparently, they'd been on holiday at a villa near Zakopane when the war broke out and they'd been forced to remain in Poland.
>
> 'I've been staying with some friends,' she added, before talking to me more quietly. 'Listen, I can help you. I know people who can get you through.'
>
> This put me on my guard again. Even if she was genuine, how could she possibly know about crossing the border?
>
> 'Thank you, but no,' I replied.
>
> 'Well, I think I know where you're going. Ask for the Methodists if you get into difficulties on the other side of the river because they'll help you.'

The River San acted as a boundary between German-occupied and Russian-occupied Poland in Przemyśl. This explained her comment about the 'other side of the river' and we soon discovered she was telling the truth. But who can you trust in wartime, especially someone you've just met on a train?

We reached Przemyśl and waited until nightfall before crossing the San, which we knew was going to be freezing. Adding to our difficulties was some waist-high barbed wire on the opposite bank and, in the event, this proved to be the main obstacle. Try jumping this stuff when you're cold and in soaking clothes! Stanisław got caught in it and struggled to break free, so I ended up ripping him out of his jacket. It was a desperate measure but there was no other way to untangle him and I was worried about Russian patrols and the threat of hypothermia if we didn't get moving fast.

Exhausted after crossing the last bits of wire, we decided to see if there really were some Methodists who could help us. Luckily, it wasn't too difficult to find them because Methodists in Poland were unusual back then and the locals had made a note of them. It turned out they were a married couple, with the husband an American who couldn't speak a word of Polish. We must have looked terrible in our tattered clothes but they took us in and made us comfortable despite the danger. I was carrying some pork fat – an excellent source of energy for such an arduous journey – and I handed it to the lady for her to cook. She added some eggs as well.

We said our goodbyes after resting a little and hurried south, crossing icy fields and getting closer to Hungary. To our great alarm, we discovered the region was crawling with Russian troops and we soon realised it was simply too dangerous to carry on. Despondent, we decided to return to the German partition and rethink our strategy and that's when our luck ran out because we blundered straight into a Russian patrol back at the border. They threw us to the ground, searched us and took us to a local prison, where we were accused of spying and questioned accordingly, with the interrogations always held at night. Thankfully, they didn't work us over too much and I told them about the remains of Stanisław's jacket, which they soon found. I suppose this added credence to our story and the interrogations came to an end. They shoved us into a room with several other Poles and promptly forgot about us because we were two little fish caught in a very big net.

I can't remember how long we spent in that place; spring came, summer came, autumn came and we just waited and waited. There were around 70 Ukrainians detained in a larger room nearby and they'd been arrested for things like petty theft or banditry. Sanitary conditions were poor, while exercise involved five or six of us being taken into a small yard and allowed to shuffle around a small circle. We were finally transported east around November, stopping first at Starobilsk monastery. It was being used by the Russians as a kind of transit centre for their next haul east and had been the site of a tragedy for Poland, although none of us knew it yet. Thousands of Polish officers, non-commissioned officers (NCOs) and border police had been held there after being captured by the Russians in September 1939 and these poor souls were later executed in a series of massacres, including the murders at Katyn, near Smolensk. I remember looking at the monastery's walls, noticing Polish names scrawled across them and I've always wondered if they knew what was coming.[9]

My destination wasn't far from Kotlas in north-central Russia[10] and we were transported there by train in miserable wagons without latrines. The Russians allowed us to jump out and relieve ourselves only when the train stopped, although you had to be careful because nobody knew how long the pause would last. As a precaution, the men hung onto carriage railings as they went about their business. This horrid journey was a taste of what was to come: atrocious conditions and hard labour. Our 'reward' for working was 'food', which was lukewarm soup that had little nutritional value and we cupped our hands together to receive this filth. If we were lucky, we'd also receive bits of fish or some rough bread.

Our barracks were falling apart and crawling with lice and bedbugs. They tried to delouse us once or twice but the damn things were indestructible. Smuggling occurred but I never fully understood the mechanics of it as nobody among us seemed to have anything to barter with anyway. Those with any sense bought themselves a small sheet of linen that they'd wrap around their heads at night, stopping the bedbugs and other insects from biting their faces.

The Russians started treating me as the head of a work group for some strange reason. Perhaps it was because I was quick to grasp the Russian language. Unfortunately, this came with a major drawback as I was often ordered to attend the commanding officer and listen to him accuse me and the Poles in general of spying. On other occasions, he simply sat around wading through files and asking ridiculous questions of no importance. Part of the problem stemmed from the nature of my capture, heading from west to east and then back again. It looked deeply suspicious to the Russians but it was a source of amusement among my fellow Poles:

> 'How did you get here?' they'd ask. 'You're from Warsaw not eastern Poland. What the hell are you doing in a Soviet labour camp?'
>
> 'Well, it's a long story,' I'd reply. 'I suppose you could say I'm a volunteer.'

Now that always got their attention and it always made them laugh when I explained the cause of my misfortune.

Our release from the labour camp came after the Russians agreed to the formation of an army under General Anders' command in August 1941. We were gathered up and told we'd been freed and the Soviet Union had forgiven us for our so-called crimes. We were then taken to a nearby town that resembled something out of the old Klondike, with artisanal miners wandering around armed to the teeth with carbines and pistols. It felt unreal to go from a labour camp into a world like the one described in Jack London's *White Fang*. However, our starving and sick constantly reminded us of the horrors we'd been through and these poor fellows were closely monitored because overeating even a small amount was potentially fatal.

The Russians and British had agreed to supply Anders' forces with clothing and equipment but most of this promised kit never arrived. However, my group was lucky because the Russians suddenly issued us with quilted coats and trousers that kept us warm. We were so far north that the temperature never went too high, even in summer. They also issued us with boots – an almost-alien concept to us in the gulag, where most of us used rags after our original footwear fell apart. The boots were called valenki and were made from compressed wool, which retained heat and proved very sturdy.

We were transported south by rail towards Uzbekistan in September and the temperatures were around 30°C (86°F), which meant our new clothes became a burden because we roasted in that heat! Confident about the future, my dreams of freedom were nearly dashed as we entered the journey's final stages. Stalin reneged on how many Poles could join Anders' forces and someone, somewhere had selected us for work on collective farms. This decision had apparently been ratified by a Polish minister called Kot in Moscow and we knew it would be a death sentence by another means,[11] so a junior officer and I decided to jump off the train and make our own way to the army. This fellow had somehow slipped through the Russian net and had a document that outlined his lawful release from hard labour.[12] It had to be presented to all prospective employers, which meant no one in their right mind would hire us. However, it was also proof we'd been freed and this was vital for continuing onwards to Anders' forces.

We eventually reached a town called Karshi[13] in southern Uzbekistan and got there by jumping on various goods trains. This could be dangerous but it was the quickest way of getting from A to B without having to pay. We met an Orthodox priest at Karshi, a Russian exile who'd been sent east during the 1920s because of his religious views. He gave me a job of putting bricks into kilns – the type Uzbeks used to warm their homes – and we were paid with food. We also performed some odd jobs, including temporary work on nearby collective farms and, again, were paid with food. It kept us going as we struggled to develop a plan to join the Polish Army.

One day, a Polish captain surnamed Bielasik suddenly arrived. He was looking for others to gather up and take to Anders' forces, although we didn't know who he was or where he'd come from. Was he one of Moscow's men or one of ours? We were initially wary of his motives but joined him anyway and left Karshi. Our first stop was a collective farm, meeting several other Poles who agreed to accompany us to Alma Ata in Kazakhstan, where a Polish consulate had been established at the Red Star Hotel. I remember we waited for our consul in the lobby, lounging in deep armchairs and killing our lice with great satisfaction. This fellow finally arrived and we explained our presence, prompting him to put us on the payroll and have us work for a relief organisation near Dzhambul.[14]

We arrived at our new 'office' to find a medium-sized room, a table and several straw mattresses to sleep on. Bielasik had left by now, while several others also came and went during this period. We were able to get supplies undreamt of in the gulags – things like fresh bread – and my job was to travel around the region, going to various collective farms to contact Polish people, including orphans. I noted their names for the official records and rode a wonderful horse who I named Czerwony Szatan, or Red Satan. We also received assistance and goods from several American charities, including tea, and we used this stuff to buy Red Satan's feed and convince those in authority to help us because almost all Soviet officials were corrupt and expected bribes.

I decided it was time to leave the office and join Anders' forces in March 1942 and I was processed at Lugovoye in Kazakhstan. On arrival, I was met by an NCO who mistook me for an officer, simply because I'd managed to get hold of clothes that were rather respectable given the circumstances: a forage cap, a good shirt, presentable trousers and some rubber boots made from bits of old tyres:

> 'Welcome sir, all officers must go this way,' the NCO said, politely pointing out the direction:
>
> 'You're mistaken,' I replied. 'I'm not an officer. In fact, I've never been in the military before.'
>
> 'What! Well, get the hell over there with the others!' he roared.

The Polish Army meant a new beginning and I'd arrived in fairly good shape, although I'd broken a few ribs not long beforehand in a riding accident. I soon realised I'd been very lucky because countless others were starving and in poor health. Medical checks at this stage were almost unnecessary because so many people were ill, underweight or simply dying, while new equipment and uniforms were supplied by the British, which we mixed up with poor-quality Russian cast-offs. We also slept in 'tents', by which I mean we'd dig a trench and cover this with some tarpaulin and call it a tent. It gave us some basic protection but it was still freezing and we often woke up with our hair frozen to the sides.

There were no weapons at this stage and our training was just a matter of marching and getting slowly organised. Initially, we were going to fight alongside the Red Army but Anders thought this was an impossible situation and pressed for our incorporation with the Western Allies. Most of us were ignorant of these important developments but everyone respected and trusted our commander. Many also knew the Russians had tortured him during his captivity in Moscow. Our first major transfer was to Guzar, Uzbekistan, near the Pamir Mountains that mark the start of the Himalayas.

Anders' forces were a great mix of people and a close friend of mine at this stage was a Jewish chap called Yochanan who came from Krakow. Officially, he was too young to serve because he was only around 16 years old. My future wife was also in Guzar but I didn't meet her at this stage. She also came through the hell of the labour camps and eventually joined the 316th Transport Regiment, driving three-ton trucks and Bren Carriers, which was a real skill. In fact, she was one of the best drivers

I ever met. Meanwhile, I applied for and was turned down by the PAF but I knew my chances were slim because my eyesight just wasn't good enough. My next stop was Yangiyul[15] in Uzbekistan, where I was posted to Battalion S, a unit designed to become an elite formation schooled in commando tactics. Much of our training was spent on an assault course and the equipment slowly started to improve but the overall quality still wasn't particularly good. However, we'd have taken anything at this stage and I vividly recall the day we received some British Army boots. These were fantastic compared with the ones we'd been wearing.

Our unit started a series of relocations from May 1942 onwards, until it was revealed to us in August that we were being transferred to Persia. Krasnovodsk was our point of departure and the Russians had one last unpleasant trick up their sleeves by transporting us on a ship that was much too small for the task. They simply shoved us onboard and sent hundreds below deck, including myself, where there was very little air and no latrines. It wasn't long before it was difficult to breathe and some people started suffocating. The strongest among us tried to smash the deck above to get extra oxygen and the Russians finally relented, allowing us up top. They were probably more concerned about their ship than what was happening to us. Unfortunately, the overcrowding on deck was now dangerous and this presented its own problems but I'm certain lives were saved by allowing us to come up. In some respects, this journey was symbolic of how we'd been treated all the way through the Soviet Union: we were nothing but livestock in their eyes.

That journey really felt like something out of Dante's *Inferno* for me because I'd contracted jaundice and was suffering acute diarrhoea and poor eyesight. Thankfully, we soon reached Pahlavi[16] in Persia, which seemed like paradise compared with the USSR. Sadly, some people died from eating too much on arrival; they were starving and the food simply overwhelmed their frail systems. As for me, I was able to recover fairly quickly because the medical attention was far better than anything we'd experienced in Russia.

Battalion S was soon transferred to Iraq and our first destination was Khanaqin. The training here was tough and all orders had to be obeyed along the lines of: 'Yes sir, no sir, three bags full sir!' We received additional equipment at this stage and I'd say the Polish II Corps started becoming a reality during this period, with units properly structured and basic training completed. After this, the various skills needed to conduct modern warfare were developed, with weapons issued in large numbers and vehicles delivered as well, including armoured cars. Battalion S was converted into the 15th Poznań Uhlans at this time. Amazingly, I also bumped into Stanisław, the chap who I'd been captured with. He was in Battalion S as well but was later transferred to the 12th Podolian Uhlans. He was a quiet fellow and a good man and he also fought at Monte Cassino.

From Khanaqin we went through Baghdad and onto Palestine, although this period proved rather eventful for me. A group of us were told to report to a transit camp near Baghdad, where a British sergeant ordered us to perform guard duty. I argued against this: 'You're not an officer and we're not here to perform guard duty. That's your job.' He protested but I could see he wanted us to do his unit's work. Some of us stayed at the transit camp, while others – including myself – succumbed to the lure of Baghdad and we hitched a lift there. It was a clear breach of the rules because the city was deemed out of bounds.

We were dropped off on the city's outskirts and soon walked past an officer from the British Military Police (MP). He saluted us but we ignored him. 'Stop!' he ordered and we all came to attention. 'Why didn't you salute?' he asked. This officer looked very smart and held what the British call a swagger stick. We all pretended not to understand English, thinking this would outfox him, but he had some tricks of his own and he started speaking to us in Russian. We didn't respond and he started speaking in French and we still remained tight-lipped. Finally, he reverted to English. 'Whenever there's group of Poles, I know there's always one who speaks French,' he said. 'I also know you've just come out of the Soviet Union and can speak Russian, while some of you understand English. I'm telling you to return to your camp and don't do anything stupid on the way back.'

We saluted and he walked off. There was a quick debate about what to do next and we decided to carry on, avoiding him by going around the opposite corner. We did this and promptly discovered he was there waiting for us; he'd read our minds and now had a bunch of MPs in support. 'Stop!' their sergeant shouted. 'Belts off! Shoelaces off! Form up in twos!' They placed us under arrest and marched us into an enclosure surrounded by barbed wire. We spent the night in the open, wondering what was going to happen and how much trouble we were in. A Polish cavalry sergeant major arrived the next morning and he wasn't impressed. 'First, you're all a bunch of idiots,' he said. 'Second, you're now in a difficult position because having something like this on your records will probably stop you from attending officer cadet school.' He would have known some of us wanted to become officers. 'However, the British fellow in charge happens to be a cavalry man and this may prove useful but you'll still need to be careful.'

Our belts and laces were returned to us, plus some shoe-cleaning kits, metal polisher and belt cleaners. It was vital to look smart and salute in the British style. Thankfully, the cavalry officer in charge was very understanding, realising we'd not caused any real harm and I suppose he just wanted us out of his hair. 'I'm getting you out of Iraq and forwarded to Polish forces in Palestine immediately,' he said. 'You'll be going by private transport to ensure this is done with the minimal amount of fuss.' So that's how we left Iraq, with no formal paperwork for anyone to worry about. It was a huge favour and I suspect he risked his neck by organising things this way. Looking back, I wish I'd found out his name and thanked him afterwards because getting the wrong kind of reputation – being arrested and punished by the British – could land you in serious trouble in the Polish Army and I think he understood this.

I applied to become an officer in Palestine and was accepted for training, scoring well in my tests. In fact, I won first place but those in command asked me to take second place, arguing I had the advantage of earlier training with Battalion S. 'First or second, it doesn't really matter to me,' I said. But it did matter; I was made second-in-command of a platoon when I became an officer cadet but first place would have given me more of a head start and possibly a better position.

The next stop was Egypt and I met my future wife near a base at Abbassia, not far from Cairo, while I was finishing my cadet officers' course. I then left for Italy, which was the Polish II Corps' next destination. We only took our personal kit as the heavy equipment – things like armoured cars – would be supplied on arrival. Our ship landed in Taranto in March 1944 and our training programmes re-started almost immediately. They wanted us familiarised with the Italian theatre at double speed and the most pressing issue was to learn about warfare in the hills because the terrain was very different from what we'd experienced in the Middle East. In Italy, you'd often reach the top of ridge and discover something completely different waiting for you on the other side.

We were then sent to a place that, roughly translated from the Italian, meant something like 'Abandoned Mountain'. The Germans didn't expect us there and we conducted a nocturnal raid, plus some other attacks and aggressive patrols. I was formally promoted to cadet officer after this and became second-in-command of the 4th Squadron's 3rd platoon, while I should add the 15th Poznań Uhlans was part of the 5th Kresowa Division. Personal equipment was excellent and possibly too much given the weight we each had to carry. I was confident because I believed in our cause and there was no question about us beating the Germans; we'd survived Russia, so anything else could be overcome.

I'd never heard of Monte Cassino before going there. Quite frankly it was a case of saying: 'Where the hell is Monte Cassino?' It was just a name on the map to us. I asked one of the officers who always seemed know what was happening but even he didn't have clue. The first thing you noticed on getting near Monte Cassino was the continuous action between artillery, although it wasn't a ferocious bombardment like you see in the movies. Instead, there would be long pauses and then: 'Boom, Boom, Boom!' This would be followed by another long pause. It was unnerving and it felt like the enemy's guns were busy being re-aimed at you. However, we were soon able to tell the direction the shells were heading and whether they were aimed high or low.

I'll never forget our arrival at Monte Cassino. Mule companies took our heavy equipment as far as possible and the main approach was under enemy fire. There were MPs present, telling the men when to move or take cover. They'd shout 'Go! Go! Quick!' and you'd march at the double or 'Take cover! Quick!' and you'd jump into the nearest ditch, streambed or whatever. I landed in a ditch on one occasion and noticed a chap was already lying there. He was a one of the men from the mule companies and was in a crouching position. The artillery fell 'Boom, Boom, Boom!' and this was followed by shouts of 'On, On, On!' I leapt up but this chap was motionless and I told him to get going. Then I realised he was long dead – a blackening corpse nobody had the time to risk moving and I freely admit this incident scared me.

We reached our positions exhausted and terribly thirsty. The Germans had us under constant observation during the day, particularly from their posts on Monte Cairo, which was one of the highest features in the area. It was a slightly different story at night because there was more opportunity to move around a bit. I can't remember who we replaced up there but it was weird because their positions were completely empty on our arrival.[17] There was also a lot of rubbish around, while the 'pillboxes' we took over were useless. We went to work on them almost straight away, otherwise the rain would have come straight through and we didn't want to be left exposed. Fortunately, it was May and getting warmer.

I think we were all powered by adrenaline during those first few days; our bodies knew we were in a bad spot and that helped us get over the initial difficulties, although the lack of water was tough. Incidentally, those who say everyone at Monte Cassino was 'so brave' and 'so strong' are talking rubbish because a man on the frontline always feels fear, unless he's so exhausted that he doesn't care anymore. That's when he becomes machine-like and it's a dangerous situation because mistakes get made and too many risks are taken. For example, my commanding officer was badly wounded not long after we arrived; he picked up a phosphorous grenade and, on examining it, mistakenly plunged the detonator. He managed to fling the grenade away just in time but he was still badly wounded in the process. That's how I became my platoon's acting commander.

Most orders arrived by telephone and one of the most miserable jobs was to go out and fix a broken line. You'd have to follow it until you found the break, which was usually in an exposed place, and it was never cut cleanly; it was always a complete mess that took time to reconnect. Another job was to collect the wounded after an attack – particularly after 11/12 May – and there were important reconnaissance patrols as well. I went on two of these during the Cassino offensive and clearly remember the one made before the attack on 17 May.

Our effort started early in the morning and our orders were to scout a quarry ahead of Monte Cairo and report back. That sounds simple on paper but, in reality, it meant crossing a valley from our position on Hill 706 almost up to the Germans' forward positions. To make matters worse, we were in the open and the area was littered with mines.

It was a ten-man patrol, with me in charge and a chap in front using a mine detector. He was moving slowly because the equipment was quite heavy, while the machine was whistling all the time because the area was covered with pieces of metal from shells and God knows what else. 'To hell with this,' he said. 'I'll just walk ahead and, if a mine blows me up, then it'll get me first.' The mine detector fellow was dog tired, I was dog tired and the others were dog tired. We'd already reached that dangerous stage of making mistakes and cutting corners.

Thankfully, we arrived at the quarry without incident but the Germans were clever because they'd spotted us long beforehand, working out where we were going and waiting for us to get well within range. Then they hammered us with heavy fire and we all dived for cover. Chunks of rock were flying all around, flung up by mortars etc. and there was nothing we could do except keep our heads down. The firing eventually died down and I can only guess the Germans thought they'd gotten us all. There was still some small arms fire from a couple of other enemy positions but they couldn't really see us and I think they were trying to flush out any possible survivors.

We were able to radio back during a lull and received a message that a second patrol was coming over to give us support. This unit reached us not long afterwards and their officer was completely exhausted. Their journey across had been horrible, with a couple of his men killed due to artillery fire. They intended to retrieve the bodies on the way back and he asked for volunteers from my group to help. One of my men, a very bright chap, offered to assist straight away. It finally started getting dark and we received orders to fall back as the Corps was preparing its next attack.

I was told the men searching for the second patrol's dead had set off a mine soon after we'd returned, killing and wounding several people. I immediately went out with some extra soldiers and we came across them and a wounded officer:

> 'There are officers here!' he shouted. 'Take the officers first!'
>
> 'To hell with you!' I said, swearing at him.

It really angered me and I told the stretcher team to take the most urgent cases first. On reaching this officer, we discovered he'd been hit in the leg and was in a bad way, losing a lot of blood. We bandaged him up and I helped carry him back, which was a tough job because he was well over 6ft-something. Our losses from incidents like this were constant and the main attacks meant the Polish II Corps' manpower was badly affected by Monte Cassino. Drivers, kitchen staff, batmen and all sorts were moved into the front ranks to make up the losses.

The next action I was involved in was after the Corps was fighting its way up the Adriatic Coast. One of the big battles was in and around Ancona, which was an important port that would prove useful for the Allies. I was sent to create a forward position for the regiment one night and we were near a village called Casenouve. I'd ordered our Bren Carriers to drive ahead and had them well camouflaged. They were useful because their low profile made them harder to spot compared with our armoured cars, which were much taller.

The morning came without engaging the enemy and, other than some sporadic incoming fire being reported, everything appeared to be going quite well. General Anders now ordered the 15th Poznań Uhlans to patrol in two sections towards Casenouve and then Polverigi. Using a mix of Bren Carriers and armoured cars, my unit was ordered to push forward as part of this reconnaissance. German resistance now stiffened, particularly on the main road, and I remember the 1st Squadron took a real beating that day, with quite a few people killed. As for us, we found ourselves pushing through some vineyards and my armoured car took the lead. Things were going okay until we got stuck in an irrigation ditch and couldn't move forward or backward. The Bren Carriers came up and pulled us out by using winches and we reached Casenouve soon after this annoyance, discovering the Germans had left it unopposed.

An order to withdraw suddenly arrived and we encountered a German with a Panzerschreck on the way back.[18] The exterior around our turret had become clogged with wire from the vineyards we'd driven through and it was impossible to rotate the turret. By sheer luck, we were perfectly lined up for the shot and I pressed the fire button of our 37mm gun. One second the German was there, the next second he was gone. The enemy then detected our presence and started to call down heavy artillery fire, which worried me because a direct hit on our armoured car would have wiped us out immediately. There was no counter fire to call on because our artillery boys were still moving up, so I decided to get going.

Unfortunately, we soon came across a halted Sherman tank lying directly in our path and refusing to budge. We couldn't drive around it because our vehicle's steering was now performing badly. I closed the turret and started listening to the radio, which was working wonderfully for a change, and tried to figure out who was ahead of us. I could hear the tank chaps talking: 'Olga 1, Olga 1, this is Olga 2; Janek is incapacitated and has lost conscious from the exhaust fumes. We're trying to revive him.' The incoming fire was growing and it was obvious Olga 2 was the tank ahead of us and I was nearing the end of my tether: 'Olga 2, Olga 2. To hell with you! Stop messing about and move out of my way!' I didn't realise my commanding officer was also listening to the radio traffic. 'Maria 1, Maria 1,' he said, which was our call sign. He then swore at me before saying I should use the correct procedure. 'Olga 2, Olga 2. Please move out of the way,' I requested. I heard the Sherman's engine powering up and the tank finally moved aside.

I remember another occasion when we were attacking some Gothic Line positions. My platoon was using Bren Carriers, with the armoured cars left behind. We'd been given tracer ammunition to target any enemy movement for some accompanying Canadian Shermans to fire upon. The job was dangerous because using tracer gave away our positions but it was important to get the enemy nicely lined up for our boys. German panzers normally came out on top in a tank-on-tank duels with Shermans, so they needed all the help they could get. Luckily, there was no fighting that day because the enemy had pulled back.

It's worth noting we liberated many towns and villages on our way up the Italian Boot but it's hard to recall their names. However, I fondly remember San Giorgio, which is where our unit was sent for a rest. It was also around this time that I was given the chance to take a promotion or receive a medal. I chose the rank but maybe I should have gone for the medal. Anyway, we were slowly pushing north in autumn 1944 and eventually reached the region southeast of Bologna, where our part of the front had settled. I was sent back to Abbasia in Egypt in December to begin work as an interpreter with the British, while my regiment was also transferred to Egypt to be refitted as a fully armoured unit before returning to Italy. This proved unnecessary because the war ended not long afterwards.

Back in Italy, I started engineering studies in Fermo, just south of Ancona, and I continued my higher education after reaching Britain. I got married and we had children but it was hard to get used to life in exile, especially at the start. Many British people thought the USSR was a wonderful place and the Poles were a problem. Still, I carried on working and completed my studies. I did rather well in business and travelled to many parts of the world as an engineer, including the Soviet Union of all places.

ALEKSANDER BOGDAN

I was born in 1925 in a small town called Grajewo in northeast Poland and attended a primary school in nearby Szczuczyn. Later, I went to the equivalent of a high school in Grajewo. We lived near the East Prussian border, which was only several miles away, and my father ran a medium-sized farm. Agriculture was the main business of our area, although many of the farms were rather small because they'd been divided and subdivided through inheritance. This was a local tradition stretching back to the 13th or 14th centuries, perhaps even earlier. The region was mainly Catholic but plenty of Jews lived in the area's villages and towns, running shops like bakeries, blacksmiths or cobblers and there were some poor Jews as well. In addition, there were members of the intelligentsia, such as scientists, teachers and writers etc.

The build-up to war created lots of commotion and there were constant discussions about what it might mean. Our area hosted some cavalry regiments and, because we were near the border, thoughts of war were often at the forefront of people's minds. The fighting started on a day like any other for us, with my family up early and harvesting potatoes when lots of aircraft suddenly appeared. We initially thought they might be ours on an exercise but people in the nearby marketplace suddenly started to scream and run. My father, mother and I just stood there flabbergasted and there were cries all around us: 'The Germans are shooting! The Germans are shooting!' My uncle was killed by these aircraft, which were attacking civilians. Much of Grajewo was damaged or destroyed by the advancing German forces, including the town's synagogue, although the enemy pushed through quickly and only a few units remained in the town. We stayed indoors and I sometimes watched them through the windows of our home.

The Germans were now focussed on attacking fortifications to the south and there were big battles for Łomża and Wizna at this point, with Polish formations halting the enemy on this line for several days until forced to retreat. I recall some German soldiers staying in our farmhouse for a night or two around this time, telling us Poland had already surrendered. But my grandfather – who'd been in the artillery during the First World War – noted the sound of shelling further south. 'So, what's all that noise about then?' he asked. They nearly shot him for that.

The remaining German units in our area weren't expecting to stay much longer, which worried us because we thought they'd be replaced by security forces, including the Gestapo. However, none of us could have predicted what happened next: our region was handed over to the Russians, which occurred on 18 September or 19 September.[1] Red Army units arrived first, with their cavalrymen entering the town followed by two or three tanks that went up and down the streets several times, trying to create a big impression. The difference in quality between the Germans and Russians was obvious, with the average German soldier looking far more professional and carrying a great deal more equipment.

The Russians' initial attitude was okay but they soon wanted to know who lived where. The NKVD was busy making lists and, I don't know why, but some Jews seemed pro-Russian when the Red Army arrived.[2] You were also expected to join the Young Pioneers, which I wanted nothing to do with because I was quite patriotic. However, my problems were small compared with those of my older brother Vincent. He'd refused to join the Red Army, which he was expected to do because we'd automatically been made citizens of the USSR. He tried fleeing into the German partition but was caught and returned to the Russian partition along with several others.[3] They promptly threw him into the jail at Łomża.

The Russians finally came for us in early June 1941, saying we were being sent east. My younger brother and sister managed to run away and remained in hiding throughout the war. I also had an opportunity to flee because the Russian commander told me to fetch my grandfather who was looking after cows in the meadows. But the thought of running away at this point just didn't occur to me. After the war, I discovered this decision possibly saved my life. The Germans rounded up and killed around ten boys of my age in our area because one of their soldiers had been killed by local partisans soon after Operation Barbarossa started on 22 June 1941. I could have easily been one of those shot in that reprisal.

Deep down, I think we knew the Russians would eventually come for us. The family had heard about the arrest and deportation of other Poles and, much later, we discovered we were part of the fourth and final wave taken east. They gave us about 15-20 minutes to gather whatever possessions we thought might be useful and then took us to Grajewo train station. There were six of us, including myself, my mother, father, older sister, baby sister and grandfather. The train was composed of cattle wagons and it took us all the way to Omsk in Siberia. The biggest problem was how to feed my baby sister because they only gave us hot water and salted fish, which made everyone terribly thirsty. Three people in our wagon died during that journey.

They put us on a riverboat at Omsk and took us north to the place where the Irtysh River flows into the River Ob. The town there was called Khanty-Mansiysk and our little barrack block was crawling with lice, fleas and bed bugs. However, it was around this time we realised something had gone seriously wrong for the Russians because of the way they were behaving and we guessed a war with Germany must have started. Indeed, it wasn't long before the Soviet Union agreed to the formation of a Polish army within its borders and they started releasing thousands of Poles from the camps and collective farms. We were freed at the end of September or early October 1941 and made our way south, stopping to work and survive at a sawmill near Tyumen during the horrible winter of 1941/42.

Word eventually reached us a Polish army was indeed being organised in the USSR and I got these details confirmed by a Polish liaison officer based in Sverdlovsk.[4] I wrote a letter requesting permission to join and they replied, telling me to approach the Soviet authorities and ask for the necessary tickets and passes to travel onwards, which is exactly what happened. It was spring 1942 by the time I joined the Polish Army at Lugovoye and my next destination was near Guzar in Uzbekistan. It was a grim journey and we often found Polish people lying on toilet floors in railway stations, starving or dying. Things were equally bad when we reached the camp, with around 300 people dying when I was there. I was almost one of them because I was going blind from the lack of nutrition and vitamins and there was an occasion when I went without food or soup for three days. A friend looked after me by taking my dish to the canteen and making sure I ate something. I got through it and, thankfully, our situation steadily improved not long afterwards.

A sergeant gathered a group of us together one day and asked all those who attended high school to raise their hands and step forward. I did this and immediately regretted it because those of us who stepped forward had just 'volunteered' for signals work. I tried to back out, claiming that – on second thoughts – I'd never been near a high school before the war. Well, the sergeant wasn't having any of it! Luckily, the signals units were based in a fairly well-organised camp, although our equipment was primitive and we spent most of our time learning the basics and Morse Code.

I was part of the transport leaving for Persia in August 1942 via Krasnovodsk. The boat was overcrowded and smelt terrible, with the odour of vomit and bodily waste almost overpowering. We landed in Pahlavi after a hellish journey and many of us fell ill from eating too much soon after our arrival. I also remember being amazed by the British greeting us with bars of soap and telling us to go wash ourselves in the sea. We were transported by road into Iraq not long afterwards, which is where our training started at full speed. I passed the various tests required for Morse Code and to become a radio operator, while my main motivation was to avoid having anything to do with telephones. Anyway, it turned out I was quite good at signals and they sent me to teach at a training section, where I was surprised to find my class was all-female. They'd been selected for General Anders' headquarters and I must say that they were clever and quick and it wasn't long before they were better than me.

I never met Anders but I saw him many times. This was mainly at church services, where speeches were also made. He was a fantastic guy and had an eye on life after the war, making sure youngsters like me learnt the skills needed for civilian life and I got a chance to attend school in 1943. You're a nobody without a good education, so it was of paramount importance. I finished my schooling in late February/early March 1944 and was posted back to my unit, the 11th Signals Battalion, which was already on the Italian front. I arrived in Taranto and was forwarded to the Monte Cassino theatre, where I was assigned to a Chevrolet mobile radio truck.

Our little team included me, another fellow and a driver and we'd often travel along poor Italian roads. This could cause valves and other bits in our equipment to shift and we developed an expression in response: 'If it doesn't work, give it a kick!' It might realign the parts if you were in a hurry. I was in direct contact with headquarters and there were several radio units like ours, linking the infantry divisions with tanks, engineers and artillery etc. We spent much of the time listening to the airwaves, trying to pick up German radio traffic and we knew they were monitoring us. In response, we developed a strict procedure for going onto the network: we'd connect, get in touch and quickly shut down. Sometimes, we'd immediately drive to another spot because it was important to keep our locations and movements concealed and we became very skilled at this.

All hell broke loose at Monte Cassino when the Allied preliminary bombardment started at around 11pm on 11 May. It was a huge effort – maybe 1,000 guns or so – and it was obvious an offensive was starting across the entire front. Every section was operational at this point and reported in. Unfortunately, our first attack didn't prove the success we'd hoped for and heavy losses were reported. This became readily apparent to me when I moved to forward positions just after Monte Cassino was captured on 18 May. It was the smell that struck you most, the aroma was of corpses and dead animals rotting in the Mediterranean heat.

The Germans often hid booby-trapped grenades under the bodies, including their own dead, while anti-personnel mines appeared to have been laid everywhere, making it difficult for our sappers to clear pathways. Looking towards the abbey, I was amazed at how much of it had been completely flattened and realised it must have provided a fantastic defensive position for the enemy. In fact, the Germans had held the abbey from February until we finally forced them out on 18 May. Monte Cassino and Cassino town were critical because they commanded the main road north to Rome, although I'm sure none our top commanders thought it would take nearly six months to break through and take the city. The Germans really were superb fighters when on the defensive.

The Polish II Corps was shifted to the Adriatic side of Italy after Monte Cassino, fighting alongside the Canadians. Radio transmissions were our main form of communication, although telephone lines were essential because they were more reliable. Messengers on motorbikes were another option as well. Frankly, the radio was seen by many as a third choice because the Italian hills often blocked transmissions and it could be really frustrating. For example, you might pick up London but find it impossible to send a message to a guy in the neighbouring valley. In fact, there were times when I'd purposefully listen for London signals and, on occasion, pick up transmissions from Warsaw and other parts of Poland. There were also two radio channels broadcasting propaganda in Polish: a German-backed 'Wanda' and a Russian-backed 'Wanda'. German Wanda was saying things like Poland had been sold down the river by Britain and the USA and it was useless to fight on, while Russian Wanda kept asking when the Poles would take up arms against the Germans.

I'd occasionally hear signals associated with the Warsaw Uprising, which was underway not long afterwords. These were transmitted from London to Poland and were almost certainly intended for our secret stations. I often felt like crying on hearing them; it felt like we were fighting for Italy's liberation but were unable to fight for own country's freedom. This wasn't long after we'd taken Ancona, which had included some tough fighting. We slowly advanced north after Ancona and eventually neared a region south of Bologna. However, I wasn't present at that stage because I'd been posted to a military college as an instructor. Our army was keeping up its manpower by recruiting Poles who'd been conscripted into the German Army and who'd managed to surrender or escape. They volunteered to serve with us and we immediately retrained them in Allied methods, which often involved signals work and required people like me to assist.

We interacted with Italian civilians quite a bit, although we could see the population was suffering and knew things like prostitution and black-market trading were serious issues. The Italian economy appeared to run on cigarettes, which were used for small things like paying for food at a restaurant. Meanwhile, I'd become preoccupied with education at this late stage of the war, knowing it was going to be important in peace time and I achieved a scholarship to attend one of our Polish schools established in Italy.

I don't recall VE Day on 8 May 1945 because it wasn't so important for us Poles. We knew the Russians were going to decide Poland's fate and it was an absolute tragedy for everyone. I recall General Anders visiting our school one day and delivering a very frank speech. 'Boys,' he said. 'If you want to return to Poland then go but I cannot guarantee where you'll end up. However, I'll try and help you as much as I can if you decide to stay.' Our collage was eventually transferred from Italy to Yorkshire, with our guns handed in once we docked in Liverpool. We continued to dress in uniform until our demobilisation, which occurred in 1947.

My family members deported into the USSR returned to Poland after the war, although my eldest sister was re-arrested by the Russians. She was given 15 years for 'sabotage' and only returned home after Stalin's death in 1953. What was her so-called crime? She threw some food to starving German prisoners in a nearby camp and that was an absolute no-no for the Russians. They sent her to various camps and she was eventually attached to some Polish girls from the AK. They'd also been detained and deported east. One of these girls was allowed to return to a town that's now in Belarus and she wrote to my parents, suggesting how they could help my sister.

My mother forwarded the letter to me and I assisted by using various channels and some Soviet-style bribery. My sister was forwarded to Grodno and had to wait for documentation to prove who she was and that she wanted to return to Poland etc. She was finally allowed into Poland after a six-month wait and, thankfully, I got her over to Britain with the help of the British government. I also assisted my younger brother in getting to Canada. My maternal grandfather remained in Poland and the authorities wouldn't budge when I tried to assist him because his surname wasn't Bogdan. My brother Vincent was released from prison after the Germans attacked the Russians and had forced them back. He'd gone to the home where my grandfather, younger brother and younger sister were. I sent as much medication and food as I could for the family members who remained, while I got a good job in Britain working at a shipping company. We transported passengers from Europe to North America and also sent Canadian soldiers around the world. I eventually became a chief accountant and was asked if I'd like to move to Canada but I wasn't so sure. However, my wife was keen to go and I ended up agreeing, although the deal was we'd try New York for the first two months.

I returned to Poland for the first time after the war in 1961. It was business trip and it was grim; people were scared to speak with me and, frankly speaking, Warsaw was quite an ugly place at that time. There was also a work trip to Gdansk and Gdynia in 1976. I was inspecting the production methods used for building new cargo vessels and was amazed how poor the shipbuilders' business model was. They purchased equipment and machine tools on the open market from places like Switzerland, while the Russians – their main customer – paid for the finished product in roubles. In effect, they were building superb vessels and selling them at a huge discount, which meant massive losses were incurred. It was problem mirrored in Poland's other manufacturing sectors and was a major reason why the country kept getting poorer and poorer. However, there was no way anyone had the power to tell the Russians to use US dollars when buying Polish output! Poland's communists were never able to solve this issue and the losses via exports into the USSR eventually meant they were unable to buy the produce needed to keep people reasonably fed. You really could tell there was going to be a revolution from the mid-1970s onwards because of that.

JAN BRODZKI

My mother was a specialist teacher who worked with blind and deaf children at Warsaw University. She continued working in this field until the age of 75 because there were very few specialists like her available in Poland. My father was a businessman and accountant but I never really had a chance to ask him about his life because he died in March 1939. I was born in Warsaw in 1923 and was a member of the Scouts as part of the 23rd Group, which was known for its broad orange scarves. My grandfather had been one the Falcon movement's founding members, an organisation run along similar lines to the Scouts but with more of a military focus.[1] He visited Chicago in 1908 and brought back the principles of international Scouting, wanting to help introduce them in his part of Poland. As for myself, well I proved to be rather hopeless as a Scout! Still, it was a focal point of my life at that time.

The situation in Warsaw was very confused when the war broke out. Fears were really growing by 6 September 1939 and there were unconfirmed rumours the Germans would kill or send all males between the ages of six and 60 to concentration camps. Panic spread that day and there was an exodus of men and organisations like Scout units and schools.[2] Indeed, I was evacuated with my Scout unit and I paired up with my cousin Bill, whose father was a diplomat and whose mother was Irish. We Scouts marched east from Warsaw and reached Brześć[3] after about ten days, with hundreds of thousands of refugees on the roads by then, all of them hoping to escape the German advance. The Luftwaffe strafed refugees and bombed villages with no military value whatsoever and we passed through several destroyed places, with many of the dead left unburied. Thinking about it now, so many decades later, I don't think we had the time to be horrified by these sights. Bill and I were stunned more than anything else. Being young and fit also helped and I suppose this allows you to get through terrible things a bit differently.

Anyway, they put us onto trains at Brześć on 16 September and I remember Russian aircraft suddenly flying overhead dropping propaganda leaflets that said things like 'your government has deserted you' or 'your Soviet friends will liberate you'. Our train journey lasted about three hours before coming to a sudden halt and they ordered us off, announcing we'd be marching back to Warsaw and rations would have to be found along the way. They broke us up into separate groups and our little band numbered around 20 people. The nights were spent in empty villages and, again, there was lots of devastation around us, including the smell of burnt buildings and dead bodies. We were soon famished and our hunger drove us onwards.

One beautiful morning, 13 of us woke up and discovered the others had gone on ahead, forgetting to tell us they were leaving. This caused some consternation but what could we do other than continue our journey west? We marched on until, suddenly, there was the gorgeous aroma of a famous Polish soup that's made from peas, bacon and butter.[4] It's very solid stuff and we immediately followed our noses towards its source. By blind luck, we'd stumbled across a unit from General Kleeberg's army in the vicinity of Kock. A young lieutenant approached us. 'Well, this is splendid,' he laughed. 'Here's a group of 13, which is a very lucky number! You'll be runners for our platoon.' We were given food, ammunition and some rifles, although I hate to think what might have happened if the situation required shooting. I'd have probably hurt myself more than the enemy.

We were waiting in line to receive additional rations that evening when a mysterious car passed us. It stopped and turned on its headlights to illuminate a nearby train station sign, which is when the firing started. We didn't waste any time hanging around and fled in different directions. I was with Bill and suddenly felt rather faint. 'Bill, I don't feel very well,' I said, putting my hand to my head – I'd been wounded and needed to lie down. Later, I was told the wound was caused by shrapnel from a rifle grenade. Bill managed to find small cart that was pulled by an unruly horse and we headed for the nearest village, eventually coming across a Red Cross station in a little hut. We clambered out and Bill now realised the cart was full of ammunition boxes. We'd have gone up straight away if they'd hit us!

Our arrival at the Red Cross station was on 4 October and the next day marked the capitulation of General Kleeberg's surviving Polish forces. The Germans arrived and took us to a hospital at Garwolin, a smallish town about 50 miles (80km) northwest of Kock.[5] We discovered people were already being deported into the Third Reich for hard labour and realised we should get moving to avoid this fate. Bill got himself a temporary job as a hospital orderly, while one of the boys who'd been with our little group also came in wounded. His mother and father arrived from Warsaw after he'd somehow got a message to them. The parents agreed to help Bill and I, although we'd have to help pay for the cost of transport and we willingly agreed. We also needed to get rid of our Scout uniforms because the Germans distrusted them and the guard was under strict orders to stop any Poles in a uniform from leaving, including Scouts. Bill managed to get hold of some ghastly-looking civilian clothes and, with a superb display of Teutonic efficiency, the guard allowed us to leave because we were no longer in uniform.

We spent two nights in a cobbler's house, waiting for some transport to arrive. Thankfully this soon came and there were no other problems, with our little party returning to Warsaw sometime between 15 October and 18 October. The city had been badly damaged but this wasn't terribly shocking to us after what we'd already seen in the countryside. More unnerving was the sense of bewilderment among people. I joined my mother and sister in our flat in Mokotów, a southern part of Warsaw, although the fourth floor had been hit and one of the rooms had been destroyed. The rest was fine and this is where they were living. Finding medical treatment was a priority because of my wound and the fact I was now running a high temperature. I was fortunate as we secured the help of a doctor who was also a family friend. It would have been very difficult without his assistance because all the hospitals had been taken over by the Germans. However, nature is a marvellous thing because, while the wound was a stinking mess, it had already started to heal. Bits of shrapnel were already being pushed out and the doctor removed them with tweezers and cleaned the wound with disinfectant.

The Germans imposed a curfew that lasted roughly from dusk-to-dawn, while the schools remained closed and I was unable to return to my studies. The winter of 1939/40 was awful, with no coal for heating and a constant shortage of food. Things were made worse by broken windows because no glass was available to replace them. The Germans finally allowed some technical schools to reopen in spring 1940 but private tuition was needed to make any real progress and this was something my mother found impossible to pay for. Fortunately, I found work as a technician in the chemistry department of a college. Working in the laboratory meant I was exempt from deportation but you still needed to be careful because no job could ever be called truly safe.

In fact, it was critical to stay constantly alert. For example, I remember walking to a hospital in central Warsaw in 1941 and spotting a line of soldiers ahead. Instead of investigating, I promptly changed direction and left the area. I later discovered this was one of the first times the Germans started grabbing people off Warsaw's streets to be sent to work in the Third Reich. Anyone they were unsure of or didn't like the look of were usually sent to the Pawiak prison.[6] It was a matter of common sense when dealing with the Germans: never argue, answer their questions clearly and try to look as unimportant as possible. You see some unusual movement on the streets? Stop and retreat or start moving sideways if this isn't possible. Get out of the area as quickly as possible but try not to look suspicious. It became a sort of automatic instinct after a while.

In the meantime, the Underground movement was starting to become increasingly well organised and we even had information bulletins clandestinely distributed throughout Warsaw. Secret radio links were also operational, allowing the London-based Polish government to communicate with the city.[7] Our social lives continued because you cannot live being completely oppressed. For example, there were lots of cafes to spend time in but we boycotted the cinemas and theatres. There were some actors who collaborated but only a few.[8] There were weddings and parties too because, as I say, you cannot live a life of misery all the time.

There was an extremely disturbing development on a scale never seen before in spring 1943: the Warsaw Ghetto Uprising.[9] We knew what had happened to the Jews and many saw they were suffering because city trams continued running through the Ghetto, although no stops were made. I often travelled on one of these routes as I had another job working at a hospital run by the Knights of Malta located in central Warsaw. We also knew the penalties for anyone caught assisting Jewish people were severe: you would be shot and your family members would probably be executed as well. Still, many people tried to help despite the immense risks. The Ghetto Uprising was truly horrific; try and imagine a part of London being walled off and its inhabitants being killed and there was nothing you could do about it. The Germans burned street after street and those trapped in the buildings often faced a terrible choice: burn or jump. It was traumatic and utterly awful.

The Warsaw Uprising started more than a year later, on 1 August 1944. My mother was in the AK but I'd not joined.[10] We knew the Germans were going to lose the war and it was obvious by summer 1944 because you'd see their lorries and cars being prepared for a massed evacuation. At the same time, Polish people were walking around carrying barely-concealed weapons. The enemy was not interested in attacking us at this stage; his priority was to retreat in good order if the Red Army advanced far enough. The fighting started just before 5pm on 1 August and I was in the centre of Warsaw, trying to make my way home. This initially proved impossible because I was in a German-held area, although there was an unofficial ceasefire after three or four days. This finally allowed me to reach my house located within a Polish-held area.

I reported to our office for propaganda and information soon afterwards and served there until 2 September, the day we received an order to evacuate our shrinking zone in the Old Town via the sewers. We were to head for the AK-held city centre and it's difficult to compare my thoughts of today with those at the time. It's also hard to compare the euphoria we felt at the start with the gradual realisation our situation was hopeless. Interspersed within all this came moments of elation. This included the times when Allied aircraft came over and dropped supplies, even though most of the cannisters fell into German hands. When I think about it, I'm not sure it truly dawned on me that we'd lost completely until almost the end, although I must have subconsciously known much earlier.

Anyway, I went into the sewers on 2 September and it was a most unpleasant experience. Quite frankly, I'm not sure how I survived because my group spent 17 hours moving through them and it all seemed so unreal. We got lost at one point and the situation appeared hopeless until we were saved by stroke of luck; someone held up a lighter and there, right front of us, was a sign pointing towards the Warsaw centre. This was enough to get us back on track and moving in the right direction. I met my mother soon after reaching the city centre and discovered she was helping to run a soup kitchen. I joined Bill's unit, which he commanded despite being wounded. My uncle was there as well because he was also in the Underground. The fighting was intense most of the time and I was in the middle of it, trying hard not to get shot.

I said goodbye to my mother and uncle when we were forced to capitulate, while Bill was taken with his wife to a hospital camp in Germany. I stayed on with his unit, which was ordered to patrol the streets in the city centre along with some Germans at the very end. We were looking for survivors, making sure the evacuation was completed and no one was left behind. This is when I saw something of the city's ghastly fate. Hitler had ordered all of Warsaw to be destroyed and the Germans were already using flamethrowers to burn houses not yet damaged. It was very painful to see and made me very angry.

I arrived at Stalag IV-B in Saxony in mid-October 1944 and was imprisoned there for several months. The camp was a large one and, alongside the British and Poles, there were American, Dutch and French prisoners of war. In a separate compound – and being treated like animals – were Soviet prisoners and they were in a completely different category of camp. I was with other Poles from Warsaw and counted myself lucky because I was with an old school friend. We tried to put on some entertainment, with some friends and I organising a puppet theatre in our barracks. I also joined a Polish theatre company and made contacts with those involved with the British theatre, which allowed me to start improving my English. I must say that the British theatre was very well equipped and they put on a marvellous show.

Unofficially, we were liberated when a jeep arrived on 23 April 1945, carrying a British brigadier and an American soldier – a fellow who promptly handed out some Hershey bars. We already knew liberation was at hand because the commandant had left and quite a lot of Polish prisoners had gone with him. They'd headed west because the Russians were also nearing our sector. I decided to stay put because I thought it was too risky outside the camp; all it would take was for a German who didn't like the look of me to shoot me out on the road. At least there was a certain amount of protection by staying.

The brigadier held a meeting in the auditorium and I understood him because I was getting better at English by then. He assured us a nearby airfield was being repaired and aircraft would fly us out, although nothing of the sort happened. The Russians arrived soon afterwards and the first thing they did was tear up an English newspaper we'd been editing. They said there was no question of flying us out and we'd have to walk around 13 miles (20km) to the town of Riesa. It was a great shock because we realised everyone was going to be screened before being sent home. I remember we reached a forest clearing and, from the opposite end, some American lorries arrived filled with liberated Russian prisoners of war. They were bringing everything with them but the kitchen sink and were promptly marched off. We were going to use these lorries once our screening was completed and I'd already obtained a false name and number, which meant I was somewhat prepared for avoiding the Russians' clutches.

I was eventually called into a nearby building and American, British, French and Russian officers were sat behind some desks in the processing room. They didn't particularly care who I was, although the Russian commissar asked me why I wanted to travel into the American Zone of Germany and not return to Poland. It took me about ten seconds to explain but it seemed like hours and I think my knees were trembling. I somehow came up with a lie that worked beautifully. 'I'm a Polish soldier who was captured in Africa,' I said.[11] 'I've been a prisoner for the past three years and my wages have been paid into a London bank account, so I'm going to Britain to get my money.' I promised the commissar I'd head to Poland immediately afterwards. 'Khorosho!' was the answer, which roughly means 'okay, good!' and I was waved away.

We were taken by lorry into the American Zone and given a thorough delousing before being put on an aircraft that took us Brussels airport, where we waited for a connecting flight to Britain. We'd been sitting around for quite some time when someone gave me a light kick; my false name had just been called and I'd not reacted. Well, thank goodness someone was paying attention! I got on an aircraft and was flown straight to London. It was 26 May and the war had officially ended on 8 May, so

I'd been extremely lucky to reach Britain at such speed. Standing in the arrivals section, I was listening to a series of announcements over the loudspeakers: 'British soldiers head to… American soldiers head to… Commonwealth soldiers head to…' But there was no category for me, so I just stood around looking rather dazed. A Waaf eventually approached and asked me what I was doing. My spoken English was still rather poor but I tried to explain my situation, mentioning the Warsaw Uprising and the Polish Home Army. She called for a Wing Commander to come over:

> 'Are you a soldier or a civilian?' he asked.
>
> Back I went, trying to explain the Warsaw Uprising again but he wasn't interested. He kept asking me this one question until the penny finally dropped:
>
> 'Ah, I'm a soldier,' I said.
>
> He smiled and became more talkative.
>
> 'Right, we're sending you straight to Scotland and the Polish authorities will take care of you from there.'

I started networking soon after reaching Scotland, contacting various English aunts and people my parents knew from before the war. I was eventually called in by the convalescent building's commanding officer. 'I don't want to keep you any longer than I have to,' he said, 'but please tell your aunts to stop ringing me!' The issue related to documents granting me permission to leave and my aunts kept phoning him to check on my progress. Roughly one month later, on 24 June, I arrived at King's Cross Station in London and went to see some family friends, one of whom included the Polish Chief of the General Staff. He advised me to prioritise learning English, which I did, and that was my war over with. Suddenly, I was in a democratic country at peace. Having lived under German Occupation, I decided to enjoy every minute of it and have done so ever since.

BARBARA BUCZEK

My father's background was German and he studied at Leipzig Polytechnic, becoming a vehicle engineer before the First World War. He fought in the Austro-Hungarian Army until he was wounded in the legs by machine gun fire. He was sent to recuperate at Skawina, a small market town southwest of Krakow, where he worked at a sawmill owned by the mayor. He fell in love with the mayor's daughter and married her and she was my mother. He was working as an engineer again by the time I was born in the early 1920s and our family lived near Będzin, Silesia. He was quite successful, which allowed us to return to Skawina a little later and I was privately tutored before being sent to a boarding school run by nuns. It was a strict place but the curriculum was good.

I remember feeling happy when war broke out because it meant our school would be closed for the foreseeable future. I was just a teenager and had no idea what the war would mean for Poland or my family. Despite his earlier injuries from the First World War, my father was called-up and served as an officer in the Polish Army when hostilities broke out. His unit was forced to retreat eastwards and was trying to reach Romania when its luck ran out and the soldiers were captured by the Germans. Along with many others, he was soon being transported by train to a prisoner of war camp. Amazingly, some of the Poles working on the train knew my father and agreed to help him escape by wrapping him in lots of blankets and throwing him off at a slow section. He had bumpy landing but was unharmed. Luckier still, he was near Skawina and returned home quite quickly.

The Occupation had already started by then, with the Germans confiscating all available cars, bicycles and radio sets. They also closed the schools and universities, with only the churches allowed to stay open. However, the awful reality of our situation wasn't wholly apparent in the first few months because the winter of 1939/40 was severe and distracted both Poles and invaders alike. I remember the pipes in our house bursting soon after the first cold snap, leaving our house icy cold.

I eventually got a job at a nearby hospital, a place the Germans were afraid to enter because, among our responsibilities, we happened to look after the district's typhus cases. Wounded members of the ZWZ/AK were sometimes hidden in the hospital because of this. Being a member of staff also meant I was protected from being deported to work in Germany, while our hospital passes allowed us to move around the town and local area after the nightly curfew came into effect. However, being out late was dangerous because the Germans often shot first and asked questions later. My job was to assist the doctors and they were soon struggling with shortages of equipment and medical supplies, a problem that lasted the whole war.

Skawina had a population of almost 4,000 people and quite a lot of people were Jewish, which was common in Polish villages and towns at that time. The Jews often ran the shops, such as the tailors and shoemakers, and usually lived in separate areas. I knew a lot of Jews because I grew up with them, went into their shops and played with Jewish children my own age. The Germans came for them in maybe the second year and I remember my father arriving unexpectedly at the hospital, telling me to return home because something bad was happening.[1] We discovered the Jews were being rounded up and squeezed into the market square before being taken away. I was watching from behind our garden fence and saw two young Jews walking along a nearby path, while some German soldiers stood near our house smoking cigarettes. Shots suddenly rang out and I looked back at the path: two bodies were now lying on it, the soldiers having killed them for fun. I went into shock and my father grabbed me by the arm, dragging me back into the house... We were simply powerless to help.

On another occasion, a close friend came to me and told me a horrendous story. He was about 16 or 17 years old and extremely frightened:

> 'I was ordered into a car with some other boys by the Germans last night,' he said. 'They took us to a place and

made us dig a big hole. A lorry filled with lime then arrived, closely followed by a lorry carrying a group of Jews.'

'What happened next?' I asked.

'They shot them all.'

He and the other boys were terrified and immediately threw up their hands. The Germans ordered them to keep silent, saying they'd be killed if they told anyone about what had happened. Some of the Jews were still alive but seriously wounded and the boys were forced to continue shovelling earth and lime onto those poor people – their bodies still moving. The grave was eventually filled, flattened and covered with branches. Much later, in 1947 or 1948, I was sent a cutting from a local newspaper that detailed this event and reported the grave's discovery.

Our lives were always in danger during the Occupation and the Germans never gave reasons for their actions. We certainly had no legal protection from them and you had to behave carefully if you spotted Germans in the street. For example, to be seen talking and laughing in public could get you into real trouble. I also remember young boys waiting near the railway line and keeping an eye open for trains carrying coal. The train would slow on its approach to the station and they'd clamber into the wagons, grab some coal and drop down again. Later, the trains suddenly started carrying coal dusted with lime and anyone caught with this type of coal – now easily identifiable – would be shot.

My father and grandfather were often taken to the local prison for questioning and sometimes they and several others were detained as hostages. The Germans did this because they hoped to discourage further acts of resistance in the area. My father was recruited into ZWZ because he'd been an officer and it was later decided I should join with other family members, such as my younger brother. My job was quite simple: I had to keep my eyes and ears open; deliver messages and papers; and make a mental note of any German soldiers and their locations. My reports were made through the doctors at the hospital.

Our knowledge of the outside world mainly came from the family's radio, which we still had access to. I should add the top floor of our house was occupied by a German officer and he'd kept the wireless for his own use. This officer would leave for work during the day, allowing us to sneak upstairs and listen to Allied broadcasts. We'd tune into the BBC for the special Polish programmes, although it was important to be careful as the punishment for illegal listening was severe. We always noted the position of the dials before using the set and then turned them back after finishing. Just in case, we also kept the volume down and a family member would stand watch on the balcony, making sure no German was approaching our house.

Signs the enemy was on the verge of defeat were obvious by the start of 1945. The military trains had nearly always travelled west to east after Hitler declared war against the USSR, carrying equipment, ammunition and German soldiers. Almost all the trains were travelling from east to west after January 1945, evacuating whatever they could salvage. It meant the Russians were closing in and there was heavy fighting when they arrived and I remember the approach of Red Army tanks, watching one of them get hit and burst into flames nearby. The crew managed to scramble out. Lots of homes in the town were destroyed and an ammunition train exploded at the station, causing additional damage. Thankfully, the Germans were pushed back after two days.[2]

The Red Army was very different from the German one. For example, the Germans almost always had rations in boxes or tins but the Russians simply brought along livestock, such as cows and pigs, and they'd slaughter these animals whenever needed. Their mentality appeared to be this: 'We're going to Berlin and nothing stands in our way.' The Russian women who followed were quick to look through empty or damaged houses, hoping to find silk nightdresses. After the war, you sometimes saw these women going out in nothing but night dresses when visiting Krakow's theatres or restaurants. At first, they wore jumpers and underclothes with the night dresses over the top because it was still cold. We weren't particularly frightened of the Russians and, in the immediate aftermath of our liberation, there was some concern the Germans might return. There were no newspapers available and information was very hard to come by at this stage but life slowly returned to something like normal.

So how did I end up in Britain? Before the war, I had met a Polish officer called Ludwik Januszewski. His unit had been briefly stationed in our town in September 1939 and my parents also knew his family quite well. He'd escaped from Poland via Hungary and had joined the Polish forces abroad. To my great surprise, I started receiving letters from Ludwik shortly after I began studying medicine at university in 1946. His correspondence made me think a great deal. He was very good at languages and had worked as a Polish Army liaison officer, making contacts among some of the British embassy staff now in Warsaw. Ludwik handed a letter to one of them, Basil Stors, asking him to forward it to our family. Basil decided to deliver this message in person, travelling down from Warsaw to Krakow. He decided to have a rest on the train and took off his jacket, visiting the toilet on nearing Krakow. On returning, he discovered his jacket and other possessions had disappeared – they'd all been pinched! This included his money, passport and other papers, so poor Basil eventually arrived at our house and had to ask my father to pay the taxi fare because of his bad luck. Really it was very funny and the first thing we did was dress him in some proper clothes.

Basil frequently travelled between the UK and Poland and delivered messages for Ludwik and me. He often came to visit the family in person, bringing us parcels and talking lots to my father and mother. He explained Britain wasn't a bad country for someone looking to settle down and this helped persuade me to leave Poland to see Ludwik again. I started by taking the train from Krakow to Wrocław and, from there, to Frankfurt on the Oder. This area had been heavily damaged during the war and there were lots of ruins, while millions of people were still travelling from east to west and vice versa at this stage. I travelled onto Leipzig, where there was a huge station packed with people waiting for trains or just seeking shelter. Many people were washing themselves with buckets, while lots of children were crying – it was like a vast refugee camp and everyone looked hungry. Perhaps the Germans were now hungrier than the Poles?

I knew the Polish 1st Armoured Division was stationed in northwest Germany and I decided to go there first.[3] They spent some time investigating me, asking me why I'd left Poland etc. They wanted to check my character and make sure I wasn't a spy. However, I already knew people in the division and soon found myself among friends.

Ludwik came out from Britain to be with me and we visited Paris to get married because I had no papers. It was very romantic but I've no idea what the registrar said because it was all in French! We stayed on Boulevard Montparnasse in the Hotel De Nice and I received my first British identity card soon afterwards, allowing us to travel together officially. It was the start of our new lives.

ANTONI BUDZYNSKI

I was born in a small village called Jastrzebia, not too far from Tarnów. My father had served in the Polish Army and was rewarded for his service with a farm, although I'm not sure if he fought in the 1919-1920 war against the Bolsheviks. My school was located about 70 miles (110km) away from our home and I was a boarder, lodging with local people and attending classes every day. I suppose it was the equivalent of the old-style English grammar school. I can't recall much about the approach of war but my father was called up to join his battalion in 1939. The invasion started when I was still at school, with Russian cavalry and soldiers eventually taking control of our area. Their appearance was not terribly impressive but they treated us okay, just so long as you behaved yourself. However, the school was closed soon afterwards and I decided to head home. I soon learnt the Russians had captured my father and sent him to the Kola region, while my older brother had been captured by the Germans. That meant only my mother and two younger sisters remained.

The Russians came for us in April 1940 at around 5am. There was a group of soldiers led by an officer and he said we were being sent east. He advised us on what to take but there was very little time to prepare – we just grabbed whatever might be useful and left everything else behind. They took us to the train station and we were shoved into a goods carriage with around 40 others, all of us packed in like sardines and struggling to find some space. The journey took 16 days, passing through the Ural Mountains and arriving at a small town on the banks of the River Irtysh. Food and water were provided at various halts during journey but we weren't allowed off the train. They'd just open the door and present us with buckets. Most of those in the carriages were either young or old but I can't recall anyone being seriously ill at this stage. My family was eventually dumped in a hamlet about 60 miles (95km) away from the nearest village and a few hundred miles away from a small town. It really was in the middle of nowhere.

One of the first people we met was a Ukrainian man who offered to take me on as a carpenter, which was very kind because I knew nothing about woodworking. Unfortunately, the job lacked the extra food needed to help feed my mother and sisters, which is why I volunteered for a work brigade that received better rations and was located about 30 miles (50km) away. My first job was to look after some cows but this work proved too much, so I requested a reassignment and the brigade commander told me to help with the ploughing instead. This involved getting up at around 3.30am and going to bed at roughly 10pm during the height of summer. I say roughly because we had no watches or clocks; we worked out the time by noting the sun's position in the sky.

Our accommodation was a simple barrack block and mealtimes involved a kind of soup poured into a giant wash basin, with all of us using wooden spoons and taking our turn. We received some bread as well but I would save this for my mother and sisters. My mother would travel to see me every month and I gave her the bread to take back. The agricultural work lasted until around mid-October, which is when winter started and we prepared ourselves to wait for the following spring. This mostly involved sitting near a special type of Siberian stove and listening to the wind howling outside, with an awful lot of snow falling as well. Parcels occasionally arrived from Poland as people were still allowed to send us goods but we weren't allowed to write back. The nearest doctor was in the hamlet and I recall coming down with something once and being taken to see him by truck. He took one look at me on arrival and said: 'Well, you look okay to me. Get out.'

Fortunately, I was in reasonable health overall and became increasingly familiar with the Russian language, helped by my having studied it earlier in school. In many ways, my mother and sisters were in a worse situation than me because they had no way of earning extra food, other than selling spare clothes or some of the goods we'd taken with us. There was no news from the outside world until late June or early July 1941, when we were suddenly told the Germans had invaded Russia. They even sent over a propaganda officer who claimed the Red Army had captured thousands-upon-thousands of German prisoners and shot down hundreds of aircraft. We all knew this was rubbish. More importantly, they didn't tell us about the Sikorski-Maisky Agreement or the formation of a Polish army in the USSR. Life carried on as before until December, when I was ordered to attend the work brigade's office. I was almost speechless when they told me I'd be leaving the next day for a Polish Army unit based in Tatishchevo.

The Russians organised everything for me and those I travelled with, including food and transport, so I have no complaints on this particular point. I tried to find out about my father on arrival at Tatishchevo but this proved difficult because so many people were still coming in. However, it wasn't long before a sergeant approached me and asked who I was. On finding out, he said my father was safe and with such-and-such unit and he took me to see him, which is how we were reunited. I was then selected to join the 5th Division. I can't remember seeing sick people at this stage but some of us were extremely hungry and you had to be careful with your bread ration. Leave it in the open and it could easily get stolen.

Originally, we were going to fight on the Eastern Front until it was decided we would join the British in the Middle East and the Soviets transported us across the Caspian Sea, landing us at Pahlavi in Persia. The ship was overcrowded but I was one of the lucky ones and got a space at the very top. We received excellent rations in Persia compared with what we'd had before but my good fortune soon ran out as I contracted jaundice almost immediately on arrival. I just lay in my tent and the effects were horrible: you go yellow and are unable to see anything. Other than keeping me under observation, there was little that could be done and it took me about six weeks to recover. It wasn't long before my unit was transported into Iraq and based near an oil refinery at Kirkuk. Our next stop was Palestine and I remember we joined a combined exercise with American, British and French units. In fact, there were exercises going on all the time, with the training taking place in the early morning or late afternoon because it was simply too hot under the midday sun. Our new equipment was marvellous and we were supplied with whatever was considered necessary, while the rations were good as well.

We were eventually transferred to Egypt and discovered the Polish II Corps was being sent to the Italian theatre. I remember my unit departed at around 2am, with rifles issued just before reaching the dockside. There were about eight transport vessels in total, with three destroyers in support and air cover provided. It was a quick journey over and we spent the next few months acclimatising to Italy and getting prepared. My role at this stage was in the brigade signals office[1] and a new name started cropping up: Monte Cassino. It was our next destination.

There were occasions when I was about 250 yards (230 metres) away from the German lines, with two primary positions opposite us: the Monte Cassino monastery and Monte Cairo. The Germans could see our every move and call down fire on us with great accuracy. Their shelling often broke our signals and telephone lines and I remember an occasion when I volunteered to fix one of them. Thinking nothing of it, I crossed a field, fixed the line and walked back in. On returning, I found my colleague looking at me white as a sheet because I'd just walked straight through a minefield and failed to notice any of the warning signs! There were some other weird events. For example, there was an occasion when I got up and left a bunker with a lieutenant following right behind me. There was no real reason for us to leave and a shell landed right on top of where we'd been a few minutes later. The three remaining occupants were killed instantly.

Those in charge were looking for a few extra military policemen at one point and someone had put my name down. Thankfully, my commanding officer refused to let me go. 'You're a signalman and will remain a signalman,' he said. My job involved using Morse Code quite a bit and we'd receive messages from the frontlines and pass them onto our officers. I was in 15th Wilenski Rifle Battalion and my unit was the link between battalion and brigade, feeding information up and down the chain of command. The big attack was scheduled for early morning on 12 May, with a barrage delivered by more than 1,000 guns firing across the whole Cassino front. Those gun flashes were so bright and so constant that you could almost pick a needle up from the ground. My job that night was to synchronise with other signals units via radio as our attack lines were drawn up. We were positioned in a small valley but had been spotted and the Germans put down some counter fire on us, which is when I got hit. I was taken to a field hospital but events were confusing because it all happened at night. Thankfully, I wasn't in bad shape and they soon patched me up and I re-joined my unit two days later. However, the level of signals work had fallen off by then.

Our attack had been extremely costly, with hundreds killed in action or wounded. Later, I recall looking through binoculars at Monte Cassino monastery and seeing the Polish flag flying. I felt immensely proud of what we'd achieved but there was little time to rest as the Polish II Corps was soon shifted to the Adriatic side of the Italian Front. The liberation of Ancona was particularly hard going and I remember getting hold of a bicycle around this time and using it to go from place to place. It wasn't a very sensible thing to do because it made me an obvious target near the frontlines. I was soon flagged down and told off: 'What the hell do think you're doing! There are Germans all over the place!'

I didn't interact with any Italians, only other Poles and sometimes the Americans or British. They were great and I only have good words for them. In battle, those fighting at your side are true friends because you rely on them and they rely on you. However, I don't remember hearing much about the Warsaw Uprising and we weren't aware of the political plans for post-war Poland. The first time I heard the full details was when I reached Britain. The Germans fought to the very end in Italy – to the last drop of blood – and one of our final goals was to liberate the city of Bologna, which we reached as the war neared its end. I remember entering the city, with most people staying indoors rather than coming out onto the street. I think they were worried about gunfire breaking out.

I had a motorbike by then and was doing well as an officer cadet. However, they'd moved me up from brigade to division and I wasn't too happy about this. I can't really remember VE Day but I do recall being sent to a camp near Imola, where my signals work continued and a lot of time was spent on postal work. We were soon offered the chance to return to Poland but we knew the country was going to come under communist control. Later, we heard some of those who returned had disappeared and had probably been shot.

Our journey to Britain started in Naples, staying at airfield until a ship arrived to take us to Glasgow. Our arrival at Clydeside was marked with a parade and we were taken to a camp. I was a lieutenant by now, although my unit had no real assistance in resettling and we were told just get on with it. Here I should add my father had been badly wounded earlier on and, after recovering, had been posted to help manage a Polish refugee camp in Tanganyika.[2] Sadly, he fell sick there and died. I was able to contact my mother and sisters via the Red Cross, learning they'd returned to Poland in 1946. I was unable to visit them and they couldn't visit me, with my mother then contracting tuberculosis and dying not long afterwards. Thankfully, my older brother survived German captivity by working on the farms. My career in Britain started by asking a Naafi manager for a job. He agreed but told me it was a three-month contract and I'd have to leave immediately afterwards. I ended up working there for 43 years!

JERZY CYNK

My family's roots are in Krakow, where they stretch back to the 14th Century. However, I was born and grew up in Warsaw. My father took part in the 1919-1920 war versus the Bolsheviks, although he was too young for frontline service and was posted to a motorised ambulance unit instead. He became a manager for Standard Mobil petrol stations and garages during the 1920s and did well until the global economic crisis struck. That's when he lost his job and it led to hard times until he became a supervisor at a Polish telephone company several years later.

I was always fascinated with aviation and dreamt of being pilot. However, I was only 14 when the war started, so I never had the opportunity. My father was in the reserves but wasn't called up because he was now considered too old to fight. There was a great deal of tension just before the war but our family wasn't directly affected until 8 September, which was my sister's name day. The Germans bombed our part of Warsaw that day, with a large marketplace behind our home set on fire. Along with many others, we were evacuated to a nearby church hall and I can distinctly recall a Polish radio bulletin at this time, telling us the Germans were claiming Warsaw had surrendered and was now in their hands. 'But everyone should know Warsaw is defending itself and will be defending itself in the future,' the announcer said.

Many Germans whole-heartedly believed their propaganda about Warsaw capitulating and, somewhat amusingly, one of their trucks sped right through our lines and drove straight into the city centre on 11 September. It was carrying spare lorry batteries and the driver was dismayed on being taken prisoner, blaming his superiors for telling him

Warsaw had fallen. Still, it didn't take long before the capital came under immense pressure, with food supplies running low and the city under constant artillery bombardment. I was searching for rations on 13 September when a particularly heavy air raid occurred killing a lot of civilians. It was very frightening but nobody I knew wanted to surrender.

My father had already left as all men capable of carrying arms and not yet members of reserve units had been ordered to leave Warsaw for mobilisation elsewhere on the night of 6/7 September. I remained in the city with my mother and younger sister, helping my Scout group with its fire-prevention patrols. All of us hoped Britain and France would launch an offensive in the West but it was a mirage and they did very little to relieve the pressure on Poland. In fact, they didn't cause the Germans any real discomfort at all.[1] Meanwhile, we still received radio announcements and news bulletins, while the city was filling up with the remnants of retreating Polish units forced back into the capital. I recall some regiments of the Poznań Army arriving on 14 September,[2] adding their weight to the defending units already in place.

It was explained to the public that Poland would continue resisting and Warsaw would hold out for as long as possible and we continued praying Britain and France would do something to relieve the pressure. Our hopes were dashed on 17 September, when the Russians invaded. To add to our misery, a heavy German air raid was launched that day as well. It was followed by a call for our unconditional surrender or the threat of utter destruction. The city rejected the demand and a series of heavy bombardments started after two or three days and one of the final air raids also occurred at this time. More than 300 enemy aircraft were involved.

Warsaw's military command sought terms on 26 September. Personally, I couldn't believe the city had fallen; I went to a nearby square and saw Polish troops throwing their weapons into a heap overlooked by the Germans. I couldn't understand why our soldiers were told to surrender when they were still capable of fighting and had their weapons. It seemed inconceivable to me and I believed we should have fought the enemy until the very end; I really couldn't reconcile myself with this outcome and I know many others felt the same way.

The Polish Underground came into being almost immediately after the surrender, with the first clandestine news sheets appearing about a week after the Germans took control. I got involved in helping distribute this material in early December 1939 because I belonged to the secret Scout movement. The Germans had also banned us from owning or listening to radio sets but many people disobeyed this order. Sadly, the arrests and executions started relatively early on. For example, the Germans thought they'd been shot at in the street on 26 December, so they stopped a suburban train at random. They hauled out some terrified passengers and executed them on the spot. The Germans represented death and it was horrible how your life hung so finely in the balance, although there was hope as well – a belief that tomorrow might be the day of freedom. That was my motivation and not a single person I knew thought about surrendering to or collaborating with the Germans.

Most of my time was spent on Underground work because the Germans had closed the schools. They didn't want the Poles to have an education – they wanted us to become slave workers. Some schools were eventually reopened but they only taught basic trades and nothing more. However, a lot of the teachers offered secret classes and sought to broaden their pupils' knowledge. This included tuition meetings in people's homes, with children and teenagers trying to study the pre-war syllabus. I don't think many people today realise the Poles created an efficient Underground state-within-a-state and, while fighting the Germans was vital, things like education and learning trades were essential for the country's future and Poland was excellent at organising all of this. Meanwhile, the Germans tightly controlled Warsaw's rationing system, so there was huge demand for food on the black market. Most of this was supplied by farmers coming into the city and illegally selling their extra produce. These people were often arrested but usually freed after a warning because the Germans desperately needed them back on their farms, forcing them to supply the Third Reich as well. The farmers knew this and, overall, the rewards for being a black marketeer more than outweighed the risks.

I was still interested in aviation and spent a lot of time in shops that sold model aircraft and drawings, including some of my own. The owners were happy to sell them on my behalf and, rather ironically, my best customers proved to be German. I suppose they liked buying models and pictures of Polish aircraft and maybe they wanted souvenirs of a land they thought had been conquered. Anyway, I was delivering some of my drawings to a shop one day and I was stopped by a fellow who asked me if I was interested in the PAF:

> 'Absolutely,' I replied.
>
> 'Well, we have an organisation that meets here and we're working to preserve the achievements of the Polish Air Force,' he said. 'Would you be interested in joining?'

I readily agreed, knowing full well this organisation would be doing a lot more than just historical research.

It was through my contacts in this group that I eventually heard about a potential uprising being planned for unknown date. It was now 1941 and the Soviet Union had been invaded by Germany, so I think our leaders were increasingly confident the Third Reich would be defeated. At the same time, they wanted Poland to preserve her sovereignty in the event of the Red Army's approach, hence the reason for a planned uprising. My group was affiliated with the clandestine Warsaw Aero Club, which conducted Underground work primarily dedicated to aviation.

I formally joined the AK's aviation unit in October 1942 and it was tasked with joint-planning the capture Warsaw's airfields and ensuring they became operational as soon as possible. I was allocated to a sub-unit that would provide ground support at Bielany airport. All going well, we'd conduct maintenance and repair for any Allied aircraft, particularly the ones we hoped would deliver units from our parachute brigade based in Britain. In fact, there was a chap working with us who'd trained as a paratrooper, helping ensure our preparations were geared towards a parachute operation's needs. We also started a clandestine aviation magazine, which I believe was the only one of its type regularly printed in Occupied Europe. Finally, I was also a member of an Underground officer cadet group.

Disaster struck for me at the start of June 1943. I'd been drafted into one of the first aid units established in response to Russia's long-range bombing raids on Warsaw. These infrequent attacks were not discussed in the wider world at the time and are not really known about today.[3] They were dangerous and an increasing threat as the war went on. I was given some medical training and my task was to assist any civilians who might have been hurt. However, a couple of our chaps gunned down two Gestapo agents in Saski Park and all of us were arrested as a result. We were in eastern Warsaw and the Germans put us on a lorry and drove us to the Gestapo headquarters at 25 Szucha Avenue. Almost everyone had clandestine papers on them and we flung these over the sides as we crossed a bridge over the Vistula. The Germans either didn't notice or didn't care. I disposed of some notes for a speech I'd been working on for an Underground club and my topic, of all things, was a comparative analysis of NKVD and Gestapo interrogation methods!

We were eventually forwarded to Pawiak prison, which was surrounded by the remains of the recently-destroyed Warsaw Ghetto. I was interrogated for more than six weeks and, after this, they decided to send my group to Auschwitz. We knew exactly what Auschwitz was because the Germans hadn't really hidden what they were doing there.[4] They transported us by train during the night and the SS surrounded the carriages with guards and dog handlers on our arrival. Then they marched us into Auschwitz I and we were given our numbers the next day. Unbeknownst to us, we'd already been given a greater chance of survival because a camp doctor – a Pole called Dering[5] – had requested our immediate secondment to the hospital. He was looking for orderlies with some basic medical knowledge and discovered we'd all been trained in first aid. It meant we weren't used for hard labour in the fields, where we'd have suffered the effects of working long hours in the cold and rain. I was allocated to one of the five hospital blocks in Auschwitz I, all of which were manned by prisoners.

I soon discovered there were several clandestine movements in Auschwitz and one of my friends was in a group that had somehow stolen a German radio set and tuned it to the BBC. He told me about what was happening in the wider world. We were also prepared to start an uprising in the camp if such order came through from our AK superiors. However, the communists were much better organised than us and their group included several Spanish Civil War veterans. They'd become experienced long-term prisoners and even produced various news bulletins, with some SS men occasionally helping them by taking materials to a communist press being run just outside the camp. It was difficult to understand how all of this worked, even at the time.

The kapos were prisoners put in charge of working groups and they were rewarded with the use of prostitutes if their unit performed well, with these women kept in a specific area of Auschwitz. The camp also had a swimming pool, built solely for the eyes of a Red Cross delegation that visited on an inspection tour. In addition, there was a boxing ring and competitions were held between the kapos and selected prisoners. Again, this was built at short notice to make things look wonderful for the Red Cross. But let me give an example of the true German mentality at Auschwitz. They wanted an extra floor added to a single-storey building and created two work groups for the task. The first group was ordered to take building materials up some ladders to the second group, which was responsible for the construction. However, those in the first group weren't allowed to come back down the ladders; they were ordered to jump from the first floor onto a concrete area below, with several breaking their legs as a result. These unfortunates were then picked up and taken straight to the camp hospital. It was complete madness.

The prisoners formed work details early in the morning and an excellent band played as they marched off. It was conducted by Franz Nierychlo[6] and I recall seeing them practise a modified version of a Straus waltz during Christmas 1943. I was listening to the melody and gazing through a window when I saw a big cart pass outside. It was filled with bodies being taken to the crematorium and suddenly skidded on the ice, with many of the corpses falling off. I continued listening to that lovely waltz as the prisoners struggled to put the dead back onto the cart.

Some SS dog handlers came into the camp two days before Christmas, although this was quite common. However, a dog vanished on this occasion and the SS were livid, looking for this animal everywhere but nobody could find it. Friends of mine in Block 28 – a hospital block that had a mortuary at the bottom – invited me over for a special dinner soon afterwards. They had captured, killed and cooked the dog and were now eating it. Another episode that gave us great satisfaction was when a group of kapos killed themselves by drinking an illegal batch of badly-distilled vodka at a Christmas party.

I received parcels about once a month from home and, in August 1944, we heard news about the Warsaw Uprising. It was a worrying time for us and many people taken prisoner during the Uprising were sent to

Auschwitz. Indeed, I even met one or two friends who told me what had happened in greater detail. The main evacuation of Poles from Auschwitz happened as the Uprising was being crushed from mid-September into the start of October. German guards had captured some partisans trying to infiltrate the camp and they were worried an uprising behind the wire was about to begin. They gathered most of the Poles together, including myself, and transported us to other concentration camps in the Third Reich. Only a small number of Poles were left behind and most of Auschwitz was emptied at the end of 1944 and into early January 1945, after which it was finally liberated by the Russians.

My group was transported to Oranienburg, just north of Berlin, and we joined a mobile concentration camp that was used to repair or rebuild railway lines.[7] Our first destination was Stuttgart, which had been heavily bombed, and we worked there for roughly three or four months. The rail network around the city had been wiped out and we were ordered to build a line through a park, bypassing much of the damage. They moved us around to several locations after this until we ended up near Offenburg, close to the Siegfried Line. The railway lines here had been tremendously bombed by the Allies, with only the sections protected by embankments left untouched. Our task was to connect all the remnants together and create serviceable routes over which trains could pass. It was the final phase of the war and not a single train came through because the USAAF would bomb everything almost as quickly as we made the repairs.

The shortage of rations in Offenburg became acute because there were only limited means to get supplies into the area. We were guarded by SS men from the Sudetenland – now part of the Czech Republic – and they were very anti-Polish. They didn't realise many of the bombed-out railway carriages we came across contained food and alcohol and they were only interested in us once we started getting hold of this stuff. They'd now stand around in silence and wait for us to pass them the food we'd scavenged, which was important because it meant we had a reason to exist. Gradually, they even became a little bit more human towards us.

One tanker wagon we came across contained wine. The SS men promptly commandeered it and used one of the Russians among us to fish out a glass of wine whenever they wanted one. He was seen heavily drinking one day and then simply vanished, with dozens of guards spending hours fruitlessly searching for him. They eventually gave up and a Pole took over the task of supplying the wine, which went well until he neared the bottom. Something was stopping him from scooping out the last dregs, so he poked his head through to see what the problem was: it was the body of the missing Russian. He must have drunk so much that he'd fallen in and drowned and it meant our guards had been drinking wine contaminated by his corpse.

I was hurt at Offenburg at the start of February 1945, when an American fighter-bomber came over and five of us rushed for cover in a signals building. Unfortunately, the aircraft's bomb hit its side, collapsing the corner and knocking me out. The others were killed. My hand was sticking out of the rubble and my friends helped dig me out and I thought it must be heaven until I realised I'd survived. They took me to a hospital and I spent about two weeks recovering, after which I was assigned to light duties and told to clean the carriages used by the SS men. They probably thought I was now anti-American or something because of my near-death experience.

We retreated as the Allies advanced and eventually found ourselves deep in Bavaria and I was liberated on 3 May 1945, a Polish national holiday that celebrates our constitution from 1791. It was morning and we were working in a railway embankment, not knowing what was happening around us. Suddenly, there was a strange noise that kept growing louder and I volunteered to climb up and take a look. I was presented with an amazing sight: dozens of tanks were moving around in the distance but I couldn't tell if they were American or not. Then a small group of Germans with machine guns set themselves up on a bridge, under which was part of our train. They started firing and I realised the tanks must be American – and there was bound to be return fire. Some of the tanks approached closer, destroying any opposition encountered, and then the firing suddenly stopped. Now came the realisation we were free and all of us started running towards the Americans and I must have been one of the first to reach them. We spoke in German and an officer told some of us, myself included, to get on one of the tanks and hitch a ride to the main American lines that were about a mile away.

On reaching safety, the Americans gave me and another fellow the use of a horse and cart, asking us to travel to Munich and report on what we'd been doing.[8] We were still wearing our striped uniforms and, at one point, reached a major crossroads. Some American soldiers were there, surrounding a very large group of German prisoners of war. Since the US Army had already liberated places like Buchenwald, they knew exactly who we were and these chaps shouted greetings to us and then started firing over the heads of the Germans for our amusement. We were given accommodation in Munich that had been used by German officers and stayed in the city for about two weeks before being sent to a displaced persons camp at Aschaffenburg. The Americans were preparing to process more freed internees and I was put onto an organisational committee of about ten ex-prisoners. Eventually, there were about 1,000 people in our section alone.

I didn't have the opportunity to send a message to my family that I'd survived, while I soon encountered some Poles under Russian command who were organising the return of Polish prisoners. I thought my first duty was to return home and help with any rebuilding effort and possibly fight the Russians. I put my name down for the first transport to return, although I was also suffering a bout of acute diarrhoea at this stage and they told me to wait for the next transport. Recuperated and still waiting, I was sent to Frankfurt-am-Main to deal with some issues relating to Aschaffenburg and this is where I met some young men who'd fled Poland:

> 'What are you doing here?' I asked. 'Why are you "escaping" when we all need to return and fight the Russians?'
>
> They laughed at my naivety.
>
> 'It's absolutely impossible to fight the Russians at the moment,' one of them replied.
>
> 'Well, we've fought the Germans and now we can fight the Russians. What's the difference?'
>
> 'Don't be so stupid,' he said. 'AK members are being arrested and the communists are searching for anybody with any connection to resistance work, treating them as the people's enemy. If you have any sense, you won't go back.'

That conversation made a deep impression on me and I decided not to return. Instead, I travelled to Murnau, which had been a Polish officers' camp in southern Bavaria. Some of the former prisoners were still there, although not too many because most had been processed to join the Polish armed forces in the West, particularly the Polish II Corps. Fortunately, I bumped into my old tutor from the AK and he placed me on the next transport to Italy. He also gave me some letters for Corps command and my destination was Porto San Giorgio, just south of Ancona. This was a recruitment station for new arrivals and I passed the letters on as requested. Someone at this place told me a funny sort of unit was looking for volunteers but he wasn't too sure what it did.

I set off to find this outfit and eventually met a sergeant standing in front of a tent and he asked me what I wanted. I explained I'd been with the Polish Underground and had survived Auschwitz:

> 'I also understand you're recruiting for a new unit,' I added.
>
> 'Hmm…Wait here,' he said.

So, I stood around for a few minutes until he returned and ordered me to follow him into a room where a colonel was sat behind a table. This officer wanted to know where I was from and asked me a lot of details about my past, which I was happy to explain. He turned to the sergeant and said he'd accept me. Well, this was excellent news – except I had no idea what I'd just volunteered for!

I soon discovered it was a Polish counter-intelligence unit. I was sent on a special two-month course and General Anders visited at the end. He selected just 15 of us, myself included, and we were assigned to an area not far from Trieste. This was disputed territory between the Italians and Tito's communists who wanted the port city incorporated into Yugoslavia. We were based at Palmanova and were the only Polish unit in the region still on a war footing because of what was happening.[9] We also had a secret frontier station and were responding to communist infiltration. Incidentally, a chap attached to our unit had been instrumental in getting V1 components flown from Poland to Britain during the war.[10] I had around 15 Italian policemen working with me when making arrests and, since I didn't have an officer's rank, I was given the pretend rank of captain simply to impress them.

House searches were detailed and time consuming and I remember one occasion when I couldn't find anything until I went upstairs to find a woman looking after a young baby in a cot:

> 'Don't touch the baby because he's asleep. Leave him alone,' she suddenly said.
>
> That was suspicious and asked her to pick up the child and she refused.
>
> 'There's nothing there!' she exclaimed.

I picked the baby up and found two guns under his pillow, so we arrested the father. Another interesting incident was my arrest of a communist Pole who I personally escorted to General Anders in Ancona. The British government had changed by now and the new Foreign Secretary was Ernest Bevin. He announced in Parliament that Polish military police were destroying good relations between East and West, by which he meant us, a group of just 15! We were withdrawn on Bevin's request.

I now decided it was best to complete my higher education, which had been interrupted since my arrest in Warsaw. I applied for and joined a Polish college in Italy, which allowed me to take my final exams. Demobilisation eventually started and I came to Britain for the first time and graduated soon afterwards. I'd already contacted my family back in Poland and discovered my father was working in the radio industry. On a final note, a driver in our counter-espionage unit decided to return to Poland in 1970. He was immediately arrested on arrival by Polish intelligence and they tried him as a British spy. He was executed as a result. This was a fate many Poles who returned from Western Europe suffered, while others were imprisoned and left to rot. I took British citizenship to return to Poland in the late 1970s, when the regime was less brutal than before and less subordinate to the Russians.

ANTONI FEDOROWICZ

I was born near Tarnopol[1] in eastern Poland, which is now part of Ukraine. I never knew my father because he died when I was just two; he'd been a woodsman for the local authorities and I'm not sure what he did during the First World War. My mother worked in a tobacco factory, while my school was good and I enjoyed being a Scout. I was only 14 years old when Poland was invaded in 1939 and I don't really recall the details about the build-up to the war. However, I clearly remember discussions about it only being a matter of time before Germany attacked. Still, I didn't expect the Soviets to invade from the east and they took over a great deal of Polish territory, including our area.

We were deported by the Russians quite early on and they took myself and nine members of my family, including my 83-year-old grandmother; my uncle's family; and the children of another uncle who'd died sometime beforehand. Some friendly Ukrainian neighbours warned us we'd been marked down for deportation but what could we do and where could we run to? Sure enough, the Russians came for us not long afterwards, arriving early in the morning and using sledges pulled by horses. They gave us just a couple of minutes to prepare ourselves and we accompanied the soldiers as they went to some other addresses in the surrounding area.

They took us to a train station filled with thousands of other people about to be deported. The Russians had already prepared some trains using cattle wagons and we only set off once they'd been filled to bursting. In fact, it took almost two weeks before our particular train was allowed to leave and no rations were distributed by the Russians during this period.

They expected us to live on the food we'd grabbed when leaving our homes. The sanitary conditions were appalling as the toilet was just a hole in the floor designed for cattle waste, although we managed to put up some blankets to allow for some basic privacy. Mealtimes occurred when the train made stops during its long journey east. We were fed with watered-down soup and, very occasionally – and only if we were really lucky – some rough bread. Our 'food' was delivered by people walking wagon-to-wagon, carrying the soup in buckets and giving us one or two cups and that was it. The situation was identical whenever we reached a train station, although we were sometimes able to get hold of boiled water. That helped us warm up a bit.

They usually let us out when the train halted and there was a guard posted on every other wagon to keep an eye on us. One of them allowed me to walk away from the railway line as I wanted to stretch my legs and I suppose he was either being kind or simply didn't care. Mind you, we were in the middle of nowhere and it's not like I could have just run off. There was one occasion when I noticed some black rocks next to the tracks and assumed they were lumps of coal fallen off a freight train. It seemed like a marvellous opportunity to get some additional heat in our wagon, so I grabbed as many chunks as possible and scrambled back on board feeling very pleased with myself. It was quickly pointed out that all I'd managed to find were some chunks of iron ore!

We travelled by rail for about a month before finally arriving in the Novosibirsk region. The station was miles away from the logging camp that was our ultimate destination, so the Russians transported us there by using sleighs. Our camp was Number 90 and near Number 36, which also contained deported Poles. There were lots of other camps dotted around the area and many other nationalities were present. Our camp was mostly Polish, although there were several Ukrainians as well and I wondered if they'd been taken by mistake. Then again – and knowing the way the Soviet system worked – that seems doubtful.

Thankfully, both branches of our family managed to stay together but my grandmother and uncle would both die in Russia. We all slept in a wooden barrack block that was infested with bugs, including lice that bit us mercilessly. The problem became so bad that those in charge eventually tried fumigating the place but the damn things survived regardless. The lice even had a favourite strategy, whereby they'd climb to the ceiling and drop down to feast on a person as they slept.

The Russians had some carpenters and joiners build a school in the camp that I was then forced to attend, despite my initial refusals. I'd been working at logging, cutting down trees and preparing them to be sent downstream and this job secured additional rations – mainly rough bread – that was vital for our family. School wasn't considered work by the camp authorities, which meant I'd receive less rations by attending. It was a potentially lethal situation because the difference between life and death often depended on that little bit of extra food. My mother backed my decision and was placed in solitary confinement as a result. The camp authorities told me she'd only be released if I relented, so I gave up in order to save her from any further punishment.

The teachers were Russian and we learnt Soviet music and studied Stalin's speeches every morning. One of the commanders even said I had the makings of a good communist. 'Like hell!' I thought on hearing this. I was given some Russian books by a teacher and helped her translate this material into Polish for the other classmates. Meanwhile, the camp had a small shop that was opened whenever anything worthwhile or not so worthwhile arrived. We'd queue up just see what was on offer, which was never that much. This behaviour probably sounds a bit odd today but it's important to remember just how different our lives were back then. We'd also receive news from Poland now and then as some correspondence with those left behind was allowed.

I clearly remember when we discovered Germany had invaded Russia. It was during the summer of 1941 and our camp commander had all the Poles assemble before him. 'You're now Polish nationals,' he declared. That was surprising because our nationality had been stripped from us after the Soviet invasion in 1939. However, it was his next announcement that really excited us: 'You're also free to leave.' There was a great deal of discussion about what to do next, with some people choosing to stay as others decided to risk heading south for the warmer weather, opting to travel towards Kazakhstan. We were part of the second group and we raised the money for our train tickets by selling all the remaining goods we'd taken with us from Poland.

It was vital to work and earn food on our arrival in Kazakhstan and we did this by offering our services to collective farms. They usually housed us in appalling conditions – often giving us just a single room with a floor of packed earth to sleep on – and we were paid in grain that we had to grind ourselves. Unfortunately, we never had enough food for the whole family and we resorted to theft on a few occasions. It wasn't a pleasant thing to do but it was necessary for us to survive. Our strategy was simple: one of us distracted the person responsible for keeping an eye on the stores, while two others raced around the back to try and find an opening. This always included me because I was the smallest and most agile. I'd grab whatever supplies I could lay my hands on, passing them back to the other person waiting outside. I'd clamber out after enough food was taken and both of us would make a quick getaway, while the person doing the distracting soon made his excuses and left. It was an extremely dangerous thing to do but it really was a matter of survival.

Word finally reached us about the formation of Anders' forces. My brother went first and I followed him about a month later. My mother, sister and the others were left behind, working on a collective farm. I thought there might be a chance of sending for them after I joined up but this proved impossible. Getting to the army wasn't too difficult because I was almost fluent in Russian at this stage. Indeed, people often mistook me for being a Russian boy and I recall a Soviet security guard calling me over and asking me where I was headed:

> 'I'm going to join the Polish Army,' I said.
>
> He looked at me mystified.
>
> 'Why? What's wrong with the Red Army? Aren't you a Russian?'

I was processed and posted to a signals company in the 5th Division, where we were trained by an old sergeant who taught us Morse Code by blowing on a whistle. We were learning the basics at this stage and it was the best he could do because there was no equipment. The 5th Division eventually secured some guns and new uniforms that weren't particularly good. Thankfully, it wasn't too long before we were shipped to Persia but the journey across the Caspian Sea was hellish. It started with the Russians telling us to hand over any Soviet currency we still possessed, saying it was considered worthless on the Persian side. This was a lie as the Persians were quite happy to exchange roubles. We were then rammed onto a ship, with no space whatsoever and nothing by way of lavatories. People who needed to answer the call of nature had to perch over the sides. Fortunately, the trip only lasted overnight and we instantly realised our new lives had started on reaching Persia.

We were almost immediately directed to a zone where we handed over our clothes and were deloused. The British then sent us to another area and issued us with new kit. Lots of people were in bad shape, suffering from disease and malnutrition and I was probably in this last category. There's a picture of me soon after my arrival in Persia – just after being kitted out with British Army clothing – and my legs look like sticks! Happily, it wasn't long before I put on some weight and I also visited my brother around this time.

Our transfer to Iraq was a hair-raising experience as we were transported in lorries driven by Persians racing along steep mountain roads. It was scary stuff with them at the wheel. My unit was then forwarded to Palestine, where we met some Jews who'd emigrated from Poland before the war and it was great fun because we could speak to each other in Polish. I then discovered they were looking for recruits for the PAF and the Polish 1st Independent Parachute Brigade (IPB) and my goal at this stage was very simple: I wanted to get home as fast as possible and I thought either the PAF or IPB was my best bet. Unfortunately, my left ear was damaged and the PAF rejected me because of its strict entry requirements, so I applied to join the IPB instead and was accepted.

The time soon came when all those selected for the PAF and IPB were told to prepare for transport to Britain. My particular group headed the list and our voyage took more than a month, with us sailing all over the place to avoid the U-boats, including a stopover in Rio de Janeiro. We eventually disembarked at Glasgow and it was a completely new experience because nobody knew the first thing about Scotland. Nonetheless, we were very impressed with the ladies and always looked forward to the dances during our time off. I made a lot of friends in Scotland and fell in love with the people there, with the IPB based in the town of Leslie. I clearly remember when it was time for us to leave; all the townspeople came to the train station to wave us off and wish us luck. It was an unbelievable experience.

Our training in Scotland was tough but it didn't take me too long to become a fully-fledged signalman. I was also sent on an intensive parachutist course at Ringway in Manchester, where the instructor in charge was a Polish officer. Here we had a chance to train and jump – or break your bones if you were particularly unlucky! Manchester was great and we'd often head into the city for fun whenever it was allowed. The local government even gave us free transport and the people there would buy us food and drinks, which was fantastic.

There were sad times too and the most difficult period was during August 1944, when we heard about the Warsaw Uprising. Joining the Uprising was the IPB's reason to exist so it was very difficult to hear about it and realise we weren't going to be deployed there. However, we had to put all thoughts of Warsaw and Poland behind us when we dropped into Driel as part of the Arnhem campaign. We had a job to do and we didn't want to fail our commander, General Sosabowski, although it took some time to enter the campaign because of constant fog at the airfields. I was scared by thoughts of what might happen and I admit that most frankly. I also prayed a lot.

My jump at Driel didn't go to plan. You were meant to lower the signal set on a line attached to your leg when coming into land and we'd been given thick rubber gloves to give us the necessary grip. Unfortunately, I'd left my gloves behind by mistake, which meant the rope slid through my hands and burned them. This forced me to drop the set far too early and it was smashed on hitting the ground. Luckily, there were enough spares to go around and I was soon given another one.

I clearly remember the death of my friend Private Nowak, which was a most terrible thing. We'd taken up position in an apple orchard not long after landing and enemy mortars had started to fall. One shell fragment tore into his stomach, leaving him mortally wounded and crying out for morphine. An object then hit my back and I thought I'd been hit as well. I started to pray and slowly turned around to see how bad the damage was… I'd been struck by a falling apple. There was nothing they could do for my friend and it was truly awful to see him that way. He's now buried in Oosterbeek cemetery.

Our mission at Driel was to get over the River Nederrijn and into Oosterbeek, west of Arnhem, where we'd support the British airborne troops fighting hard to hold their perimeter. However, the Germans covered the river with machine guns, ready to stop anyone from crossing. They even had special lighting to help their spotters and I remember the tracer bullets flying around and incoming mortar fire. The British eventually gave us boats that weren't even fit for recreational fishing.[2]

I never knew just how bad it was for those boys in Oosterbeek until afterwards, while contact with the British XXX Corps seemed very poor and I can only recall one occasion when a jeep pulled up carrying a British officer. He quickly explained we needed to hold our lines because the armour was about to arrive. It all seemed so disorganised. We remained in the Netherlands for some time after the Arnhem campaign and were then taken by lorry to a nearby port and departed for Britain by boat. We had little interaction with the Dutch, although I remember Cora Baltussen helping our troops a great deal, particularly the wounded. She owned a jam factory in Driel.[3]

General Sosabowski was relieved of his command at the end of 1944 and I now know there was a lot of politics behind this decision.[4] The IPB joined the British Liberation Army in 1945, which then became the British Army of the Rhine. I wasn't too keen on dealing with the Germans but we remained fair. We were based near Osnabrück, which is where I met my wife; she and her family had been deported by the Germans and she'd been sent to work on a farm. I met her at a dance held by Polish families at a nearby camp. By the way, a lot of Russians were present as well. Most of them had changed their nationality to Polish on hearing they'd be repatriated to the Soviet Union by the British and they knew this would amount to a gulag sentence.

I married my wife in Germany and we eventually resettled in Britain, which wasn't easy to begin with. Jobs were offered to us but mostly in mining, heavy industry or textiles. I took a job in the textile industry, working on the looms for several years. Then I became a specialist builder, helping with the construction of a power station and eventually becoming a foreman. My brother survived the Italian campaign and we helped each other, buying a property together for both our families. I didn't know what had happened to my mother and sister at war's end and I wrote to the Red Cross, asking it to contact the family on my behalf. They found them in 1946 and I received a letter explaining the family had suffered badly in Siberia and had arrived home to discover almost all the Poles in our region had been forced to move westwards.

They'd followed my sisters – the ones who'd avoided being captured by the Russians – and resettled in Silesia. My mother visited us in England in the 1950s and brought us lots of apples, having been told by the communists that the British people had nothing to eat!

The first opportunity I had to visit Poland came in 1961. It was a difficult journey because you had to register with the local authorities at regular intervals, telling them where you were going and when you'd be leaving. It never worked according to plan and I got into some difficulty after being unable to register my departure. It wasn't my fault because the woman in charge of processing British passports was having her lunchbreak. The family wrote to me after I returned to Britain, explaining this failure meant the communists now considered me a spy! It was wonderful when Poland secured its true independence after 1989, although it would have been so much better if it had been a free country after the war. Today, we know Stalin outplayed the Western Allies at every step in the negotiations for post-war Europe. Meanwhile, I will always feel grateful towards the Dutch people. They honoured Sosabowski and the IPB with awards in 2006, formally recognising our efforts at Driel. That was truly a great thing.

ZBIGNIEW GONDEK

My friends call me Bob and I was born in Przemyśl, which is now in southeast Poland and near the Ukrainian border. My father was a policeman who'd served in the Austro-Hungarian Army during the First World War and my mother was a housewife, while I also had an older brother. I did well at school but I didn't really hear much about events in the wider world at that time. I was a Scout and recall how proud we were every 3 May on Constitution Day, with parades and the Polish Army present. 'Gee whizz, we've got a lot of horses,' I thought. We had no clue about what was happening in the weeks leading up to war and knew little about the events of 1 September 1939 or just afterwards. I heard bombs exploding one day and I wondered what was happening and that was about it.[1] The Russians then arrived; they were poorly dressed and took anything they wanted, particularly watches.[2]

We soon discovered you needed communist-issued coupons to obtain food and you needed to work to get the coupons. About five or six of us found jobs at a local sawmill and I was almost 16 at this time. My father was hiding at home because we sensed the Russians would target him as an 'enemy of the state' and, sure enough, he was arrested in early February 1940. The Russians arrived at 2am or 3am and took him away. Much later, we discovered he was murdered by the NKVD in May, so he only survived for four months after his arrest.[3] They returned several days later, giving my mother and I just a few minutes to pack a couple of suitcases. Everything else had to be left behind. They took us to a goods station, where thousands of Polish people were already waiting to be deported in trains composed of cattle wagons. My mother then told me we had no bread and I managed to slip away, going to a shop and buying some. They wouldn't let me back into the station and I had to explain what had happened. 'My mother's right there!' I ended up shouting.

Our journey east took about a month and we'd often stop in railway sidings overnight. The conditions were awful and there was no toilet – it was just a hole through the floor. The doors were closed all the time and could only be opened from the outside, while a single stove had been installed to keep us warm. I was standing next to it during one of the stops when the train suddenly started moving and I was thrown backwards, falling on the stove and getting burnt in the process. I was eventually moved into another wagon, where a doctor was located and where I could sit down. In addition, the door could be slid open, so there was some fresh air and I stayed like this for a couple of days before being moved back again.

Our final stop was in Kustanay, northwest Kazakhstan's largest town. All the surrounding villages had been collectivised and we were told where to stay, ending up in a place that was almost totally Kazakh – who I found to be excellent people. The authorities said the Poles would never see their homes again and we needed to work if we wanted food. It was simple as that. One of my jobs included ploughing, where I created immense lines in the earth that stretched for something like a couple of miles. I had no farming skills when I arrived but I soon learnt to shout at the oxen to get them moving in the proper direction. We also tilled the ground and looked after the crops as they started growing, working from sunrise to sunset.

The toughest time was during harvest season, when we worked in the fields without any breaks. The food we received was just soup and bread and we were supposed to earn money as well but you never earnt enough to cover the cost of your rations. Indeed, they once told us we were in debt because we hadn't worked hard enough![4] The homes were made of earth and you'd sit on the floor, while winter conditions were fierce and involved lots of snow. In fact, there was so much snow that the homes would become obscured – you'd just see a rooftop or chimney with some smoke floating up. The Kazakhs were generous people and they often shared their flatbread and tea with us. I was sent to work with another family at one point and they were responsible for stabling some cattle. I helped them with the cleaning etc. and the start time was around 4am, although this family occasionally let me sleep just a little bit longer.

I came down with something bad on one occasion – an awful cold or flu – and the collective's manager came along:

'What's up with you? Why aren't you at work?' he asked.

'I'm really sick,' I said.

'You're not sick,' he said, before walking off.

Within a month, I was ordered to attend court in another village and there were maybe ten of us present. A person's name would be called out and someone else would shout 'guilty!' Then they'd read out a pre-determined sentence and they certainly didn't ask anyone what had happened or whether any special circumstances were involved. I ended up receiving five months in jail.

The prison was located in Kustanay and I had to walk there, with the journey taking about two days. The conditions were bad and there were about 40-50 persons to a cell that should have held maybe ten or 12. There were Russians, some Kazaks and a couple of Poles. Wardens would come in every now and then, looking for people to clean other parts of the jail or to perform some manual labour. Lucky prisoners might also be taken outside and allowed to walk around for a bit but I was never allowed out. Mealtimes involved a slice of bread and something they pretended to call tea. I'd dip my bread in this 'tea', trying to bulk it up and hoping it would fill my stomach just a little bit more.

The cell's beds had been taken by others long ago and you started out by sitting next to where people went to the toilet. You'd move to a better spot as people were released or taken elsewhere, while the next person got the place you'd just left. Later, you might get some space on a bench. I remember a few of the guys shaved themselves by using shards of glass but I've no idea how they got hold of these 'razors'. I don't remember us washing at all, while I recall another room nearby held children, maybe around 30 or 40 boys. They finally let me go after six months, telling me to find my own way back.

It was now summer 1941 and I think Germany had invaded the Soviet Union by the time I got out. There were certainly some rumours going around but nothing definite. I eventually heard an invasion had indeed occurred and a Polish army was being formed in Russia, with the authorities suddenly announcing all Poles were free to go. Most of us moved southeast, to places like Tashkent, but I can't recall the details of our journey there. Unaware of his fate, we also hoped my dad might turn up. One day, I told my mother that I thought it was my duty to join the Polish Army and that I needed to go. She stayed behind because we didn't think they'd allow her to accompany me. Getting to a recruitment centre involved jumping on various goods trains and I joined up at Lugovoye on 2 February 1942. I later discovered some of the guys had taken family members with them but I didn't have enough time to return for my mother. That's because an order suddenly arrived putting us on notice for departure to Persia. Regarding the short time I was in the army in the USSR, well the conditions were very, very basic and almost every day involved us trying to get rid of our lice.

The journey to Persia wasn't good and many people were suffering dysentery. In addition, a lot of people ate too much on arrival in Pahlavi and got sick, with some even dying because of this. I recall eating some eggs and having a little brandy on arrival. The British told us to strip soon after we arrived, directing us to some showers and then telling us pick up our brand-new uniforms. Overall, I felt happy because I didn't think any Poles would ever make it out of Russia. From Persia, we went to Iraq and then Palestine. I was in the 6th Battalion of the 2nd Carpathian Rifle Brigade, itself part of the 3rd Carpathian Rifle Division. We started our proper training at this point, assisted by guys who'd been in the Independent Carpathian Rifle Brigade that had fought at Tobruk during the famous siege in 1941. I was promoted to corporal and attended an NCO training course soon afterwards, so I was well prepared to command a small unit in combat. We were then transferred to Egypt and told we were going join the Italian campaign in November 1943.

We arrived at Taranto and stayed in the area for quite some time because a lot of organisational work was required. I recall meeting quite a few locals during this period, learning a little bit of Italian and getting on with them quite well. Some of them were upset when it was time for me to leave, warning me not to go to war. 'Well, I've got to,' I said. They were sending us to the frontlines and our new positions were near the

River Sangro. We experienced incoming artillery maybe once or twice a week and I remember there was a rationed shot of rum every night.

Most of our efforts at this stage involved reconnaissance of no-man's land, with the Germans sending out their own patrols and there'd be some small-scale fighting every now and then. Most local people remained in the area and you'd occasionally see them as well. Patrols involved maybe 15 guys and you'd cross the Sangro using a little boat, with the contested zone lying beyond and roughly several miles deep. There were times when we'd stay in a building and wait, just keeping an eye on things and engaging the enemy if we spotted him. Contact usually involved throwing a grenade or two and firing our small arms, with the Germans then disengaging. We'd leave a little later and it felt almost co-ordinated in some respects.

Now for Monte Cassino. Had we heard of it beforehand? Yes, because our artillery and other heavy stuff had moved up first and we followed not too long afterwards. We were helped by some mule companies going in and we soon changed over with those who'd been up there beforehand. All of this was done at night and people spent quite a lot of time sorting themselves out, although you needed to be quiet because sounds could invite enemy fire. Smoking at night was strictly forbidden as the enemy was looking for glowing cigarette ends to target. The ground was rough and stony but I eventually found a soft spot that didn't seem too bad. The next morning, I discovered this 'soft spot' was a dead body buried in a shallow grave and this came as a real shock. The patrols soon started again, with my platoon going out maybe two or three times before the offensive started. You'd take off anything that could make noise, including boots that were exchanged for plimsols. There was one occasion when we took some incoming fire and both the platoon leader and I ended up scrambling into the same hole to take cover. Sometimes, we'd reach a position and it would be close enough to hear the Germans talking.

I remember our artillery going in on 17 May, with a huge volume of fire, while our assault was aiming for Massa Albaneta beyond Point 593.[5] Someone told us it had been taken but it hadn't and we received incoming fire from our rear as we advanced. So much stuff was now flying around that you could hear it going over your head, making a metallic zinging sound. I had something like ten guys with me and all of us were keeping our heads down. Then I saw the Germans pulling out maybe 50-100ft (15-30 metres) away but we couldn't fire on them without revealing our position. That would have invited enemy fire right on top of us and we'd already suffered lots and lots of wounded. In fact, our company was down to just 17 people when the attack ended. I thought we'd be taken out of the line – or maybe some replacements would be sent over – but we were told to stay put and prepare ourselves for another attack. It was important to take care as we waited in cover because the Germans had left behind lots of mines and booby traps. Pick up something interesting and there goes your arm or even worse. I think it was around noon or maybe 1pm when we saw the abbey had been taken – with British and Polish flags flying – and we were so happy.

Piedimonte[6] was the next target, although I wasn't involved in the fighting because our unit had been taken out of the frontline. We had about two weeks rest and needed to replace our losses. The Corps was then shifted back to the Adriatic side of Italy and this period involved my unit pushing forward in jeeps, jumping out and fighting German rear guards as their forces were pulled back. We then reached a strongly-held town called Loreto on the way to Ancona. Two battalions had been deployed, with some tanks and heavy machine guns in support. We needed to cross a river and advance on the other side but our unit got pinned down by some machine gun nests. Under fire, I crawled closer and closer with grenades and bombed two of them out, which allowed our troops to push forward again. Enemy mortars then started to fall and I got badly hit; the Germans must have called in strikes very close to their own positions, if not right on top of them.

Another guy – not so badly wounded – was with me and we were eventually taken into a nearby house, where an Italian lady was crying. My left hand was gone and my leg was in bad shape with some bone showing, plus my body was full of shrapnel. I was later awarded the Virtuti Militari.[7] I was transported to a field hospital and they worked on me very quickly. A priest arrived not too long afterwards and asked for me by name and I started to worry, wondering if he knew something I didn't – and that he might be about to deliver my last rites! It was the one thing that truly scared me. I spent six months in a hospital to the south and my surgeon was very good, working hard to save my leg. They even used maggots at one point to eat away the wound's infected parts.

I also received penicillin and the doctor told me I probably wouldn't have made it without this, while those maggots helped me keep my leg.[8] They got most of the shrapnel out of me but years later, in the 1960s, I started experiencing some pain and went into hospital. They did a thorough examination and discovered some additional shrapnel, warning me that taking it out carried the risk of paralysis. I went ahead with the operation and they got a lot of it removed. On another occasion, at a health club, I saw some blood and then noticed some more shrapnel had fallen out of my body.

Anyway, back to that hospital in Italy. They asked me if I wanted to wait for a skin graft or travel to Scotland and receive my treatment there. I knew my brother had reached Scotland and I decided to transfer there. I went via a Red Cross ship but I can't really remember the voyage. It was Christmas 1944 by the time we docked and I was taken up to Scotland on a military train, staying in two or three military hospitals and then recovering in Glencoe, which is a beautiful place. There were six or eight Poles with me and one of them was a pilot who'd lost both of his legs. My brother was with the Polish 1st Armoured Division and he'd already been deployed to Northwest Europe but his wife came to help me and I went to stay with her and her parents for a time.

The war then ended and my brother discovered our mother had made it back to Poland. I got married in 1948 and my wife and I resettled in Canada in the mid-1950s. It seemed like a dream place because it was a country where you could afford a car and own a home. I visited Poland in 1973 to see my mother. My hometown now seemed so small, with the big streets of my youth tiny compared with the cities I've since lived in or travelled through. I did a lot of work with war amputees in Ontario and eventually became a director for the War Amps charity, with several people working for me at one point. I still try and help war amputees and I also talk with school children about my experiences. I could talk to them for hours and they always ask lots of questions like 'were you afraid?' and I honestly have to say no, not really.

EUGENIA JARKIEWICZ-WERYNSKI

My maiden name was Hucyło and I was born in Augustów in northeast Poland. I had two older brothers and I was the youngest. My father was an office worker but died when I about six and left no pension, so my mother found work in the meat and butchery trade. We lived near my school, while one of our neighbours was an ethnic German woman. My mother could speak German reasonably well and she'd ask this lady about Hitler and what he'd been saying, trying to discover what the Nazis were really up to. The woman's husband didn't like this and they left for Germany soon after the invasion. This lady visited our town after the war and I talked to her about what had happened to them. Their son had suffered as a hunchback and, very sadly, he'd been taken by the authorities and murdered. The Nazis did this to many disabled and mentally-ill people.[1] Her other son was conscripted into the German Army and was killed within months of joining. In fact, she lost her boys within a three-month period and her husband was killed during an Allied bombing raid.

I remember the start of the war quite clearly; I was at home and it was at about 5am or 6am when enemy aircraft flew over on their way to bomb Grodno. German forces eventually reached our city, with their first units arriving on motorbikes and bicycles. However, they didn't stay long as some Russians arrived on horses just before 17 September, the day they formally announced their 'intervention.'[2] A Red Army commander ended up living nearby and a strict curfew was imposed, with nobody allowed out after 8pm. They also took whatever contents they fancied from the stores and shops. Our school remained open but they started teaching us in Belarusian, plus language lessons in German and some Russian and French. There was no mention of Poland or the Polish government and our history lessons were all about Russia.

My brother René was detained in Grodno prison. He'd been captured by the Germans and handed over to the Russians during an exchange of Polish prisoners based on where they lived before the war. My eldest brother Edward had also been taken prisoner by the Russians and both were detained in the same place for a short while. My mother was eventually arrested, although she avoided deportation to Siberia. She was imprisoned in Brześć and returned to Augustów after the Soviet Union was invaded by the Germans. Edward was unlucky because he was deported deep into Russia but he later joined Anders' forces after changing his name to Edmund and lying about his age. He eventually fought at Monte Cassino, while René was taken by the Germans after they invaded the USSR but he managed to escape from them.

A neighbour warned me I'd been placed on a deportation list in June 1941. She was a Russian lady with small children and I often visited her and she asked me to stay overnight one day. I never normally did this but I listened to her for some reason. I then returned home to discover the authorities had been looking for me as they started deporting people from the region. Incidentally, this wouldn't be the last round-up of Poles in Augustów. They took away hundreds of Polish men from the city in July 1945 and nobody knows their fate.[3] Anyway, this Russian family helped me and I ended up being hidden by some friends.

The invasion of the Soviet Union started early on 22 June 1941 and the Russians killed prisoners in the local jail before fleeing, with the Germans taking photos of this massacre as evidence.[4] The schools were closed by the Germans and we were forced to work in labour groups instead. They sent us into the woods to pick herbs and berries or they had us plant trees and vegetables. They also made us work at a nearby military barracks and I was often made to peel potatoes in a kitchen or help clean the local hospital. I received a notice to report for work in Germany in early 1943 and some men came to arrest me but I pushed one of them away and ran off, hiding in some nearby bushes. They didn't see where I'd gone and started looking for me in the next street. Later, I attended church and that's when the Germans arrived and started taking people away, including myself and a pregnant woman. A group of us were sent to a small camp in Augustów, working in the forest and helping dig out tree stumps. This lasted about two months. Then they took us to Grajewo and put us on a train. Two or three wagons were for prisoners, while the rest was for regular passengers in normal carriages. They gave us a warning beforehand, saying the Gestapo would burn our family homes and everything in them if we tried to escape.

They took us to Stutthof concentration camp and, thankfully, let the pregnant woman go.[5] Marching music was played on our arrival and we had no clue what was going on. They started by registering our names and taking our clothes, giving us striped uniforms in return. Other personal items were seized and we were each given a piece of soap, a toothbrush, some toothpaste and a comb. They checked our hair but didn't cut it there and then. That happened a few days later and I can't describe what that was like… It was early spring and raining quite often but we had to work outside whatever the weather and there was nowhere to dry our clothes on returning to our barracks because it was so crowded. The main job at this stage was to shovel sand used to cover vegetables; there would be a layer of sand and then a layer of carrots or beets and then another layer of sand etc.[6] We'd also sort the good vegetables from the bad. Male prisoners were used to fell trees outside the camp and drag them back. Someone threw a carrot on the ground one day and a man picked it up. He was spotted doing this by a German guard who walked over and shot him on the spot. The guard then stepped on his neck to finish him off and I saw it all.

Our rations comprised two potatoes and a ladleful of 'soup' which was just hot water with some vegetable bits floating in it. There were Red Cross inspections every now and then, which is when the Germans gave us macaroni and meat. 'Oh, that tastes nice,' the inspectors would say. They'd also tour the camp but we were ordered not to speak with them. My mother tried to get me released because I was under 16 and, in theory, shouldn't have been taken. My name was called out during a morning roll call one day. 'Your mother was trying to get you out,' a German announced, 'but you're not going home because we've told her you're not here!'

I sometimes worked on nearby farms, driving a horse and wagon at one place to help collect the hay. The farmer turned out to be an important Nazi – a Gestapo guy – and he had about 40 people working for him. He asked for my name and number, saying he'd get me transferred to work on his farm fulltime. However, they never let me out after this and, instead, ordered me to patch uniforms and clean the lice off them. Incidentally, lice were everywhere in the camp. We'd take off our clothes and try to delouse them and the guard assigned to our block would sometimes wolf-whistle at us all. We didn't care by then. Later, they arranged a disinfection bath, handing us soap and exchanging our clothes. We were okay for about two or three weeks but the lice soon returned. I should add we slept in shifts and I worked at night, sleeping a little bit during the day.

We were transferred to Ravensbrück about a month after this and they took us there by train, giving us our original clothes for the journey. We returned these on arrival and received camp uniforms once more. I was okay health-wise at this stage, while our first job was to fill potholes on the main parade ground with sand. A female guard watched over us, standing there with a dog. These women were bad – much worse than the men – and one of them was a real sadist.[7] She gathered us together one day and took us to a crematorium, where she pointed out the remains. 'You'll all end up like this,' she said.

Ravensbrück was large, with about 18 barrack blocks in my part of the camp alone. Morning roll call started at 4am and could last a long time because they insisted on counting everyone. I was at Ravensbrück for roughly six weeks. All the prisoners I'd arrived with from Stutthof were examined during this period – hands checked and ages verified – and then forwarded elsewhere. Soon, I was the only one left from this group and they eventually selected me for a work party being forwarded to a nearby aircraft factory.

The managers told us we had around ten days to learn our jobs and we'd be shown how to use the tools. I was on the assembly line using this or that, with a foreman keeping an eye on things. He asked me to use some heavy machinery but I couldn't lift it, so he pushed me out of the way in frustration and a guy came over from a welding unit. 'Come with me,' he said. This fellow showed me how to weld and it became my job. I'd weld cockpit frames and did this by cutting tubes and fitting them. Everyone had a number and mine was 99. If something happened – say a mistake or sabotage – then the Germans could potentially discover it was you through that number. We worked on small bombers for Heinkel,[8] although we never saw the completed aircraft because they took them out of the factory and hid them in the nearby brush and woods.

We were detained in old army blockhouses and worked from 7am to 7pm, with French prisoners of war taking over for the night shift. We had no contact with them, other than walking past each other when the shift was changed. However, there was a day when someone said hello and the Germans got angry, forcing us stand still for a roll call that lasted quite some time. The woman in charge of our block was often upset with us, punishing people by forcing them to hold their shoes with arms outstretched. She'd start shouting if anyone's arms started to sink. We eventually complained about her behaviour to our foremen and they reported her to our overseers because the factory didn't want exhausted people – they wanted us working and they were paying the German government to lease us as forced labourers.

We were targeted by Allied aircraft one day, the sirens coming on just as the bombs started falling. All of us were in the factory when this happened and they opened the doors, with everyone running outside. It took about three days before the workforce fully returned. Amazingly, the factory wasn't damaged but all the finished aircraft that had been prepared for delivery were destroyed. I suspect the Allies knew prisoners were working in the factory and the aircraft outside were a good target.[9] The food wasn't much better at this place compared with Stutthof or Ravensbrück and there was an occasion when they sent us a batch of spinach crawling with worms. We tried returning this filth but they refused to listen and we waited three days before any new food arrived.

We weren't supposed to work on Sundays but the guards always had us do useless stuff like moving rocks after midday. They turned off an electric fence one Sunday and ordered us to weed the surrounding ground and got upset when one of us discovered some edible wild plants. They shouted at us to put them back! We never received any outside news at this stage, other than when some people suddenly arrived from Warsaw. They'd taken part in the Uprising and told us how bad it was but they were afraid to talk too much.

The Russians were approaching by April 1945 and that's when an evacuation order arrived. I was with about 80 people at the factory gate and we were told to hand out the remaining food to those marching out.

This was just some bread and cheese. We then followed and soon started coming across dead bodies lying in the road. These were people who couldn't keep up and the guards simply shot them. We passed a small town not long afterwards, with German children and others waiting for us; they spat on us and called us shit this and shit that. They also threw stones.

We stopped in a forest after about three days of walking, sleeping in some hay. I woke up to discover there'd been a bad frost and my throat was so sore that I couldn't speak. Someone had also stolen my clogs and I was forced to use a pair of old slippers I had with me. Unfortunately, they weren't good enough for cross-country walking and my feet were soon bleeding. The guy in charge had us stop at some barracks, telling us not to enter the homes of a nearby village and warning us booby traps had probably been set and any remaining food would be poisoned. Unfortunately, some of the prisoners didn't believe him; they snuck into a house and got caught in an explosion.

We were heading towards the port of Rostock when a Russian motorcycle suddenly arrived and this was our liberation, with many of our guards fleeing. However, some of the Germans gave up and decided to stay with us. The Red Army took us to a nearby barracks and gave us new clothes – and then decided to take them back! We were afraid of being detained by the Russians and they started questioning us individually, wanting to know who we were and what we'd been doing during the war. I remained in Russian hands until 29 June 1945, when I was suddenly told to join a group of freed prisoners leaving from a nearby station. It was taking German machinery to the Soviet Union and I was told to get off when it stopped Poland. They also gave me some paperwork.

The train halted in Poland not long after crossing the border and some guys from the Polish People's Army were standing outside on the tracks. They told us to get off because the train would head straight into Russia, with no extra stops on the way. We ignored them because someone else said the train would stay put for a few days, which meant we had some shelter for a little while yet. Unfortunately, a group of thugs came onboard that night; they were carrying guns and didn't speak a word. They took everything from me – all my remaining possessions – and I couldn't believe they were stealing from people just released from a concentration camp.

Several of us got off the train the next day but none of us had any money. We went into the station and saw they were selling buns and hot drinks and a lady there gave us some free coffee. Then I got another train to head home. It was overcrowded and I didn't have a ticket, so I sat on the roof. We reached Warsaw and I saw it was in ruins, with rubble everywhere. I got on another train – back on the roof again – and reached a place called Sokółka. It wasn't too far from Bialystok and I had a friend there who offered me a place to stay overnight. He escorted me to the marketplace the next day and helped me find some other people going my way. I started talking to a boy in an adjacent wagon, telling him I was going to Augustów and he joined me because he was heading there as well.

Unfortunately, our wagon stopped with around 25 miles (40km) to go, which meant we had a long walk home. We left early in the morning and neared the town at around 9pm, meeting some people from the Underground in a forest along the way. They asked me where I was going to in Augustów. 'You won't find anyone there,' they then warned me. 'You should stay here.' However, we carried on and I noticed only a few houses remained on my street, the rest having been burnt or destroyed by the Germans. Fortunately, my home had survived; my mother had saved our property by throwing up wet blankets and pouring water everywhere. Strange as it may sound, but the Germans had converted most of our home into a bathhouse/sauna and they'd cut holes into the floor into which they placed bathtubs. Next door had been owned by some Jews and they'd burnt the property because of this.

My mother was at home when I arrived. She'd restarted her butchery business but had been forced to kill cats for meat to sell on the black market. I already knew she was alive because she'd been able to write to me in Germany and, on occasion, even managed to send through a few parcels. One of them included some dried bread and biscuits and she did this thinking it would help preserve the contents. She didn't realise I had neither the time nor water in which to soak them in. One of the female guards at Ravensbrück spotted me walking around with some of this dried bread and seized it from me, throwing it to a camp dog. The dog refused to eat it, so she stamped on it until it was crushed.

I now needed to register my presence with the Russian commander in Augustów and he took one look at my paperwork and promptly binned it.

Then he sent me to a room for further registration and I sat there waiting and waiting, with no food or anything. It started to get dark and I began to worry it was a form of confinement, when a guy opened the door and told me to leave. We still didn't really know what had happened to my brothers at this stage, other than René was in Polish People's Army and Edmund was with Anders. I also discovered a guy called Mieczysław Borowski had reached Augustów. He'd been at Ravensbrück – one of the few male inmates detained there for any length of time. He'd arrived at the camp with four other men and only he'd survived, with the rest dying from exhaustion. 'Things are not going well here,' he told me. 'We've got to leave Poland.'

My mother had a cousin who owned a wagon and horses. He had us dressed up like farm labourers and we got out of Augustów with him. This was just before the round-up that targeted the men. We were dropped off on a highway and hitched a lift with some passing Russian troops who offered us ride in their truck. They took us to the edge of Grajewo and, from there, we took a train to Bialystok and then a train to Elbląg, where we met some camp survivors Mieczysław knew. I decided to return to Augustów in September for reasons I'm still not sure of. My younger brother René arrived almost as soon as I returned and we discovered he'd been stationed in Krakow and had just become an instructor at a military school on the outskirts of Lodz.

René stayed for three days, along with a German shepherd dog he'd brought with him. He decided to go to a dance in Sokółka and was wearing civilian clothes. He wanted to take the dog but it refused to go and my brother eventually gave up. We were later told some policemen had burst in on the dance. 'Hands up and show us your papers!' they shouted. My brother was near the door and a policeman – who was later found to be drunk – shot and killed him. None of this would have happened if my brother had been wearing his uniform and I swear that dog knew something bad was about to happen.

Regarding Edmund, someone who'd been there said he'd been killed at Monte Cassino but my mother kept praying he was still alive. A letter from the West arrived for me around Christmas 1945 but it was no longer there when I went to retrieve it. Another letter came a little later and I was able to pick it up. It was from Edmund, informing us he was in a British hospital. He'd been badly wounded and they'd operated on his head, taking out a piece of shrapnel but another piece remained. He enclosed a picture of himself when his head was wrapped in bandages. His next letter told us he was relocating to Argentina and he invited me to leave Poland and live with him. I went to the Argentinian embassy but they said I could only visit and not emigrate, so I decided to stay.

I got married and had two children after the war, with my husband working as a cryptologist in an army intelligence unit that covered our region. However, he really wanted to study medicine and, for whatever reason – probably because of his work and the things he knew – they suddenly made him disappear. The authorities told me I was now a widow. I was contacted by an old childhood friend in 1960. He'd reached Britain during the war and served in the PAF before emigrating to Canada. He'd talked to some Polish people who'd recently arrived in Ontario from Augustów and asked them if they'd ever met me. Amazingly, they'd sold me a piano just before emigrating, so they were able to give him my address. He proposed marriage but the Polish government didn't like this, issuing me a passport but stating I only had two weeks in which to leave. In addition, I could only take one child. My other child would follow 'within two years' or so they promised. In fact, they were lying and we had to get the Canadian Foreign Ministry involved for them to keep their word.

I took my younger daughter and we arrived in Canada with just $10, the maximum a person was allowed to take out of communist Poland. They'd also forced us to buy return tickets, knowing we'd never use them. I couldn't speak English on arrival, so I paid for a quick language course. There was no government assistance for new immigrants back then and my first job in Toronto was working for a Jewish hatmaker, putting feathers into men's hats and being paid 25 cents an hour. Then I worked at Simpson's department store before retraining as a bookkeeper, which I'd done back in Poland and that became my new career.

GRAŻYNA KOPEĆ

I was born in Dąbrowa Górnicza, near Katowice, and I was an only child. My mother was born in the village of Gidle in the district of Radomsko and my father was a mining engineer and surveyor, with our region known for its coalfields. He was also a reserve pilot in the PAF. I heard quite a few stories about the mines and what daily life was like for the miners, which was tough and nothing like the standard of living we enjoy today. My parents had decent accommodation in an apartment building in town and they sent me to a private school run by a director called Maria Szulc.

The government had installed loudspeakers in the larger towns, usually in the market squares, over which important news was broadcast and there was an occasion when I heard Hitler making a speech. He was yelling and shouting and we youngsters were pulling faces and laughing. We really thought Poland was strong and was going to show Germany a thing or two. Today, everyone knows our armies were not as well prepared as originally thought. We toured around Poland's part of the Baltic for our summer holiday in 1939 before returning home, with my father called up for the PAF just before the end of August. Meanwhile, my mother and I travelled to Gidle to stay at my grandmother's house, thinking it would be safer there. My aunt and cousins were staying at the house as well, along with her dog and our dog. We didn't really understand the gravity of it all; we believed the Polish government when it said Britain would help us and the war would probably be over in a few weeks. We all thought Poland would win and there was great deal of excitement and gossip in the village on 1 September 1939, with plenty of people milling around. There was no electricity in Gidle and nobody had a radio, so there was no current news about what was actually happening.

The Germans arrived on 3 September, passing through the village with motorcycles, tanks and soldiers – and they didn't look friendly! Gidle has two churches and a monastery and we all ran to one the churches for safety, hiding in its basement. There was a mass going on and our dogs started howling every time the congregation started singing. Then we fled to small village nearby, going over bad roads covered with sand. The people in this village had placed their furniture in the fields, covering it with hay and hoping it would be safe if the enemy started burning down their homes. Some of the villagers helped us, letting us stay overnight in one the houses.

German motorcyclists approached not much later, although they kept getting stuck on the sandy road and we were looking at them through the windows. It was getting dark and we didn't know what was going to happen next. Fortunately, we were fine but we saw several fires burning on the horizon early the next morning. The rising sun was an almost brownish-crimson colour because of all the smoke and it was a scary sight. We soon discovered parts of Gidle had been burnt, including my grandmother's house, while I also heard gunfire and screams coming from another nearby village. A machine gun firing in the distance sounds like a machine gun but several firing at once sounds a bit like boiling water, which I thought was strange. We later heard the Germans had seen a man holding a razor for shaving and decided it was a 'weapon', which is when they started shooting people.

We stayed with another aunt who also lived in Gidle and whose home was untouched. Then I heard people were going into the village where the massacre had taken place to bury the dead. Other details also reached us. For example, some people had hidden in a well and the Germans threw a pig down to try and drown them. There was no communication with the outside world at this point and my mother decided we should return to Dąbrowa, so she hired a man with a horse and buggy and it took us two days to get there. We didn't meet anyone on the road and there was no traffic at all.

Things sort of settled down after this but there was no word from my father. We were then kicked out of our apartment because the better homes were usually nearer the centre of Polish towns and the Germans wanted them. We moved to an area at the end of a tram line in a building called Koszary, which means 'barracks' because it was said to have been used by the military at some point. It was quite a lengthy place and it didn't have proper windows, while its entrance was via a large backyard that contained two or three European poplar trees. We had no indoor conveniences and had to make do with a water pump and an outhouse in the backyard. The Germans almost immediately confiscated people's radios and my mother surrendered ours because she was worried someone might tattle on us. They also wanted luxury items, including things like skis. My parents used to go skiing quite a bit near Zakopane, so she chopped up their skis and threw them in the fire. 'I'll be damned if the Germans get our skis!' she exclaimed. However, she had some difficulty burning my father's set because they had metal edging.

My mother had no income to begin with and sold items here and there. The area we lived in was badly polluted from the heavy industry, although this had always been the case. In 1941, she decided it would better for me to live with my paternal grandparents and my uncle in Brzeszcze, which is close to Oświęcim. It was near to where the Germans built the Auschwitz camps. I was accompanied by Wanda Górecka, the daughter of my grandparents' upstairs neighbours. She lived in Katowice and her father was Polish, while her mother – who I always knew as Mrs. Górecka – was German. Maria Górecka helped a lot of prisoners in Auschwitz, cooking soup and bribing guards etc.[1]

Wanda and I changed trains at Katowice during that first journey to Brzeszcze and we saw trains of cattle wagons going past with people in them. We also changed trains at Auschwitz and I could see people being unloaded – getting yelled at, being pushed around and whacked with sticks. The people were subdued and quiet… Did we know what was happening? Absolutely. You couldn't miss any of this or fail to understand what it meant. I made this journey a few times when visiting my mother and I'd often return with Wanda. There was an occasion when our connecting train to Brzeszcze was badly delayed. 'Why don't we just walk home?' Wanda suggested. So, we took a road straight through the camp, with barbed wire on either side and guard towers occupied by men with guns. In addition, there were big signs saying things like 'no stopping' or 'no photographs'. There were also a lot of fields around us and people wearing striped outfits were working in them and it felt like someone was watching us all the time. Incidentally, prisoners would escape every now and again and we'd hear sirens going off. The guards would search the local area with German Shepherds and Dobermanns, although these incidents eventually ceased. Today, we know the reason why: the guards would execute all the people in the escapee's dorm, so the prisoners stopped trying to get out.

The Germans had prisoners build a kind of electricity station not far from my grandparents' windows, while other prisoners worked in the local mines. In a way, they were better off because the miners gave them food, although most of them were scared because they had no previous experience of working underground in dangerous conditions. Mrs. Górecka even had some prisoners visit at her home after she bribed their guards. They wrote things like letters or personal accounts and Wanda took these to Katowice, placing them in jars and then burying them in her backyard. I heard a book was later published compiling many of these accounts. Mrs. Górecka needed cigarettes for bribery and I'd often sit with her rolling them using a little tin box. It's strange because I've been to Auschwitz three times since the war and the museum appeared to have no knowledge of her. I've since seen her name in a book about Auschwitz, while my uncle's friend Doctor Zieliński was also mentioned and I saw a photo of him in the museum. He was one of those who helped with things like securing medicines.[2]

I was about 12 or 13 by now and I wasn't going to school and things were getting much worse around us. The crematoria at Auschwitz couldn't keep up with the number of people being killed, so they started burying the dead in shallow graves and the atmosphere all around us started to smell. I was then told the Germans were piling the bodies into big stacks, dousing them with kerosene and setting them alight. Most of this information came from Mrs. Górecka but you could tell what was happening from the stench. In fact, everyone knew because it was so obvious and you should never believe anyone who says 'well, I never knew.' No, that's not the truth – it was unmistakeable.

I returned to Dąbrowa but my mother didn't want me attending school because the Germans would know when I turned 14, which is when you could be deported to work in Germany. The schools that remained open were very basic anyway, only teaching simple subjects. However, Maria Szulc organised a clandestine school, with classes of no more than three to five pupils held in different places at different times. It was risky and we tried not to be seen, hiding our books in pouches under our coats, while there would be one teacher for maths and another for biology etc. In-person lessons took place about once a week. Meanwhile, our rations were based on a coupon system but I don't think anyone could have lived off this alone. Most people cultivated little plots of land to grow things like vegetables. Also, a lot of stuff was traded on the black market.

With regards to Dąbrowa's Jewish people, the Germans had been quick to round them up and deport them, including our family dentist. My mother later told me Jewish parents had been told to send their children away first and they'd be following them soon afterwards... Dąbrowa was not part of the General Government but neither was it in the part of Poland seized by the Third Reich. It was a sliver of territory that fell into a kind of border/mixed category, albeit with the signs and placenames changed to German, so Dąbrowa became Dombrowa.[3] However, you could still speak Polish on the streets without being challenged. By contrast, you had to be careful in Katowice because it was within annexed territory and its name had been changed to Kattowitz. All signs and placenames had been changed to German and speaking Polish was not allowed in public, otherwise you'd get your face slapped. The Hitler Youth were also about and they were little terrors.

My mother eventually found work at a photography studio through a couple who were family friends. The lady had worked as an accountant at Maria Szulc's school and her husband was an artist who worked on retouching negatives. He taught my mother how to do retouching work and she caught on quickly, securing a job at this studio as a result. Dąbrowa originally had three studios but they'd been seized from their owners and combined into one business, with a Romanian woman put in charge. She was an alcoholic who loved Hitler. She also claimed to be a pure Aryan and that she'd been tested to make sure of it. Apparently, they'd taken blood from her left ear as part of the process! In fact, the Germans appeared to have a thing about left ears because the identity card, the Kennkarte, often included a photo of a person's left profile, with the ear clearly visible.

One day, this lady decided the studio's workforce should go to the cinema with her as a 'treat'. This caused some consternation because there was a boycott of the cinemas by Polish people and no one wanted to watch German newsreels or propaganda films. There was even a ditty that went something like this: 'The pigs sit in movies, while the Poles sit in Auschwitz.' Anyway, all employees had to attend and my mother came home, saying she felt ashamed and hoped nobody had spotted her. There were a few people – very few – who willingly claimed German ancestry and were considered traitors as a result. They received more rations and better treatment as Volksdeutsche. One of my aunts, Zofia Kuś, lived in Sosnowiec and her husband was taken to Gusen concentration camp. They had twins, a boy and a girl, who were about six years older than me. The Germans demanded Zofia claim Volksdeutsche status because they wanted the boy for the Wehrmacht.[4] She refused and they really gave her a grilling and called on her several times, saying her husband would be freed from the camp if she relented but Zofia categorically refused.

There was a day in 1943 when a neighbour and I were visiting a friend. There was a curfew, which meant you had to be careful about coming back on time. We were returning when it was getting dark and my neighbour's older sister raced over. 'What the hell are you doing walking around!' she exclaimed. 'Someone killed a German near here and things are not looking good.' The Germans were already knocking on doors, interrogating people and slapping faces but they didn't get to us. People started to worry and a rumour went around they'd take people out of our building and hang them on the poplar trees out back. Thank God this didn't happen. Several months later, we heard a shot and then someone moaning – another German soldier had been targeted and this time it was just outside our building. I'm not sure why they went for him because our resistance people usually took on the Gestapo or people like them, not ordinary troops. We turned off the lights and heard the Germans arrive and start their interrogations. There was quite a lot of commotion and it was very tense. Even our dog who always yapped at noises and strangers was silent.

There was another occasion when a rumour went around that the Germans were going to hang people from trees lining a nearby tramline. My mother sent me to Sosnowiec to stay with my aunt and I was later told ten people were indeed hanged, although I don't know who they were and I presume they'd been taken into Dąbrowa to be executed. A boy I knew was also murdered. He worked at a nearby foundry and, if the German foremen didn't like your behaviour, then your card was marked. Three marks meant you were taken to a concentration camp and this fellow got into some kind of trouble at the foundry, escaping into the General Government by using false papers. He entered a village where his papers were checked and found to be fake and he was taken to the side and shot.

Polish-language newspapers were produced by the Germans and ignored but some people had clandestine radios, so news from the wider world was getting through. However, I didn't know about Anders and the formation of the Polish II Corps or Monte Cassino, although we knew about the Allied air raids and sometimes heard aircraft high above making a kind of droning sound. We also heard about Katyn because the Germans published details about it, including the names of those they'd identified. The Soviet Union denied any responsibility for years to come. The Germans also highlighted their victories but not their growing number of defeats and there was one occasion when I was at a railway station and saw trains coming back filled with wounded from the Eastern Front. News about the destruction of the Warsaw Ghetto reached us in 1943 and then, more than a year later, details about the Warsaw Uprising.

The Russians finally neared us in early 1945. They used smaller aircraft that fired machine guns a lot and there wasn't too much destruction, although a bomb dropped by one of them struck a nearby backyard and made a big hole. You'd listen out for these aircraft if you needed to get water during the day and were safe after they flew away, although you still needed to keep your ears open. Five massive Tiger tanks parked near our building not long before the Germans retreated. 'Oh great,' we all thought. 'When those aircraft see these tanks, well that's when they'll really start dropping bombs.' These tanks were so tall the Germans could peer through our second-floor windows.[5] Thankfully, no planes came over and the Tigers soon moved on.

It was obvious the Germans were going to leave by the start of February. For safety, we'd go to the rear of the building at evening time, meeting our neighbours and sharing news. Some German units with horses, buggies and wagons had gathered around the back one evening and were preparing to go. I looked at the soldiers and realised they were roughly the same age as me, which was about 14-16. It was the first and only time I felt sorry for them because it was winter, it was cold and they were miserable – and they were just kids. It was also around this time I heard a new poem and its opening lines went like this: 'We are waiting for you, you Red Pestilence.'[6] I was worried because everyone was united against the Germans during the Occupation but what about the Red Army and their Polish supporters? Will they be for or against you? Are they really communists or not?

We returned to our part of the building that night and the Germans were gone by the time we woke up. The area was covered by snow and there wasn't a sound. This peace and quiet lasted for a whole day, with the Russians arriving the following morning. They were triumphant, chasing women and seizing bicycles and watches. They looked like a bunch of hobos but they were beautiful singers. I also recall a Red Army solider ordering a talented artist and painter we knew to hand over a briefcase he was carrying. The artist said no, so the soldier shot him and took the case. That was our liberation.

School had restarted under Maria Szulc in autumn 1945 and life was carrying on. There had been indications my father was still alive during the war, including anonymous correspondence from unusual places in Africa. We'd also receive small parcels containing goodies, with one sent from Turkey. A young Polish soldier suddenly arrived on our doorstep one day and told us my father was alive and had reached Britain, joining the PAF there. This fellow said my father had decided he couldn't return to Poland under communist control and that we now had a choice: join him in the West or stay put. The decision had to be immediate, so we packed a suitcase and left with the soldier who also visited a young woman and her daughter and told them similar details.

The only place we could cross into Germany was at Świnoujście[7] on the Baltic Sea, which had a small railway station and was packed with Germans heading west. However, there was only one train a day and Polish guards – members of the Railway Security Guard (SOK) – were walking around and keeping order. The train arrived the next day and rapidly filled up but it proved impossible for us to get on and the guards started worrying about our safety. They knew we wanted to join our relatives in the West and told us we could use their hut to sleep in, so all five of us went into one small room and slept on the floor. One of the guards said he'd make sure we'd get on the train the next time. It eventually arrived and, although there was lots of yelling and pushing, the guard kept his promise and managed to squeeze us aboard. We halted for several hours at one point and were all standing up like sardines, with my mother almost fainting. There was another occasion when we were almost detained by the Russians for being in their zone of Germany. However, my mother was very mild mannered and good at talking. 'We're going to Berlin to look for some relatives,' she said, an answer they accepted.

We reached a town near the border zone – I think it was called Heiligenstadt[8] – and noticed German refugees everywhere. I also saw some bodies, with people dying out in the fields. The Russians had stolen our only suitcase by then and we'd been without money and food for about three days. I also had a bad cough, probably from sleeping on floors every night. We were worried about crossing the border, when someone told us it was guarded by Germans who only carried sticks and took two-hour lunch breaks. There was a crowd of people walking through the woods and fields at around midday and that's how we made it over.

The young soldier accompanying us eventually found a telephone and contacted my father, notifying him we'd arrived. My father picked us up in a jeep the next day and it turned out he was stationed at Quakenbrück airfield, near Osnabrück, which is how we ended up there for about a year. The airbase hosted Polish squadrons under RAF command and personnel there often travelled into Belgium or Holland to buy bags of coffee and smuggle them over the German border. They'd exchange this for food from the local farmers, supplementing the British rations assigned to the Polish units. It was illegal but it worked very well. Anyway, my father soon explained what had happened to him during the war. He'd left Poland on one of the last aircraft leaving for Romania. He then went to France and was later based in Africa – somewhere like the French Congo.[9] He was stationed in Britain afterwards, including the far north of Scotland, and he was a technical officer responsible for the maintenance and repair of aircraft. There were times when pilots had accidents on landing and, while most of the pilots and aircrew were very brave and very dedicated, a few of them also tried to sabotage their machines so they wouldn't have to go on operations.

There was no school at Quakenbrück, so I learnt lessons from various people on the airbase. There were also some gliders and I started hanging around them. Those in charge eventually said I could have a go, pulling the glider using a machine. Then I did hops, with the machine pulling again and I did quite well. The main instructor said I'd need my father's permission to take off because I was only 15. After a week of crying – because my father initially refused – I managed to get his permission and ended up becoming a qualified glider pilot and I still have my certificates.

Our next stop was York in Britain and I attended a private school run by nuns and didn't know a word of English, so I had to start from scratch. York was beautiful and I saw a ruined cathedral one day and asked if it had been bombed. 'Oh no, that was Henry VIII,' someone said, explaining what had happened to the monasteries all those years ago. After York, we lived in Woodbridge, near Ipswich, and then London. My father decided we should emigrate to Canada on his demobilisation in 1947 and he had two choices: become an agricultural labourer or put a down a C$2,000 deposit and buy a farm. He decided to buy a farm near Wellanport on the Niagara Peninsula. The neighbours helped, lending us horses etc., and I also learnt how to milk a cow and drive a tractor. Looking back at life when a war is going around you… well, of course it changes you. Sometimes you'd stop and think maybe you'll be next but you had to carry on. In a way, it puts things into a certain perspective, especially when I hear people say: 'Oh, you shouldn't do this,' or 'this will damage you,' or 'you should see a counsellor immediately.' Occasionally, I want to say: 'Oh, for heaven's sake!'

ZBIGNIEW KOWALSKI

My father worked in the finance department of the Ministry of Defence and it was decided all military institutions in Warsaw were to be evacuated just before 5 September 1939. I remember he and I were waiting at the train station when my mother arrived together with my two sisters; she was wearing a Red Cross armband and told us she'd been mobilised for work in a hospital. My mother stayed behind and it would be many years before I saw her again. Our train left Warsaw and was bombed by Stukas soon after leaving the capital. Thankfully, they missed us and we reached the Lwów area on 14 September, which is where my aunt lived. My father decided it would be safer for my sisters to stay with her, while he and I continued south.

We had no idea our government was planning an evacuation via Romania at that stage, although we soon found ourselves heading towards the border town of Zaleszczyki.[1] The train stopped at a railway junction near a small village just before we got there, allowing passengers to buy some last-minute supplies. I stayed behind with an army captain just to keep an eye on things and was given a rifle with five bullets 'just in case'. Stukas suddenly came roaring overhead and dive bombed us. I remember the railway tracks being blasted into the air and then falling to the earth. Amazingly, none of the bombs damaged the train or the line it was on and, being a silly young teenager, I decided to return fire. The passengers came rushing back after the air strike, concerned the captain and I might have been hurt. They noticed my hand was bleeding – I'd cut it working the rifle bolt – and I had to keep telling them I wasn't hurt and it was merely a bad scratch. We eventually crossed into Romania and ended up in a border village that had a large Polish population, which meant the locals were friendly towards us and we stayed there for quite some time.

I clearly remember the day I was asked to join the Polish Army because it was 11 November. This is Armistice Day for many people but it's also Independence Day for Poles. My father and I attended a church service and an officer approached us. 'Don't you think it's about time you joined the army in France?' he asked me. Then he looked at my father who bowed his head in agreement and so that was it; I travelled to Bucharest and waited there for an official call-up through the Polish legation. My father accompanied me and we stayed in the Romanian capital for about three weeks until my official summons arrived. Then I went straight to the legation and was sworn in. They informed me the next shipment of Polish volunteers was leaving from Split, in what was then Yugoslavia, and our destination was Marseilles. I was given the appropriate documents and said goodbye to my father. He went onto serve as well and ended up working in a Polish military hospital in Britain after the Fall of France.

Our voyage was uneventful and the new recruits were put straight onto a train heading north soon after disembarking at Marseilles. They took us to a camp on a mountainside – just behind the town of Avignon – and it wasn't long before they gave us modern French uniforms, by which I mean the brown colour rather than the famous horizon-blue ones of the First World War. We also wore special brown berets because we were part of the 5th Malopolski Regiment, an infantry formation in the Polish 2nd Division. Our commanding officer arrived for an inspection one day and promptly 'volunteered' me for a heavy machine gun section. Our division was sent to northeast France after basic training and my unit was housed in an old farm that had holes in the roof. We slept on straw and would wake up covered in snow.

All of this was during the 'Phoney War' and our pay was miserable at one franc a day, which wasn't much even for the time. However, this region had a sizeable Polish immigrant community, with many Poles working in some nearby mines and one of these miners asked me to write a love letter for him to his sweetheart. Quite a lot of people were still illiterate in those days, so his request wasn't that unusual and he took me to the local café and bought me some warmed wine as payment.

He must have been happy with my effort because he told others and word soon spread that Zbigniew Kowalski wrote the best and most beautiful Polish letters. People would buy me drinks for helping write their letters and the more people who came, the more drinks I had!

Our rations were often poor quality and I'll give you an example of how bad it could get. I'd just been forwarded to a training centre to become a lance-corporal and there was an occasion when I was ordered to help unload some frozen rations. I noticed all the loaves were labelled '1918' and the meat stamped '1915' and realised the French were supplying us with frozen surplus left over from the First World War. The meat was so tough that we cut it into fine pieces and made a kind of goulash out of it.

Our sister division, the Polish 1st Grenadier Division, was north of Nancy when the Blitzkrieg started on 10 May 1940 and the plan was to rush us into the same theatre so we could fight together. They loaded us onto trains heading north but a decision was then made for us to back-track south to Besançon. This is a picturesque town in the Franche-Comté region, not far from the Swiss border, and we ended up billeted in an old garrison near some railway lines running into the town. Soon enough, some German aircraft flew over on their way to attack the nearby train station and we had no time to get our machine guns on their supports, so we used a fence. I suppose it was overly optimistic to fire but we were keen to score a victory.

Our battalion was deployed a little further north after a few days and my unit was sent to guard a bridge near Port-sur-Saône, a village in a mountain valley. We were dug in some way back from the bridge and saw the Germans prowling around on the opposite riverbank. We received orders to relocate to Montbéliard the next day – the main area of operations – and we heard lots of firing on our approach. Some Polish motorcyclists suddenly raced towards us and we flagged them down, asking what had happened. 'Run away!' they shouted. 'The battalion has surrendered!'

It was decided our unit would retreat with the motorcyclists and then regroup with any remnants of the battalion in some nearby woods. Here an officer gathered us together and laid out the facts as he knew them. Losing the battalion had been bad enough but we were shocked when he told us the Germans were approaching Paris. It meant France might fall and we'd known nothing about this. 'From now on you have three options,' he said. 'First, you can march through the mountains and head into Switzerland. Second, you can march to your homes in Poland.' That got a bitter laugh because the prospect of seeing our country now seemed more remote than ever. 'Third, you can join me and head south.' All of us decided to join him and, passing back through Besançon, we drove past some German sentries guarding a bridge. They even presented arms to us and I can only assume they had no idea we were Polish or that any of our units were still in the area.

Our luck ran out on a mountain road after one of our lorries broke down. There was a steep incline on one side of the road and the other side had a sharp drop, which meant none of the vehicles behind could pass. Our troops were trying to push this broken-down lorry into the escarpment when shots rang out and we all scattered. I ran into the woods and climbed a tree, waiting for the firing to die down. I returned when I thought it was safe but suddenly heard someone walking right behind me; it was German officer holding a revolver in one hand and a stick grenade in the other. I offered no resistance and walked slowly ahead of him back to the road, where I saw the rest of my unit had been rounded up. They all began shouting at me to drop my weapon and I didn't understand them at first. Then I realised my rifle was still in my hands and I set it on the ground, joining the others. We were no longer soldiers but prisoners of war.

The Germans were short of transport and drivers, so they made us use our remaining lorries and we returned north under the glare of enemy guards. However, we hadn't gone too far when they called a halt in an area that seemed a good place to try and make an escape. I also noted – and don't ask me where it had come from – a large vat of marmalade standing beside me, the type they used in the canteens. I decided this would offer the perfect distraction if I tipped it over and ran in the opposite direction. I did this when the Germans became engrossed in conversation and dashed down the roadside slope into some nearby woods. My heart was pounding but nothing happened; either the Germans hadn't seen me or didn't care I'd run off.

I heard everyone leave about ten or 15 minutes later and returned to the road, walking south and eventually coming across a barn that that seemed like a good place to stay overnight. Unfortunately, a dog started barking furiously just after I'd settled down and this alerted the farmer to my presence. He burst into the barn, demanding to know who I was and wanting me to leave straight away after I explained. 'The Germans are near and they'll execute me if they find you here,' he said. I begged him to let me to stay overnight. 'Okay,' he said, 'but you leave at 5am.' This farmer came back at dawn with some coffee and sandwiches and said 'bon voyage' after I finished my breakfast. That was my cue to leave.

I continued walking and reached a place called Morez and then went further into the hills, inadvertently nearing the Swiss border. I even came across a guard post and a Swiss soldier appeared, shouting for me to come over, but the idea of spending the rest of the war stuck in a neutral country didn't appeal to me. I turned away and continued walking until I reached a small town called Gex. Now starving, I found a restaurant and just stood in front of its window, looking at the customers eating and a man eventually came out and asked me who I was. I explained and he bought me a meal and then took me to a nearby nunnery, where they gave me a bed and I slept for 24 hours straight.

I decided to head for Marseilles, which I knew had a Polish consulate, and hoped they'd help me get out of France and into British territory. I was lucky enough to hitch a ride on a truck to Annecy, a town near a large lake and where I discovered crowds had gathered in its market square. The French tricolour was being lowered and many people were openly weeping, so I asked what had happened. They explained Marshal Pétain had signed an armistice and France was going to be divided in two.[2] It was alarming news that spurred me on and I was lucky enough to catch a bus at Ugine, a village not far from Annecy. The driver allowed me on for free and a Polish immigrant passenger gave me her sandwiches and some cash. This allowed me to pay for a bus ticket onto Albertville.

Unfortunately, I was arrested almost immediately on arriving in Albertville and taken to a police station, where I told them my story. I was wearing civilian clothes at this stage, although I can't remember who gave them to me or when I had changed into them. The policemen detaining me held an animated discussion, which was followed by a gendarme ordering me up and out of the building. Marching in front of him, I heard his footsteps becoming more distant and suddenly realised he was purposefully hanging back for me to escape. I saw some bushes and darted off through them.

From Albertville, I continued past Grenoble, down through Sisteron and then onto Manosque, a village with a railway junction. I managed to jump onto a goods train bound for Marseilles and reached the port city not too long afterwards. The Polish consulate was shut and a sign had been posted that said: 'Closed until victory'. I knew there was a Polish legation in Toulouse, so I decided to board a passenger train and try my luck there. The carriages were overcrowded, which stopped the inspectors from doing their job and that was good news for me because I didn't have enough money to buy a ticket. Then I noticed an airman talking in broken French about bombing the Germans and I shifted up to him, asking if he was Polish. 'Of course,' he said, introducing himself as Marian Jakubowski. 'We'll travel together and I'll make sure you're all right.'

We discovered the Polish legation was still open and they found us a place to stay. They also supplied us with passports and visas for Dutch Curacao, which was our cover because we'd head for whatever British territory was nearest once departing Vichy France. Our ship was to leave from Port-Vendres, just south of Perpignan, which we reached without any problems. We'd just boarded when some officials turned up and decided they didn't like the look of us. They threw us off the ship and we decided to try the overland route across Spain and into Portugal, where we hoped to find assistance to reach Britain. However, we knew it was going to be risky because Spain's fascist dictator General Francisco Franco had no love for Poles, some of whom had volunteered to fight for the Republicans in the Spanish Civil War. This included quite a few Polish communists I might add.

The terrain wasn't too difficult crossing into Spain but I took a tumble at one point and cut my leg quite badly. I hobbled to a stream and tried to stop the bleeding but it didn't work, so Jakubowski came over and told me to pull down my trousers. I thought this was a very odd request given the circumstances but I followed his instructions and he then urinated on my leg! It was very painful but it helped stopped the blood flowing.[3] Moving on, we eventually came across a woman washing some clothes in the river. Hungry and needing help, we stumbled towards her shouting 'Mademoiselle!' Unfortunately, three Spanish border guards appeared at that precise moment. We were immediately detained, although they proved to be pleasant fellows and shared their lunch with us. They took us to Figueres after their shift and marched us through the streets up to a castle,[4] where I was taken to see a captain and quickly explained who we were. I surrendered my passport and other documents and we were detained with three others, including some French foreign legionaries. The camp authorities hoisted the Spanish flag every morning in the castle courtyard and took it down every evening, performing a small ceremony in the process. We were forced to attend and shout: 'Viva España y Viva Franco!' It sounds ridiculous now but it was deadly serious at the time.

They eventually took us to the nearby station and put us onto a train, with someone telling me they were taking us to a concentration camp[5] and I decided to escape again. The train was moving very slowly south through the countryside when we stopped at around 4am at a station in Badalona, a small town near Barcelona. Some soldiers were patrolling the side of the station where dawn shadows fell, while a group of workmen were checking the rails on the lighter side. None of the guards had their eyes on me because it was still very early, so I took my chances and climbed down from the carriage and then casually walked past the labourers, reaching the platform's end and then exiting the station.

I'd been incredibly lucky and I walked for some time through fields of sugarcane. I stopped to rest and, after a while, picked myself up, dusted myself down and got onto the road to Barcelona. Nobody travelling that day seemed to notice me or stopped to ask me who I was. I discovered Barcelona had an honorary Polish consul – a Spanish businessman – and it was this fellow who opened the door and bluntly told me to return at 3pm. I walked around doing nothing until the appropriate hour. The consul's Polish wife opened the door this time and I explained who I was and she allowed me to stay at their house as documents were obtained. These papers allowed me to continue onto the Polish legation in Madrid.

I went straight to the legation after arriving in the Spanish capital and was interviewed by its head, only to be shocked by his attitude. 'Why did you bother coming?' he asked. 'Don't you know I've had all sorts of trouble from the likes of you?' I couldn't believe what I was hearing – I thought I'd break down and cry right there and then. Later, I discovered he was very pro-Franco and didn't want to annoy the regime by helping Poles who'd fought for the Allies. I spent three weeks waiting in Madrid, first at the legation and then at a Jesuit abbey on the city's outskirts. I returned to the legation after they'd organised documentation and passports for me and a couple of others. Together, we boarded a train bound for Portugal, although something went wrong at the Portuguese border and an official ordered us off the train before taking us to a nearby tavern. Thankfully, I was allowed to phone the legation and ask for assistance. They told me they'd send help and, sure enough, some policemen and a legation official turned up the next day. They stamped our documents and announced we could continue into Portugal.

We reached Lisbon without any bother and discovered the Polish legation there had already prepared more documents for us. Finally, we boarded a ship that took us to Gibraltar, where we transferred to a vessel that joined a convoy sailing deep into the Atlantic because of the U-boat threat. It was a very circuitous route, taking us past the USA's Eastern Seaboard, past Iceland and then down into Liverpool and it took roughly 20 days. I was immediately posted to Biggar in Scotland, which was where most Polish forces in Britain were based. My father was stationed at a military hospital nearby and he already knew I was okay because I'd sent word to him via the legation in Madrid. I was transferred into the 1st Highland Battalion formed out the surviving units that had fought at Narvik and our duties during this period included watching Scotland's east coast, preparing for a possible German invasion via Occupied Norway. We'd spend 24 hours on watch and then 24 hours back at our camp.

I was asked by my commanding officer to join a recruiting mission to Canada in summer 1941. We were desperate for more manpower and Canada and northern USA had large Polish communities that were obvious places to seek new recruits. I stayed out there for a year and returned to Britain in summer 1942. I re-joined my unit, which was now incorporated into the Polish 1st Armoured Division and we spent the next two years preparing for the liberation of Europe.[6] We weren't in the first wave to land in Normandy and our unit was transported over on 31 July 1944. The division came under the overall command of the Canadians and our morale was high and I thought – most of us thought – that we'd drive all the way through Germany and onto Warsaw. However, there was also great sadness at this time as my best friend Jozef Rudnik was killed on 8 August.[7] I took part in the ceremonies to mark the

60th anniversary of the Normandy landings and found the time to visit his grave. Mistakes were made as well. For example, we were hit from the air by our own side just before advancing on 14 August.[8] The lead aircraft dropped its bombs on our lines and the following aircraft copied this, their bombs falling into the dust thrown up by the first explosions. The jeep carrying our regimental standard was hit and only parts of its pole remained.

I was an NCO by now and in command of a three-inch mortar platoon. Our unit was part of a support group that helped with the taking of Hill 262N, close to Chambois. Anyway, my mortars were in a nearby wood and I was giving the order to fire and dropping my arm at the same time. I'd just done this when I heard a 'paf! paf!' sound. The first sniper's bullet pierced my helmet and scratched my head, while the second shot went straight through my arm. I was taken to a field hospital, where Canadians, Poles and Germans were all being treated and, from there, I was returned to Britain for a slow recovery. The damage was such that I was declared unfit for frontline duties.

I became a 2nd Lieutenant after being commissioned on 1 November 1944 and was asked to become an instructor, although I was also given an opportunity to focus on my education. In my heart, I knew my war was over and I applied for and was accepted into Oxford University. I studied law and followed this by studying economics in London. My mother and sisters were eventually allowed to visit me, while my father decided to return to Poland permanently in 1966. However, he found it hard to adjust to life under the communists and died soon afterwards. As for me, I married and settled in Britain. Years later, I was awarded the Croix de Guerre.

ZBIGNIEW MIECZKOWSKI

Our family estate was the manor at Dzierżanowo in central Poland, roughly 60 miles (95km) north of Warsaw, and I was born there in 1922. We were part of the Polish gentry and the family owned an estate that required a sizeable workforce to look after its horses and livestock. My father's immediate ancestors came from Cibórz, which was in German-occupied territory before Poland's independence in November 1918, while my mother's side, the Chamskis, came from the Russian partition of Poland. An uncle on my mother's side served with the Russian Guards, while an uncle on my father's side was in a Prussian unit raised in Danzig/Gdansk. However, lots of Polish families had members who fought on opposing sides during the First World War and we were all united when Poland achieved independence and had to fight the Bolsheviks in the 1920 Polish-Soviet war.

I had two sisters, Dana and Elżbeita, and my youth was a wonderful period. Apart from going to school, I really enjoyed riding and visiting relatives on their estates and vividly recall trips to the home of my father's cousin, Wacław Mieczkowski of Niedźwiedź. He collected artefacts, antiques and suits of armour, although these metal guardians scared me when I was very young because I thought they contained ghosts. Wacław also owned magnificent examples of furniture, paintings and porcelain and he was declared a 'Pole of the knightly estate' when the German occupation started. That meant he was allowed to stay put, despite the Nazi policy of 'Germanising' the region and evicting thousands of Polish people from their homes and land. Sadly, all that remained of old Niedźwiedź was destroyed when the Russians arrived and the communists took control just after the war.

My father was dedicated to running his estate and learning about the latest agricultural techniques. He often took over from the chauffeur, making everyone nervous by enthusiastically pointing at the fields and paying little attention to the road. Our chauffeur, Machnacki, became the post-war administrator of Dzierżanowo after the large farms and properties had been nationalised and he secretly assisted my parents. Other servants also helped and this included Latka, the coachman. He saved my mother and sisters' lives when the Gestapo came looking for them one day, while the cook, Matuszewski, helped feed the family after the Germans occupied Dzierżanowo.

People were uncertain about Poland's prospects in the period just before the war. True, we'd received guarantees from Britain and France that they'd attack Germany if Hitler invaded Poland but what if he took that gamble anyway? How would Britain and France really respond? The answers to these questions came at the start of September 1939 and, with the benefit of hindsight, our country's defensive strategy was flawed; we spread our mobilised forces too near the borders and across too much territory. However, the government wanted aggressive contact maintained with the enemy from the start, ensuring Britain and France honoured their commitments to Poland, which they did on 3 September. I suspect our government was also concerned Poland would become another Czechoslovakia if we failed to fight back and fight back hard. In the event, our forces were engaged but had little by way of defence lines to retreat to. Meanwhile, there was no offensive in the West, except for a small push by the French into the Saarland.

My departure from Poland was more through circumstance than by design. Dana was heavily pregnant when the Germans invaded and her husband, Stas Dziewanowski, had been called up and was fighting at the front. My father decided it would be best for Dana to go to Warsaw, where maternity care was much better. However, Machnacki had also been called up, so he asked me to do the driving and the journey wasn't too difficult because the roads were still comparatively clear at this stage. Sadly, Dana's husband was mortally wounded during the defence of Modlin and his daughter Zosia was born in Warsaw shortly after his death.

The PAF requisitioned the family car soon after my arrival in the capital and I threw my hat into the ring by volunteering to drive it. The offer was accepted, which meant I became a temporary chauffeur and it wasn't long before I was needed to take some officers east, to airfields untouched by Luftwaffe bombing. There had been talk of French fighter aircraft being flown into Poland but this proved to be wishful thinking. The Russians invaded on 17 September and an order to evacuate via Romania came through immediately afterwards, so we raced south and had soon crossed the border. I was processed with few questions asked and minimum paperwork requested, probably because Romania's bureaucracy was overwhelmed by the arrival of so many Poles all at once. They also classified me as a civilian refugee, which meant I could travel onto the Polish embassy in Bucharest without interruption.

I was keen to join the Polish forces being formed in France but I discovered the waiting time for my provisional passport was going to be about two months. Funds were not a problem at this stage because my father handed me a lot of cash before I left for Warsaw, possibly sensing my journey was going to be long and we might not see each other again. Thankfully, the Romanians were still happy to exchange my zloty at the normal rate. People today forget Poland's pre-war currency was quite strong and readily welcomed abroad and I was selling zloty on the black market after its exchange was officially ended by the Romanian authorities.

Getting around was made easier by my fluency in French, taught to me by my governess. It was the lingua franca of educated people across Europe in those days, including Romania, and there was an interesting incident when my knowledge of it came in handy. The Romanian police had been making money by requisitioning Polish military and government vehicles and selling them on and they were keen to get their hands on my father's car. In fact, I was forced to attend a local police station to prove the vehicle was mine to keep – that it was privately owned and didn't belong to the Polish government. However, I knew it was only a matter of time before they concocted a watertight excuse to seize it.

Standing outside the police station and mulling things over, I suddenly noticed a high-ranking Romanian Army officer. I raced over and, speaking in French, asked if he wanted to buy a car. I explained its condition and that I was its lawful owner, with all the necessary documents to prove it. Although taken aback by my sudden offer, it turned out he was looking to buy a car for his brother. High-ranking officers were treated like kings in Romania back then and there was no way the police could argue points of 'law' with this man and he brought their protestations to an abrupt end by advancing on the most senior policeman and landing a blow to his face. This army officer got the vehicle at a heavy discount from me, of course, but it was good to have some extra money in my pocket and get one over those corrupt policemen.

My temporary passport was eventually ready and I travelled by train to France overland via Yugoslavia and Italy, with both countries still neutral at that stage. However, I kept my mouth shut just to be on the safe side. I joined the Polish Army in France and was soon posted to an infantry unit based at a satellite camp near Coëtquidan in Brittany. The conditions were dreadful as our barracks were summer huts and the winter of 1939/40 was particularly harsh. It was also difficult to switch from my pleasant civilian clothes into the rough-and-ready uniform of a soldier. Incidentally, we were supplied with surplus materiel left over from the First World War and our weapons… well, we were initially trained with wooden sticks! I can laugh about that now but it was desperate stuff at the time.

I'd just missed an intake for officer cadet training, so I was sent on a machine gunner's course and promoted to lance-corporal instead. I then applied for officer cadet training with Polish armoured units and my request was accepted at the start of May, just before the Germans launched their Blitzkrieg of the West. A lot of our tanks and training facilities were in southern France and I made a quick stop in Paris on the way, meeting some family members who were also serving in Poland's armed forces.

The invasion of France started just as I reached my new unit and I soon found myself involved in the preparations to evacuate.[1] We were all shocked by the speed of the French collapse and my unit managed to reach Saint-Jean-de-Luz, near Bayonne, by taking various forms of transport until it had to march on foot. A boat was already waiting dockside, the *Sobieski*, and I had tears in my eyes on seeing this vessel; after so much chaos, we were greeted by a Polish ship with banners flying and trumpeters signalling. It was magnificent and a complete contrast to the defeatism we'd experienced over the previous weeks.

We eventually docked in Plymouth and were met by some charming ladies who gave us tea and biscuits before we were entrained and sent to Scotland. We had another wonderful greeting there and were deployed soon afterwards, helping guard Scotland's east coast because the British were worried about a secondary invasion from Occupied Norway.

My unit was held in reserve, guarding an area that would become a defence zone if the units ahead had been broken. There was very little equipment in Britain at this point because the country had lost an awful lot of materiel in France, although our particular situation was made easier because we'd managed to keep three French heavy machine guns. Technically, they should have been returned to the French under the terms of the armistice agreed between Pétain and Hitler and, when helping lug these things up steep slopes, I sometimes wished they had!

Our lives dramatically improved once things settled down in Scotland, including dances to attend and local ladies to meet during our free time. My first girlfriend tried writing a letter to me by using an English/Polish dictionary and I still have it, while my English at this stage was not particularly good and I probably failed to learn it as quickly as I should have done. My second girlfriend spoke French very well, so my incentive to learn English with her was not so great. In addition, my education was now focussed on meeting the standards to become an officer and I attended a Polish Army school in Scotland to achieve this.

There were plenty of military exercises during our time in Britain and the training for what became the Polish 1st Armoured Division was comprehensive. The Poles worked with several tank types as the years progressed because the British were constantly developing their armour and trying to produce better machines. However, we were primarily equipped with the US-designed Sherman by 1944, although it wasn't a particularly good tank at that stage of the war because it was outgunned and outclassed by most enemy counterparts. It was almost useless against the dreaded Tiger and destroying one of those machines was very tricky because the best spot – perhaps the only spot – our shells could penetrate its armour was at the rear. Unfortunately, there was no way to ask the enemy to kindly do the decent thing and turn around for us!

The only good thing about the Sherman was its soft armour, by which I mean enemy shells often passed straight through without a lethal splintering effect. That meant one or two people might be killed,

Right: Map of Interwar Poland partitioned. The absence of arrows emanating from the USSR is an interesting oversight. Source: McInnis, Edgar, *The War, First Year* (Oxford University Press, 1940)

Below: German soldiers torch a Polish village during the September 1939 campaign. Polish civilians faced extreme violence from the moment the war started. (Author's collection)

A wrecked PAF aircraft. Polish pilots put up a brave-but-forlorn fight against overwhelming enemy numbers. (US National Archives)

Contemplating defeat. The Germans captured around 420,000 Polish soldiers, with only a few allowed to return home. Most were used for forced labour in the Third Reich and thousands died as a result. (Author's collection)

The Luftwaffe launched indiscriminate airstrikes across Poland during the September 1939 campaign. Travelling along the roads became dangerous as a result, with many horrifying sights visible along the way. (Author's collection)

Smiles all round as German and Soviet allies meet in Poland. (Author's collection)

Warsaw formally surrendered on 28 September 1939, with German forces entering the Polish capital from 1 October. (Author's collection)

Polish Prime Minister and Commander-in-Chief General Władysław Sikroski and President Władysław Raczkiewicz review the Polish 1st Division in France on 3 May 1940. (Narodowe Archiwum Cyfrowe)

Life continues in Warsaw amid the damage of war. The city lay within the General Government, a German-created fiefdom designed for ruthless exploitation. (Author's collection)

German soldiers check civilian papers somewhere in Occupied Europe. In Poland, having the correct paperwork – or good forgeries – could mean the difference between life or death. (Author's collection)

Rations were cut to near-starvation levels in German-Occupied Poland and the youngest often suffered most. (Author's collection)

The chances of survival in German captivity often depended on the camp. All were grim but some were exceptionally vicious and their gruesome reputations well known. (Author's collection)

Above and right: Photos of Auschwitz I taken during author's site visit in 2004. This part of the camp complex was where the first gassings took place. The Auschwitz II-Birkenau death camp was built 1.5 miles (2.5km) to the east. More than 1.1 million people had been murdered at Auschwitz by the time it was liberated on 27 January 1945. (Author's collection)

Top: Equipped with the Wellington bomber, four PAF squadrons played a vital role in RAF Bomber Command's efforts from 1941 into 1943. (Author's collection)

Above: Men of 305 Squadron pose in front of a Wellington. The heavy casualties proved unsustainable for the PAF and only 300 Squadron would remain with Bomber Command until war's end. (Pilsudski Institute of London)

Left: White-hot shrapnel and tracer fills the night sky over a heavily-defended German target, almost guaranteeing a bomber will suffer some form of damage. (Author's collection)

Between 1 million and 2 million Polish citizens were deported into or conscripted by the Soviet Union and they died by the thousand. These Polish children have all been orphaned. (Pilsudski Institute of London)

Anders' forces were formed after the 'normalisation' of diplomatic relations between Poland and the USSR in July 1941. Conditions were harsh during winter 1941/42 and the Soviet-supplied equipment was basic. (Narodowe Archiwum Cyfrowe)

Polish II Corps artillerymen prep a 5.5-inch gun in the Italian theatre. The first attack on Monte Cassino was preceded by massive front-wide barrage. (Author's collection)

Above: The Polish flag and Union Jack were raised at the abbey of Monte Cassino, marking the Polish II Corps' famous victory. Many more battles were to come. (Narodowe Archiwum Cyfrowe)

Left: A Polish signals unit at work during the Battle of Monte Cassino. A lot of effort was needed to establish decent communications in this unforgiving terrain. (Pilsudski Institute of London)

Anders and senior subordinates inspect the battlefield of Monte Cassino. The monastery is in the background, reduced to an imposing hulk during the fighting. (Pilsudski Institute of London)

Above: Taking the salute of Polish II Corps soldiers in Italy in September 1944. Anders (left), General Kazimierz Sosnkowski (centre), Field Marshal Alexander (just behind) and King George VI (right). (Pilsudski Institute of London)

Right: A Sherman tank from the Polish II Corps' 4th Armoured Regiment. Probably the Western Allies' best tank when introduced in 1942, it was becoming outclassed by summer 1944. (Author's collection)

Polish Prime Minister Stanisław Mikołajczyk (right) meets Roosevelt on 7 June 1944. 'I will see to it that Poland does not come out of the war injured,' the US President claimed. (Author's collection)

Above left: General Stanisław Maczek looks at the camera as his subordinates ponder a problem. The Polish 1st Armoured Division won its spurs during the battle to close the Falaise Pocket. (Narodowe Archiwum Cyfrowe)

Above right: Infantry support was vital for the Polish 1st Armoured Division, although manpower was a perennial problem. This Pole is firing a Bren light machine gun. (Narodowe Archiwum Cyfrowe)

Remains of German vehicles in the Falaise Pocket. The carnage was such that pilots could smell the decay hundreds of feet above. (US National Archives)

Farewell parade of the 1st Independent Parachute Brigade in Leven, Scotland, in June 1944. The unit joined the ill-fated Arnhem campaign in mid-September. (Narodowe Archiwum Cyfrowe)

A clandestine AK unit parades in the months before the Red Army swept into Poland and neared Warsaw. There was a dearth of available weaponry before the uprising. (Author's collection)

A badly-wounded AK soldier receives medical assistance during the Warsaw Uprising from August-October 1944. (Narodowe Archiwum Cyfrowe)

Civilians are evicted from Warsaw in the wake of the Uprising. Many thousands were sent to German concentration camps or deported to work in the Third Reich. Behind them, German demolition teams started destroying all that remained of the city. (Narodowe Archiwum Cyfrowe)

A wirephoto of Warsaw central railway station taken not long after the city's liberation in 1945. The Polish capital had been reduced to a shell of its former self. (Author's collection)

Poland's post-war fate was finally sealed at the February 1945 Yalta Conference, with Churchill and a visibly-ailing Roosevelt accepting almost all of Stalin's demands concerning Poland. (US National Archives)

Liberated prisoners at Sandbostel. Thousands died in the war's final months as the Germans evacuated their camps in the east and force-marched prisoners into overcrowded western camps. (Author's collection)

The remains of Hitler's Berghof mansion. VE Day occurred 8/9 May 1945, although the Poles had little to celebrate in the aftermath. Their country was now dominated by Stalin's puppets and decades of Soviet control would follow. (Author's collection)

Two faces from the Warsaw Uprising Memorial. (Author's collection)

INTERVIEWEES

Stanislaw Adam

Alexander Bogden

Barbara Buczek and Ludwik Januszewski

Antoni Budzynski

Jerzy Cynk

Antoni Fedorowicz

Grażyna Kopeć

Zbigniew Kowalski

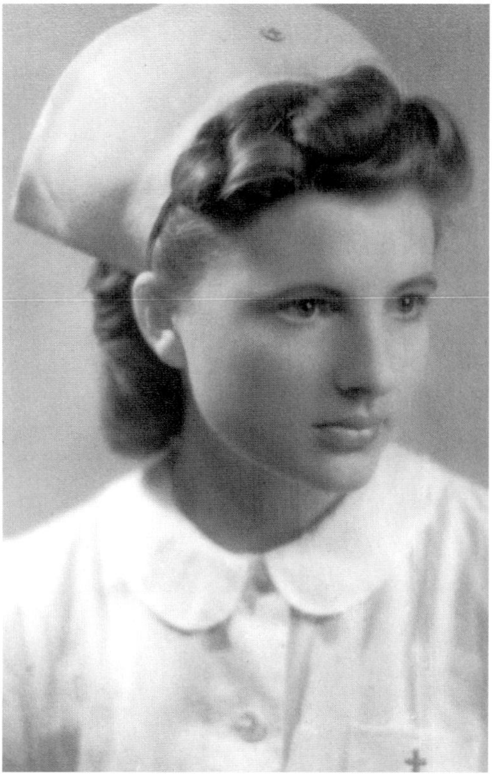

Elizabeth Piekarski

Marcelino Ostrowski

Alicja Sieciechowicz

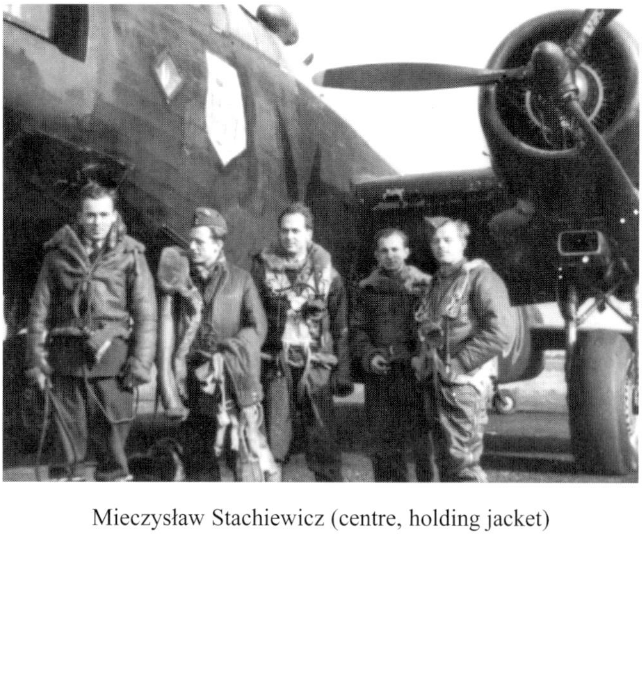

Mieczysław Stachiewicz (centre, holding jacket)

rather than the entire crew. However, an intense heat was also created and this could radiate out and burn the occupants or cause items in the tank to combust, including ammunition. It meant a crew usually had to get out fast after being hit and I saw the results of burns first hand on 18 August 1944 during the closing of the Falaise Gap. We were receiving incoming fire from a Tiger tank using some woods as cover about 1,000 metres away and the squadron commander ordered Slomki, or Straws, to the front. This was our call-sign for the Firefly tank, an upgraded Sherman equipped with a British 17-pounder that could engage the enemy at longer ranges and packed a greater punch because of the gun's higher velocity. Anyway, a Straw had just passed my vehicle when there was a colossal bang that left me feeling like I'd just been bashed on the head.

The Straw had taken a direct hit and its commander bailed out, closely followed by its gunner, Corporal Oleksy. The radio operator was already dead but the other two – the driver and loader – were still alive. However, they were unable to escape because the vehicle's turret was not straightened. In training, gunners were always told to straighten the turret if the crew needed to bail out but in combat and having just received a direct hit… well, it's not so easy. Oleksy quickly realised his mistake and rushed back, scrambling up the tank and moving the turret with the hand knob. This allowed his other crewmates to save themselves. I saw Oleksy the next day and his face was unrecognisable because it had been burnt by the heat radiating from the shell penetration. His situation was very difficult because there were no medical supplies at this stage and we couldn't send serious cases like his to the rear. The pain must have been excruciating but he survived and was later awarded the Virtuti Militari.

But I'm now getting slightly ahead of myself. As I said, our training was comprehensive and continued almost until we departed for Normandy, with the 1st Armoured Division transported over the English Channel at the start of August 1944. We were rapidly integrated into the Canadian II Corps, which was part of the First Canadian Army. British and Canadian efforts in Normandy had largely been contained by the Germans across June and July but the enemy's front was slowly cracking by the time we arrived. Just as importantly, the Americans were starting to achieve excellent results in western Normandy.[2]

Our first engagement was on 8 August and it was a beautiful day, with breakfast cooked in the field as we waited to attack. The plan was for Allied heavy bombers to hit the enemy first, softening up our path ahead, but their strike fell short and fell into our lines. Despite the bombers' failure, the order to advance remained in place and my regiment, the 2nd Armoured, sent in its 1st Squadron and 2nd Squadrons into to battle. My unit, the 3rd Squadron, was held in reserve. Our units advanced under fire from three sides and the Germans knocked out 26 tanks from our regiment alone in about 45 minutes. It was horrible.

The Falaise Pocket took shape not long after our initial operations and an order came through for the Poles to advance on Chambois. We had two rivers to cross and, using a rather brilliant plan, a battlegroup comprising our regiment, the 8th Infantry Battalion and some support units advanced in a formation that mimicked a German column in transit.[3] We approached the first crossing at night and the enemy gave us road priority! Perhaps they couldn't believe Allied units had penetrated their positions to such a depth. A Kübelwagen[4] swung into view at the second crossing and two enemy officers jumped out, approaching a friend's tank just ahead of me. They started shouting at him, demanding to know what kind of panzer he was driving and they were shot down as a result. Thankfully, there were no sounds of alarm in response and we continued through enemy territory.

Unfortunately, it wasn't long before we became uncertain of our direction and someone found a French farmer and asked him for directions to Chambois. Maybe this fellow didn't understand us properly, or maybe it was our Polish accents, but he mistakenly thought we wanted to go to Les Champeaux and directed us there instead. On arrival, we stumbled across the 2nd Panzer Division's headquarters and forced it to scatter. This division had been involved in the invasion of Poland in 1939, so it was a slice of revenge that tasted very sweet indeed. However, we now realised our battlegroup was completely in the wrong place and it didn't take long for the enemy to counter-attack at full force.

It was one Polish tank regiment and an accompanying infantry battalion against what, at first glance, seemed like poor odds for us. Adding to our difficulties were the narrow roads and the surrounding countryside being wooded and hilly, plus there was a railway embankment that interrupted our views. My tank was firing to the left of the German attacks and the 2nd Squadron was able to fully deploy a little bit later, helping ease the situation. We also suffered a ground attack by the USAAF. They probably assumed we were an enemy formation and I suppose their confusion was understandable because we were out of position and well behind enemy frontlines. Thankfully, the attack didn't cause too many casualties among those in the tanks but our infantry suffered some losses.

A wounded German was lying near my position before this air strike. Part of his leg – maybe all of it – had been shot off and he was trying to staunch the bleeding by using a large duvet that was originally white and soon coloured red by his blood. There was nothing we could do to help because we were in the middle of a fight and had no supplies or medical personnel available. The USAAF then hit us and we looked to see how he was doing afterwards but he'd been blown to pieces.

It was now a good time to disengage and get moving and the battlegroup started falling back. Three enemy lorries were spotted as we were driving along one of the narrow roads and one of our squadrons opened fire. The resulting explosions were terrific because these vehicles had been carrying ammunition and we were forced to wait until the pyrotechnics ceased. We then approached the wrecked vehicles and pushed them out of the way, travelling for several more miles before our petrol started running out. We paused for a resupply column to reach us, while wounded soldiers were now being treated by some captured German doctors and medical orderlies but, as I've said, we lacked the necessary supplies and personnel to properly assist.

People took advantage of the lull to cook some hot food because everyone had been living off sandwiches for quite some time. Each tank had a little stove for tea, soup or other rations but our vehicle had run out of spare water and a crewmate and I went to collect some from a couple of huts I'd spotted in the distance, just down a slope. The huts were deserted but we found a couple of buckets and filled them with water from a nearby pond. Heading back up the slope, we heard the sound of an engine approaching; two Germans suddenly appeared on a motorcycle and we swung about, raised our guns and forced them to a stop. They promptly surrendered and handed over their weapons.

I pointed to the buckets because they could do the heavy lifting as far as I was concerned. Then I ordered them to get moving in German and threw in a couple of stern Polish words for added effect. One of the prisoners stopped, looking bemused and suddenly spoke to me in Polish: ‘Sorry Sir, but are you a Pole?’ It turned out he was a Silesian who’d been forcibly conscripted, which meant I’d just captured a fellow countryman. This chap later explained he was a driver and we immediately recruited him and put him in one of our uniforms. He was ordered to drive a jeep because one of our men who performed this task had been wounded.

In fact, quite a few of Silesians joined us during the Northwest Europe campaign and the division established a training school after the Allied advance came to a halt in the winter of 1944/45. I became the commander of a week-long gunnery course and about 40 Silesians were among the intake, some of whom joined us after being taken prisoner, while others had fled their Wehrmacht units specifically to reach us. These men were important replacements because we had almost no reserves left and they were excellent soldiers. However, they behaved differently when carrying out instructions by retaining German modes of discipline, such as clicking their heels together when receiving an order.

But back to Normandy. We’d received more petrol and supplies and our formation prepared itself to move to the Mont-Ormel ridge, although we came under fire at this point and the 1st Troop’s commander was killed. We discovered the position on Hill 262 North was a good one and later learnt it had been carefully chosen by General Maczek, although he was physically absent from the battle. He clearly had a superb eye for geography just from map reading alone and he realised parts of Hill 262 – the contours resembling a mace, or maczuga – would give us excellent fields of fire. He was correct: the Mace allowed us to dominate the countryside for miles around but we had little time in which to prepare as the enemy was soon attacking us at full force.

We represented a threat because the Germans’ main exit routes through the Falaise Gap out of the Falaise Pocket skirted our positions. However, not everything coming our way wanted to engage us and a lot of the enemy tried to avoid battle. We attempted to pin these units down as well, hoping to stall as many German formations as possible but it was a difficult task given their large numbers. In addition, we didn’t know gaps still existed to our south. The attacks on our positions came from the west and east – inside and outside of the pocket. The enemy was desperate to push us aside and screen their retreating forces, although the Germans were hampered by having to fight uphill. Their infantry also pressed forward to join the attacks and they were tough opponents.

Some 2nd SS Panzer Division units were striking us from behind and, at one point, my squadron moved up to help repel them. The chap who commanded our mechanised artillery was standing next to our tanks, seeking a better position to spot for his guns. A small enemy panzer suddenly pushed through and he was gunned down. We immediately engaged but our infantry was very close. This German tank reversed and ran over an infantryman's legs in the process and then it caught fire. Stuck under the tracks, the man screamed for help and his cries were simply chilling and they lasted for some time but there was nothing we would do because we couldn't break position.

Canadian units arrived in force around midday on 21 August, with the fighting ending that afternoon. Our relationship with the Canadians was very good, despite there being some language problems now and then. A lot of our men had been killed or wounded during our battle to close the Falaise Gap, including some good friends of mine. My driver and gunner went to inspect some of the destruction after the action and they described it as terrible: the bodies of men and horses were everywhere and, in the August heat, the smell was indescribable. The Germans were still heavily dependent on horse-drawn transport in 1944, using it to help move artillery, ammunition and supplies. Our unit was stuck in its position for some time because there was so much devastation around us and a bulldozer eventually arrived and helped push the carnage aside. I'm told pilots flying over the Falaise Pocket could also smell the battle's stench in their cockpits.

Incidentally, our aircraft were very helpful throughout the campaign, particularly machines like the ground-attack Typhoon. The little observer aircraft that helped direct artillery fire were also very helpful.[5] We liked seeing them because the enemy's heavy guns always fell silent whenever one flew towards their positions. The Germans were worried about being spotted and hit by counter-battery fire or air strikes. However, it was time to watch out when the little aircraft turned back because it meant the enemy would resume his shelling.

The German retreat out of France and into the Low Countries came not long after Falaise. The French never hung out their flags – possibly because they were frightened the Germans might return and exact revenge – but the Belgians and Dutch always seemed eager to put up their bunting. That made life a bit easier for our reconnaissance units because it helped them identify which villages and towns the enemy had already retreated through. Still, the Germans would put up stiff resistance every now and then, often in the form of a well-placed 88mm anti-tank gun that would try to hold us up and cause maximum casualties. They also put aerial bombs under the roads and detonated them beneath our tanks, rather like the improvised explosive devices used more recently in Afghanistan and Iraq. Sometimes, the resistance was much broader and involved heavier fighting and this happened at Ypres, the town that saw so much devastation during the First World War. We also continued listening to news about the Warsaw Uprising on the radio, thinking a great deal about what it meant for us personally and Poland as a whole.

The Western Front started to settle by late autumn, after we'd advanced well into the Netherlands and liberated several important places, including the city of Breda. The Dutch countryside was flat and often waterlogged, with plenty of canals and other features to slow us down even further. Our next task was to help guard the River Maas, monitoring and engaging enemy positions across it, while I was fully commissioned during this period as well. There was a sudden move around Christmas time in response to the Battle of the Bulge but this crisis soon passed and we returned to watching the enemy over the Maas. I was in command of a troop of tanks in 1st Squadron and recall our efforts on Kapelsche Veer.[6] Three tanks had sunk into the mud there and were being manned as pillboxes, with the crews regularly rotated. There was no heating in the tanks because the batteries were long dead and everything around us was covered with snow, which meant we spent most of our time feeling half frozen.

A humorous incident occurred a little later at Bockhoven, when my troop was seconded to a Canadian unit. Their battalion commander wanted us to destroy a bunker on the other side of the river and I positioned my tanks on an embankment. Then I went to observe the enemy's frontage from the loft of an adjacent building. Unfortunately, the Canadian command post was in a nearby house made from rickety timbers and the shockwaves caused by our salvos caused its roof to collapse. Thankfully, nobody was hurt but our services were suddenly no longer required!

The drive into Germany started in the second week of April 1945, with the ground still saturated in many parts of our sector. In fact, the rivers and canals proved serious obstacles and almost all the bridges had been blown by the enemy. By 12 April, part of our division was using the Dutch village of Ter Apel as a base from which to scout the territory near Germany or just inside it. News of a camp just across the border at a place called Oberlangen reached Lieutenant-Colonel Koszutski and he was keen to investigate, although there was nothing much by way of men or machines available because all units had been committed to other operations. So, he rustled up a tank, some jeeps and a few motorbikes and had them go investigate. They were amazed to discover more than 1,700 women from the AK were being held at this camp as prisoners of war. They'd fought in the Warsaw Uprising and it was a beautiful moment – Poles liberating Poles on German soil.

The enemy was now on the verge of defeat but it's important to remember the fighting was still heavy. For example, there were particularly tough clashes at Bourtange and Rhede and sometimes it appeared the enemy was going to contest every mile. Rhede was particularly grim and about 80 Germans were killed there. There wasn't much enemy armour as most German tanks were either out of action or out of fuel. They relied on their anti-tank capacity, including anti-tank guns, Panzerschreck bazookas and Panzerfausts, which was an early type of rocket-propelled grenade. There were also the usual road-side bombs and booby traps to worry about.

German resistance finally collapsed in late April and early May and this is when we made good progress through enemy territory. Our war ended with Wilhelmshaven's capitulation on the North Sea on 6 May, with Colonel Antoni Grudziński overseeing the formal surrender.[7] It was an important location as it contained German naval shipyards and a series of dry-docks that helped build and repair U-boats. It was also a base for many Kriegsmarine surface vessels and Wilhelmshaven was heavily defended as a result, with almost 40,000 Germans taken into captivity on its surrender.

All of us were relieved when the war officially ended on 8 May because we were tired of the fighting. However, we also knew post-war Poland was going to be dominated by the communists and it meant our efforts to preserve a free and democratic Poland had failed. Our country was badly let down on the international stage; I think Roosevelt admired Stalin and there was little Churchill could do about their decisions. Stalin got everything he wanted and the Polish communists – and their Soviet masters – got on with murdering those they considered a threat, including former AK members, the ex-landowners and many of the surviving intelligentsia.

The Polish 1st Armoured Division was incorporated into what became the British Army of the Rhine until our demobilisation in 1947. This two-year period involved some good times and I did quite a bit of horse riding, helping represent the division in show-jumping contests. Incidentally, one of our riders was Colonel Michał Gutowski who'd been a member of the Polish equestrian team at the 1936 Berlin Olympics. I also managed to contact my family; both my sisters took part in the Warsaw Uprising, with Elżbeita marrying a doctor who ran a hospital during the fighting. He also helped Dana after she'd been injured by a wall collapsing on her. Elżbeita lived in Lodz after the war, while Dana remarried and lived in Sopot. My parents were evicted from Dzierżanowo and they managed to get by with assistance from family and friends, including former servants. However, my father's health was poor and he died in 1954. I was unable to attend his funeral because Poland was still under the control of a Stalinist regime, while my mother died in 1965.

I resettled in Britain after my demobilisation. Most of us knew heading home was too risky because of the communists but some people needed to return because their families were struggling. I initially gravitated to London and rented a place at a very good address, albeit with a major catch: the 'property' was a disused lift on the top floor, positioned next to a bathroom! My first jobs were varied and included selling sandwiches and tea from a mobile canteen and a stint at an ice cream factory. I eventually found work in the packaging industry and worked for the Douglas Company, although I went onto establish my own business in this sector.

My first opportunity to visit post-war Poland was through the Douglas Company after it had been purchased by the Food Machinery and Chemical Corporation (FMC), which had numerous branches and subsidiaries in various countries. I attended a trade fair in Poznan in 1958, representing some Belgian factories under the FMC umbrella.

That trip was the first occasion when I could meet my family and it was wonderful, although the Polish secret police monitored my movements and I was interviewed by them at length at their Mostowski Palace headquarters in Warsaw. I was surprised by their knowledge of my family and our pre-war lives. I travelled back regularly over the coming years and brought consumer products that were almost impossible to buy behind the Iron Curtain. Back in Britain, I sought to increase my circle of English friends and met Caroline the daughter of Lord and Lady Grenfell in 1963. We married in 1964 and have a son and a daughter.

MARCELINO OSTROWSKI

You could say I'm a multinational because I hold Canadian, Brazilian and Polish citizenships and the cause of this stretches back to my grandfather's time. He went to university in St. Petersburg during the Tsarist era because the Russians had closed the universities in Congress Poland.[1] He was a clever fellow and became a financial minister but the Tsarist security agencies started closing in on him for political reasons sometime around 1900. My grandfather and his family emigrated in response, staying in Britain until their right to stay was eventually rejected. He then took the family to Brazil, with one of his sons born on the ship during the voyage. It meant my uncle became a British citizen and, incidentally, he received call-up papers from the British embassy in Brazil during the Second World War – just because he was born on a British-registered vessel! He was around 40 by then and the embassy quickly realised it had been a mistake, so he was excused service.

The family settled in southern Brazil near Curitiba, the capital of Paraná state. My grandfather started out by planting an orange orchard and setting up lots of beehives. In fact, producing honey became the main part of the family's business and we did quite well. My father was about seven when he arrived in Brazil and he eventually found work with a Brazilian railway company. He was in charge of around 20 workers and they'd go into the forests to cut down a special type of oak, the wood from which is very dense and was perfect for constructing the train carriages built at that time.

I was born in a place called Rebouças and attended a local school established by my grandfather and father. I was there for about three or four years before attending a high school that prepared its pupils for entry into university. The threat of war was growing in Europe by then and a strong fifth column of Germans started to make their presence felt in Brazil. In fact, one of our neighbours was a German and he used to come around every so often to have strong tea, chimarrão, with my father. They'd sometimes get into arguments and this man got very angry on one occasion. 'We're going to hang you all when we take over Brazil!' he shouted. I heard this and it was a real shock to me.

I was studying economics at the university in Curitiba by 1941 and one of my friends there happened to be an English guy. He'd been born in Britain and had just received his call up papers and was preparing to leave. 'I'll come with you,' I said. I talked it over with my brother Edmund and he wanted to go as well, although we soon realised a person couldn't just leave Brazil for Britain. Our country remained under the influence of the German fifth column and President Getúlio Vargas still leant towards the Axis. There were also strict neutrality laws that Brazil wanted to maintain. Anyway, I managed to gather my documents – including my passport etc. – and presented myself at the Polish consulate in Curitiba. The consul made a big secret out of things, not even letting his secretary know the details of what we'd discussed. We didn't tell the family our plans either because, while my father would have supported us, my mother would have almost certainly objected.

We started our journey by taking a 'trip' to Uruguay during the next university break and, from there, travelled into Argentina and then boarded a ship for Britain. I wrote an explanatory letter to my parents just before leaving and I also wrote to the Polish consul, asking him to visit them and talk things over. Incidentally, Brazil was firmly in the Allied camp a year or so later, having declared war on Germany.[2] I presented myself at the Brazilian embassy in London not long afterwards, telling them I was a Brazilian citizen in the PAF. I was worried about a clash of interests and the possibility of being declared a deserter by default. The ambassador promised to look into the matter and eventually referred me to a treaty signed between Britain and the Empire of Brazil at some point in the 19th Century. Under its terms, Brazilian or British citizens fighting for the armed forces of either nation was not only permissible but counted as military service by the two countries should they be at war against a common enemy. To cut a long story short, the embassy told me to stay put and gave me the certificates I needed.

I didn't arrive in Britain without any military experience whatsoever. Before the war, students entering Brazilian universities were automatically enrolled as military cadets; you'd study and serve at the same time and, on graduation, were automatically awarded the rank of 2nd Lieutenant. Quite a few people went onto serve in the armed forces but most of us went into business etc. The important thing was all graduates left university with some form of military training, myself included. So, it was a little frustrating when I reached the Polish forces in Scotland because they had me do basic training all over again.

I was soon assigned to the 67th Battalion of the 16th Brigade and my unit used Churchill tanks – slow-moving but well-protected machines. However, I wasn't with the tanks for too long because I'd volunteered for the air force and was transferred into the PAF for basic training in Blackpool three months later. They really needed air gunners at this stage, so I took a three-month air gunnery course and was then forwarded to an Operational Conversion Unit. I joined 301 Squadron after another three months and my first mission was the 1,000-bomber raid on Cologne on the night of 30/31 May 1942.

The Wellington was the best British bomber available until the Halifax and Lancaster types were introduced and could carry a bomb load comparable to a B17 Flying Fortress. Because I've always been statistically minded, I noted 32 crews were on the roster when our crew arrived. Within ten months, only 1.5 crews remained and most of this was due to losses – either from enemy action or because of mechanical failure. However, some were shot down and later reported captured, while others were rotated out after their tours were completed. My squadron was eventually stood down in April 1943 and converted into what became No.1586 Flight, which was transferred to Brindisi, southern Italy, for special operations. This included supply drops during the Warsaw Uprising, while it was reformed again as 301 Squadron towards the end of the war.[3]

The tail gunner occupied a dangerous position because night fighters often targeted the bomber's rear first. The reason for this was simple: destroy the rear guns and the enemy can attack without the threat of return fire, which meant rear gunners had to pay attention all the time.

I had two encounters with night fighters and I saw them closing-in from quite a distance on both occasions. The big problem was the lack of defence because our aircraft were designed for dropping bombs and certainly not aerial combat. We had four Brownings in the rear, while enemy night fighters usually had cannons in the nose and four machine guns across the wings. Not only that but a night fighter's weapons could score hits at a range of almost 800 yards (730 metres), while our Brownings were good for about 400 yards (365 metres). That meant the bomber had limited options when engaged; the pilot could either break off or lure the enemy closer, allowing the tail gunner to fire at a shorter range in the hopes of shooting him down.

The pilot and tail gunner worked in unison during an encounter and we trained many hours for this, with the gunner requesting the aircraft move left, right, up or down to help get the best angle of attack. Photos were automatically taken when the Brownings were fired and these allowed us to study any encounter afterwards, observing what went right and what went wrong. The two encounters I experienced went well because the attackers fell away on each occasion. One of them was a Ju88 and I'm almost certain I scored a hit because he immediately banked down into the clouds. In total, I completed 30 missions and had two cancelled – one because of technical issues and the other because a recall order was received over the Netherlands.

You needed a photo of the bombs falling towards the target for your mission to count, with a flash going off and a series of pictures automatically taken as the bombs fell. You would be considered a 'freeman' of a city or target if you completed three missions over them and I became a 'freeman' of Bremen, Essen, Hamburg, Dusseldorf and a few other places. There was also a mission against Turin and the defences were noticeably lighter and I don't think the Italians were expecting us. It was a very different over Germany's urban areas and industrial regions like the Ruhr Valley because they were heavily defended. They even had anti-aircraft batteries that came with synchronised searchlights and getting picked out by the beams was a terrible experience. We got caught once and our pilot started performing evasive manoeuvres, taking the aircraft down until we were flying over the rooftops. We escaped but our machine suffered quite a lot of damage from shrapnel. In fact, shrapnel was a very serious threat, especially if it hit important lines or other bits of vital equipment. The petrol tanks were surrounded by thick rubber, which helped absorb shrapnel and kept the damage sealed.

There was plenty of tracer fire too and, if you've ever seen a photo of this, it's obvious your aircraft is going to hit by something over a heavily defended target. I once counted 42 holes in the aircraft after we'd landed back at base and I knew it was just blind luck none of us had been hit. There was also an operation over Essen when some shrapnel took out the base of an engine, which meant we only had one left. Our aircraft was at about 25,000ft and gradually lost altitude because a single engine wasn't going to get us back home. It meant taking emergency measures to lighten the aircraft, so we started throwing everything out, including the tail guns. We only just made it over the English coast and landed at the first available airfield – it was a very close shave.

There were several occasions when I was able to shoot out enemy searchlights. This involved us flying low, with me in the fore-gunner's position keeping a very sharp eye out; you had to hit them before they swung a beam onto your aircraft, otherwise the pilot would get blinded and it would be almost impossible to see anything. There was another time when I was in the fore-gunner's position and the pilot realised he'd forgotten his oxygen kit. I left the turret and gave him mine. 'If I die, then it's only one of the crew,' I thought. 'If the pilot goes, then what about the rest of us?' You see, the aircraft back then were basic and oxygen masks were essential at altitude. A lack of oxygen will affect your performance and can play tricks on the mind, while we weren't in pressurised conditions. I think this incident went towards my being awarded the Virtuti Militari.[4]

Heating was supplied by electricity from the aircraft and through leads into your flying suit, although these wires could sometimes burn out and leave you in temperatures of -40°C or even -50°C (-40°F to -58°F). That's when you really froze and, to this day, I can feel areas on my body where the cold really got to me. I remember we'd also wear silk gloves, followed by woollen gloves and then heavy leather gloves that had wool lining. It made things awkward when firing because your hands felt so huge. Radio silence was maintained during a mission because the enemy listened in and guided night fighters onto any aircraft engaged in radio chatter. The only time radio silence was broken was to issue an SOS.

For obvious reasons, it was important to be aware of German tactics and we studied these quite a bit. One of their methods was to approach underneath a bomber and use upward facing guns to take out the tail gunner and then move in for the main attack.[5] We encountered regular enemy fighters as well and I remember a 'gardening' mission when our aircraft got bounced by some, with our pilot taking us almost down to water level.[6] The enemy gave up and there were two reasons for this. First, it's difficult to pick out a target just above the sea at night. Second, a fighter aircraft has less draw when pulling up out of an attacking dive. Inexperienced pilots often misjudged this and, with no room left to pull out, they'd end up crashing into the water. A skilled enemy will pull back early and then make a new approach, fire off some shots and start the process again. That's when it becomes a game of cat and mouse, although the fighter pilot needs eagle eyes to track a bomber's silhouette.

Bomber Command aircraft sometimes released bundles of foil strips over enemy airspace to improve our chances on missions. These would scatter through the air, getting picked up by German radar and looking like lots and lots of aircraft on their screens, confusing them.[7] There was also a system of flares and you'd fire one on spotting an aircraft you weren't sure of. The colour had been pre-determined and you'd assume the other aircraft was the enemy if they didn't reply or used the wrong colour. However, it worked both ways because your aircraft could be the one spotted and expected to respond, so you had to remain focussed.

Most missions lasted seven or eight hours and they'd leave you utterly exhausted most of the time. There were also occasions when it would be one operation immediately followed by another and, sometimes, it might be three nights in a row. That second mission was always the worst – that's when you needed matchsticks to keep your eyelids open! Strangely, the third mission wasn't quite so bad but it was still very trying. There was a Naafi in which to relax on the base, plus we had one week of leave for every six weeks of operations, although we were always on call just in case the squadron needed us. That only happened once to my crew, when we'd gone into Bradford and they called us back within a day.

I was fortunate to fly with a good crew. My pilot was skilled and had started his training back in Poland, while my navigator was unusual because he was around 40 years old when most of us were in our 20s. He was eventually promoted upwards and out of the crew. Officers were usually in their late 20s and early 30s, with the senior officers a little older than that. I was also teamed up with other aircrews and, overall, completed about 17 missions with my crew and the rest with others.

One of more unusual events I witnessed during the war occurred in 1943 at RAF Hucknall near Nottingham. I saw a Gloster Meteor jet aircraft taking off and I couldn't believe its speed and rate of climb – I thought I was suffering double vision or something! The Germans had their own jets, of course, and these became a growing threat from 1944 onwards but I was no longer flying over enemy airspace by then. I'd been transferred to gunnery instruction after my 30 missions and this lasted about three months. I was then forwarded to an officer cadet school in Scotland and sent to a piloting school after this. I was comfortable with my training because I'd already had some flying lessons back in Brazil. In fact, I was flying solo on a Tiger Moth within six hours and I then trained on Harvards and Oxfords. I also made good friends with some Canadians around this time. They taught me how to play 'chug-a-lug', which is where you have a double whisky and a beer chaser. The people around you would chant 'chug-a-lug' as you made your way to the beer!

Time off occasionally involved heading to London, where you could visit the opera or the cinema. I also remember the start of the V1 rocket attacks on the city and they made a noise that was rather like a train and a weird sort of droning sound. Then the engine would cut out and the missile would wobble and fall, exploding on impact. There was an occasion when I was on the fourth floor of a building one evening and we heard a V1 approaching, so we raced to the rooftop and watched it fly past. London was still showing signs of the Blitz and other attacks at this stage but the British always tried to clear the rubble and keep up morale.

I graduated as a pilot in early 1945 and was asked if I wanted to convert to fighters. I declined because I felt more comfortable with bombers, so I piloted multi-engine aircraft and helped instruct Polish pilots who'd recently been freed from prisoner of war camps. The war was coming to an end but the Polish Government-in-Exile[8] suspected conflict with Russia might happen sooner rather than later and we should get our personnel back up to speed concerning the latest aircraft, bombers included. All this came to an end by 1946, when I was posted to the Polish Air Ministry as it prepared for demobilisation.

My demobilisation came in January 1947 and they issued me with a funny kind of suit that felt uncomfortable because I'd become so used to military clothing. I was married to my wife Halina by then. She was a Waaf[9] and had been an equipment officer at RAF Newton, which is where I met her. She came from eastern Poland and had been deported into the Soviet Union, while her father had been murdered in the Katyn massacre. Cruelly, many families were told they were being deported to be reunited with their loved ones, even though they were already dead. She was taken along with her sister and mother.

My son was almost born in Britain but we left for Brazil when Halina was seven months pregnant. The reunion back home was fantastic and around 200 people came to see me. My grandfather and father were very proud because they were Polish patriots and saw my service as a duty to Poland. Even my mother had come around to things. However, there was also great sadness because Edmund, my brother, had been killed during the war. He'd been sent to pilot school soon after our arrival in Britain because he'd already done quite a bit of flight training in Brazil. He was in 305 Squadron, flying Mosquito aircraft, and their squadron had been involved in sweeps of northern France in early 1944, mainly targeting German vehicles out on the roads. They even had special rockets to make their ground attacks. Anyway, they were sharing their aircraft with an RAF squadron during this period. The British guys would conduct a sortie and return, with the aircraft checked and – if needs be – quickly repaired. The Poles then took over the machines and flew their mission, which meant it was an almost-continuous effort.

The British guys came in one day in February and Edmund went to check his aircraft after the mechanics had worked on it. This was standard practise and a way of double-checking things. Tragically, one of the wings fell away soon after take-off and Edmund didn't have a chance... It was a critical stall and he crashed straight into the ground. Afterwards, they discovered some of the hooks attaching the wings to the fuselage had been shot through by enemy fire during the previous mission. The mechanics probably saw the opening created by bullet holes but they failed to check beyond the superficial damage to discover the real problems lying beneath.

I lived in Brazil for eight years after the war, working as an accountant for a pharmaceutical company that was a subsidiary of the Rockefeller organisation. So how did I end up in Canada? My mother-in-law had resettled in Toronto and was going to have a serious operation on her stomach. This was in the 1950s, when major surgery was much more difficult than today, and she asked to see her daughter beforehand. I took some vacation time and we came over. Then my wife said she wanted to stay and help her mother, which meant I suddenly had a big choice to make. There were no problems between Canada and Brazil with regards visas etc. back then and I started working as an accountant for the City of Toronto's roads and traffic department. I eventually specialised in municipal accountancy.

ELIZABETH PIEKARSKI

I was born in Warsaw but grew up near Wilno, not far from the River Nieman. My father was a landowner who bred horses for the Polish Army, although he had other livestock as well like pigs and cows. I attended a boarding school near Warsaw but I'd go home during the holidays. One of my fondest memories was when I was 14 or 15 and my father bought me a little gold watch and gave me a horse that was half Arabian. I called her Carmen. She was delicate thing and wasn't suitable for military service and I spent my holidays riding her or taking other horses to the river on hot summer days. We heard lots of news about the approach of the war on the family's radio, while my father and his friends talked about it all the time. My sister and I were probably too young to understand the dangers, plus I was on holiday in summer 1939 – riding horses and enjoying this more than anything else. However, we all knew something was wrong in late August, when German engineers in charge of installing some nearby fencing suddenly left for home. They simply vanished, so they must have known something was about to happen.

The fighting broke out on 1 September and there was the terrible noise of aircraft flying overhead as the sun started to rise. Everything shook because they were flying quite low and everyone in my family jumped out of their beds, exclaiming 'what's that!' I can't remember how many aircraft there were because so many were passing overhead. One of their targets was a nearby factory that made wooden spools for use in textile mills across Europe. It was an important employer in our area and many people from the surrounding villages worked there. Unfortunately, there were large stockpiles of dry wood at this place and the fires started by these bombers were horrific, igniting thousands of spools and killing around 60 people.

My father wanted to find out what was going on and tried turning on the radio but its battery was flat, so he left for town to get a replacement once it got darker. All the lights were out and he fell over when returning, twisting his leg badly. In fact, his foot swelled up so much that he couldn't put a shoe on, so he used rubber boots that were rather like wellingtons. Anyway, it wasn't long before we discovered the war was going badly for Poland but none of us expected the Russians' arrival. They detained my father almost immediately after reaching our area but my mother avoided being arrested because she was at our neighbours, helping one of their daughters who was giving birth and in some distress. A lieutenant among the Russians tried grabbing my gold watch and ended up hurting my hand, not realising it was held in place by a clasp. I kept trying to tell him this but he didn't understand. He eventually gave up and I still have this watch – and scars from the cuts on my wrist.

A group of Polish communists carrying rifles arrived not long afterwards. They'd been going from one estate to another, stealing and killing at each place. They forced 17 people to dig some graves just beyond our property line before shooting them and I saw this happen. Then they decided to come to our house, getting angry when my father's favourite dog tried to jump on them. They put my sister and myself in front of a wall, standing there laughing at us and we didn't know if they were going to shoot us as well. The Russian soldiers who'd taken our father suddenly turned up again and stopped these bandits. Sometime later – and after I'd learnt to speak Russian – I realised the solders told them it wasn't right to kill us because we were young enough to be 're-educated' as Soviet citizens.

Weeks later, some other Russian troops and communist militia arrived to take our pigs for the Red Army. They didn't shoot the poor animals but used axes instead, with the blood going everywhere. Then they loaded the carcasses onto their trucks, leaving us a few pigs that were killed when even more bandits arrived. These men also released the cows, which was terrible decision because lots of clover grew in the fields during summer and too much clover causes gas that can burst a cow's insides and kill them. They also torched the silos and barns, destroying the wheat, rye and barley harvests and you wouldn't believe how it burned. Then they plundered our icehouse, stealing the milk, cheeses and meats that had been carefully stored. Finally, they decided to chop down some oak trees behind our house. There was one large and beautiful tree that withstood their efforts to destroy it, although they caused so much damage that it fell in strong winds a few weeks later.

Our thoughts often turned to our father at this time. We knew he'd been taken to a school the Russians were using as a detention centre and we took him some cuts of chicken and a pair of shoes because he was still been wearing his wellingtons when taken away. Incidentally, my mother asked us to kill and prepare the chicken but we were terrified, not knowing how to do this. I told my sister to hold it by the neck over a chopping block. Then I closed my eyes and used the axe to cut off its head. My mother went to this school and was told my father was about to be taken elsewhere. They handed back his boots and took the replacement shoes.

People later told us they'd seen my father in a group of around 40 men being transferred the next day. This was our last confirmed sighting of him at this time. Two of my father's friends provided some additional details after finding me when I was in the Polish II Corps and stationed in Palestine. They'd been with him and soon realised they were part of a wider haul of officers, policemen, border guards and intelligentsia. After the war, we discovered the landowners were murdered separately within the Katyn massacres – not with the executed officers – and my father's bones have never been found. His friends had been extremely lucky, surviving only because someone in the NKVD had ordered them taken away for special interrogation just before the massacres started. This inadvertently saved them and they were still being questioned when the Germans invaded Russia in summer 1941. They were released because of the Polish-Soviet agreement and it was just sheer luck they survived.

We were evicted from our home at the start of November 1939. Nearby villagers had been giving us food to survive but more Polish communists arrived and said our estate was being turned into a collective farm. 'Just get out,' they said. 'We don't care where you go.' We headed to the nearby village, leaving our sister with a former servant because she wasn't feeling well. My mother and I then walked to Wilno, which was about 22 miles away (35km). We walked and walked and slept in some straw overnight in a village. We finally arrived the next morning and those who knew our family were suddenly afraid to associate with us because we were landowners.[1] All their doors were closed to us.

Only one person helped us: a poor Orthodox Jew who did business with my father. He'd come to our estate to buy hides and furs from the foxes and hares killed during an annual hunt on our lands. His cart was pulled by an old horse and he'd always keep to himself, eating onions and only using his own cup. My father eventually gave this fellow as many onions to eat as he liked. We decided to ask for his help and it was almost dark by the time we found his place. 'Oh, what has happened to you!' he exclaimed on seeing us. We explained our situation and he took us into his home, which was a tumbledown shack that had just one room. It had a huge bed in the middle, with springs coming out of the mattress, and he gave us some tea and shared a bread roll that I'm quite sure was his supper. His wife and baby boy were already in the bed and he told us to sleep there. He introduced us to a Jewish businessman who also knew my father the following day. 'I can take your daughter to a commissar in the town hall but I can't take you,' the businessman told my mother. 'You're a landowner and that won't work.'

This commissar was sat a big desk and had lots of medals on his uniform. The businessman told him about my father and how he'd helped poorer Jews in the area. He also told him who my mother was and what had happened to us. 'Okay, they shouldn't have been thrown out,' the commissar said. 'They can remain on the collective farm but they'll have to work like everybody else and get the same amount of food as everyone else.' He pulled out some papers and promptly signed and stamped them. 'Now go back to where you came from,' he said, handing me these documents.

We returned home, picking up my sister along the way, and my mother presented the paperwork to the collective's leader. He wasn't happy at our return but there was nothing he could do because it was a direct order from the Russians. They even gave us a small pig – one that had survived the earlier slaughter – and a few chickens. They never gave us any rations after this but they hadn't discovered the place where our family stored preserves and jams, so we lived off these. Friends from the village also came over and passed us food through our window.

The Russians eventually came to take us away in February. The people who did this were nasty, not allowing us to take anything for the journey. I was surprised when we reached the railway station because other members of our family had been taken as well: my grandmother, grandfather, an uncle and three aunts. My uncle had worked in the diplomatic service in Hungary and was married to a Hungarian lady, although she'd had a heart attack and he was forced to leave her behind. He escaped before our train reached the Soviet border and was never heard from again and I can only assume they caught and killed him.

There were numerous trains at the station and they were all packed with people. I don't recall how many were in our wagon but it was probably about 50 people. These wagons were designed to transport livestock and there was almost nowhere to lie down. My grandfather was the first to go, dying soon after boarding. My grandmother was French and she stopped talking Polish and started mumbling in French only. She died as we entered Siberia. Others went as well. For example, there was a family of a policeman: a mother, twin daughters and a boy. They'd been allowed to take a lot of possessions by the Russians who must have felt sorry for them. This included pots, pans, a camping stove and some barley. This lady would gather some snow whenever the train stopped and boil it in a big pot, putting in some barley to make a kind of porridge. She was boiling some water when the train shook as it got started and the little boy fell forward, cashing into the pot headfirst. He was killed instantly.

They came to take the bodies of my grandmother and this little boy at the next stop and we saw it was snowing outside. They stole my grandmother's ring and put her body onto a snow heap. Then they took the child, picking up his body by a leg and throwing him onto the same snow heap. All the policeman's family perished on that journey; it was as though they could no longer cope after the baby died. We covered their bodies with some bedding an aunt had brought and then, one by one, my aunts died as well. One of them begged us to brush her hair nicely if she went. We tried after she died but it was impossible in those conditions. There was nothing left to cover her with, so we used a bit of torn sheet...

We were shocked to discover many of the Russians in Siberia were poorer than us and some even begged us for help. Our first job was to help build a railway line and they put me in charge of six oxen, dragging a huge piece of wood with a broad metal edge to level off the ground. I was warned I might encounter an insect rather like a horsefly – only much bigger in Siberia. The oxen hated these things and could bolt if they heard it buzzing near them. 'That's when you'll need to run the other way,' I was told. 'Don't try and stop them because they might hurt you.' I was also instructed on what words to shout to get the oxen to turn left, right, move forward or stop. Well, I was shouting these orders and nothing happened. Then a very old man came up to me – one of the old-fashioned Russians – and he was very polite. 'Swear at them and they'll go,' he said. It was a miracle because they started moving as soon as I did and that's how I learnt how to swear in Russian!

Our next location was a collective farm, although they took my sister and other youngsters away. After the war, I discovered she'd been sent to a coal mine and suffered terrible lung damage as a result. Her hands were also filled with coal splinters after an underground explosion. She managed to protect her face but her friend – who I met some time afterwards – wasn't so lucky and suffered permanent disfiguring. My mother eventually tracked my sister down and they returned to Poland together.

I remember being told about the Sikorski-Maisky Agreement. We were clearing some things up when the head of the collective came over. 'Have you heard the news?' he asked. 'The Poles have been freed and are going to fight with us. You can go now.' It was just like that, without any further details. The only radio we could listen to was played in a meeting room and the content was almost always propaganda or Soviet news, which is how we heard a Polish army was being formed in Buzuluk. But I can't dwell on Russia anymore… Let's just say I reached and joined Anders' forces. My transport to Pahlavi was in April 1942 and it was awful. We were greeted by the British and they were shocked by how we looked. They didn't have any clothing for women, so we were given men's outfits and, because everyone was so thin, all of us selected the smaller sizes. There's a picture of me at the time and my clothes look so baggy! It was weeks before the British were able to get enough clothes for women.

It was decided those of us under the age of 17 would be sent to bases in Africa or India. However, most of us didn't have identification papers, so we lied about our ages and said we were older. All of us wanted to help and do our bit and I lied as well, saying I was two years older. My mother was shocked when she found out many years later because it meant I'd been 'born' before she and my father were married. She cried and I couldn't make her understand it really didn't matter. Anyway, I volunteered to do nursing because I'd already helped people in Russia and they immediately posted me to the Red Cross in Tehran for training. I took some exams and passed them.

The second major transport of Poles arrived in Persia in August 1942 and we returned to Pahlavi to assist. It was dangerous work because our patients were often sick and could pass diseases onto us. For example, typhoid killed one of my nursing friends. Thinking about it now, the second transport was probably in worse condition than the first because those people had been in Russia that little bit longer. Everyone was being forwarded into Iraq, although our unit was left behind to look after the serious cases and we only started preparing to leave when three or four patients remained. We left Persia being driven through some large mountain ranges but the roads were dangerous and one of our ambulances fell into a ravine. There was no way to reach the wreckage and check for survivors and there was nobody available with the necessary equipment to help. We carried on, spending a night here and there on a journey that took quite a long time. We eventually reached Iraq and were stationed at hospital that was quite large. It was now late autumn 1942.

I saw Wojtek the bear at this stage. He was born in the Persian mountains and his mother had been killed. Someone had traded him to Polish artillerymen who wanted a mascot. Well, he'd become a huge thing by the time I met him! He needed lots of water to drink and cool down in because it was still quite hot and his handlers dug a hole, lined it with canvas and poured in some water. That meant he could have a good soak. Wojtek was friendly with dogs, playing with them and pretend fighting, while he also liked wrestling with the soldiers and he never hurt anyone.[2]

The next important event was a New Year's Eve party for 1942/43, with senior officers also in attendance, including General Anders. He came over to me and I was rather nervous. He suspected I'd lied about my age to serve and I mumbled some excuses. However, my name and a friend's name were called out the next day and they told us we were being immediately sent to a cadet school. We didn't want to go but I now realise it was very important and we eventually matriculated. I returned to my unit in late 1943, with our hospital already on notice for being sent to Italy.

We spent the Christmas period getting everything ready and left via Port Said in a convoy, with destroyers and mine sweepers covering us until we reached Taranto. The Luftwaffe bombed the port soon after our arrival and destroyed many boats, including our vessel. Thankfully, we'd already disembarked but our equipment was sunk and 16 beautiful Alsatian dogs were also lost. We ended up stationed in a huge hospital near Taranto and it took about three days before we were given any new equipment and proper rations. In fact, we were still missing things for quite some time afterward.

Most of the Polish II Corps had been transported from Egypt to Italy by the time we arrived and we soon discovered lots of different medical equipment and skills were needed for coping with wounds or problems stemming from operations in a colder climate compared with North Africa. Two major issues were soldiers suffering from freezing weather at higher altitudes and the problem of mud, which could get into open wounds. We were then given notice Monte Cassino was about to happen, with the people in charge telling us to expect lots of wounded and to prepare ourselves as best we could. We were also told to find lodgings in the surrounding area because every room and every tent was going to be needed.

Sure enough, cases started arriving by ambulance and there were many horrible sights but there was no time to rest. You can cope with these things when you're young but it was still very sad. It was especially hard to see other young people in the hospital, including boys who'd lied about their age to get into the Polish Army. There was no penicillin at that time and infections and gangrene killed so many. We used a powdered disinfectant and that's about all we had. I cried a lot… I was one of the first to hear about the poppies at Monte Cassino, which would become the subject of a well-known Polish song *The Red Poppies of Monte Cassino*.[3] A dying officer cadet told me about them. 'Sister, sister, there are so many poppies there – red like a carpet,' he said. Another patient explained he'd been wounded in a field of them and that's what he was telling me about. His mother came to visit two weeks after he died; she worked with the Naafi and was told I'd looked after him. She spoke to me to find out more details. 'He would have been 17 next week,' she said.

Those not working on the wards – or busy with other hospital duties – attended a mandatory church service every evening and a list of people who'd died that day was read aloud at the end. The expression in English is 'killed in action' but in Polish it is more like 'died on the field of honour' and it was a moment we all dreaded because they might announce someone from your family or someone you loved. You'd sometimes hear weeping in response to a name being called out. The lists were long during the fighting at Monte Cassino and just afterwards and it was terribly sad. I'd listen out for my fiancé's name. He was from the 3rd Carpathian Division and I'd met him at the wedding of a friend, where I was a bridesmaid and he was an usher. I married him almost immediately after Monte Cassino in a church in Palagiano.

There was a scary occasion when my husband was involved in a terrible accident in Matera. He was scheduled to teach a class about mines and a live example had been placed on a table, with the soldiers standing around it waiting for the lesson to begin. An officer then arrived and started touching it, with people pleading for him to stop. It went off and killed almost everyone there – it was like a massacre. My husband was about to enter the room but turned back because he'd forgotten some notes. That's when the mine went off.

We had to deal with the aftermath of this accident. The bodies had been placed in large army canvas bags and one of the dead was someone I knew, a young officer who'd been badly wounded during the Monte Cassino offensive. It took him about two months before he could walk around on crutches. He was such a sweet person and everybody liked him and he'd been forwarded to Matera for light duties and to recover some more. His body was covered in blood and sent to the mortuary. Some of us went to see it after helping the badly wounded, wanting to discover what exactly had happened. The body had been cleaned and there wasn't a scratch on him, which was perplexing. A doctor took a closer look and pointed to a small black mark that was no larger than a pin head. He called for a scalpel and discovered a splinter – about the length of needle – had gone straight into this fellow, through his lungs and into his heart. It would have killed him instantly.

I continued with my hospital duties in Italy almost until the end of the war. I was suddenly ordered to join a transport to Britain in spring 1945, assisting a group of soldiers who'd lost legs, arms and eyes and we arrived on VE Day itself on 8 May. We came into port with the lights on because we knew the war had ended and our next stop was a special hospital in Scotland. It was a sad occasion for me because we knew Poland was going to be run by the communists. I suppose it was all very hard in hindsight but you need to be tough to work in a hospital and, quite frankly, you can't escape the effects of death during wartime. But it was very, very hard when people you'd cared for went back to the front and ended up being killed.

MARZENNA MARIA SCHEJBAL

I was born in Włocławek but came to Warsaw when I was seven and lived in the city until the end of the Uprising. My father was a businessman who ran an interior design company for commercial buildings and the inside of Warsaw's main post office one of his biggest jobs. There wasn't much talk about the possibility of war and it came as a surprise for me when the fighting started. We had an apartment in a large building and it was hit during the siege of September 1939, with our family moving into my uncle's house in the city centre. We lived in its basement because we didn't have proper bunkers and I remember crying and thinking the world was coming to an end. However, we talked about how Poland had survived other occupations in the past and then things seemed a little brighter.

The siege ended in late September and I started secondary school soon afterwards, although it was closed during winter 1939/40 because of the terrible weather. We'd only just restarted when the Germans closed the schools again, re-opening them with a restricted curriculum a few weeks later. Traditional subjects were banned and only technical or vocational lessons were allowed, with my school focused on sewing. However, everything had been prepared for clandestine lessons, allowing us to learn the usual subjects at a secondary level. My school was then closed a third time because it was situated in an area that became part of the Warsaw Ghetto. The school kept in contact with all its students and organised lessons in private homes. Meanwhile, my uncle's house fell into the area of where the ghetto was being created, so we moved into an apartment my father found in Warsaw's Old Town area. He'd been forced by the circumstances to become a decorator and renovator at this time. This flat was on the fourth floor of a building, adjacent to the ghetto, and the street below was divided by a wall. We could see over this into the area beyond from our windows.

I eventually received a letter ordering me to report for work in Germany and my father quickly found me a job at a workshop processing plant seeds, which meant I could remain. Unfortunately, I couldn't continue with my education. Life was hard during the Occupation but I was never targeted on the streets by the Germans, although the risk was always there, especially if they were angered by an act of sabotage or resistance. That's when they took people from the streets and shot them. I don't think the stress affected us as much our parents because we were young. For example, we'd visit people's houses and had fun if there was a name day or a birthday and you'd stay overnight if you weren't going to make it home before the German curfew started. My father was in the Underground and held meetings in the flat but he told my sister Ewa and I not to get involved. He also warned us to be very careful when speaking to people about these things because they might let slip details to the Germans or inform on us if they were arrested and interrogated. We simply couldn't run that risk. However, my father agreed that we could join or help any uprising when the time came.

Heavy fighting occurred during the Warsaw Ghetto Uprising during April-May 1943 and we couldn't go to the front of our flat because it was too dangerous. For example, the windows and balcony shutters had been destroyed, although we eventually looked outside and saw terrible things: dead bodies lay in the street and there were so many of them… Now and then, someone would come out of their basements, probably thinking the German units had gone but they hadn't and we saw people being shot. We also witnessed people leaping from windows… it's very difficult for me to describe.

News from the wider world was difficult to come by during the Occupation but it was obvious the Germans were losing by summer 1944. Their vehicles started leaving the city during June and July and we knew the Russians were getting closer. Most people thought a city-wide uprising might last for three or four days and the Red Army would reach us within that timeframe. I was visiting a jewellery shop with my sister on 1 August, buying some rings that had dates stamped on them to share with friends. It was the afternoon and we were coming home on one of Warsaw's main streets, Marszałkowska, when we suddenly heard shooting. The Uprising had started and people were trying to move away from the fighting. It took me three days to return home but I can't remember the details of where we slept or how we managed to get back.

My mother was home but my father had already left to join the Uprising, while the rest of the building was almost empty. My sister and I told her we were going to join the fight – as our father had agreed to earlier – and we left to find the nearest place accepting volunteers. It was easy to enlist because everything had happened so quickly and many people were unable reach their units' rendezvous locations, so they were forming independent groups and accepting recruits. My first job was to gather medical supplies from pharmacies and chemists or anywhere else that might have stocks. I did lots of different things afterwards, like carrying the wounded to various hospitals or working as a messenger. I was praying almost non-stop – praying to God I'd survive and still be able to help.

Our positions in the Old Town were slowly collapsing and it was decided we should evacuate through the sewer system on 2 September. Casualties were given priority and they were taken via the larger tunnels and some of them by stretcher. I didn't go this way but knew about it because my sister had been wounded and already evacuated. Besides, it was impossible for our unit to reach the main sewer tunnels because of where we were situated and a Scout informed us of an alternative route, one with an estimated journey time of around three hours. Our commander agreed and we soon joined the queue for this exit. It was only when we climbed down the rungs of this sewer entrance that we saw how tight the space was: something like 70x80 centimetres (27x31 inches), which meant it was more like an enlarged sewer run and nothing like a tunnel. You had to crawl on your hands and knees and there was certainly no space for standing.

There was a bad accident at the start. One of our friends didn't realise there were only small steps going down and she slipped and fell, landing on a boy just below her. He had a helmet on and the blow wasn't too great but he went into shock and fainted. We were all frightened because the Germans might attack us at any point and both this boy and girl had to be taken up and out, which meant our company was delayed in starting and only 39 of us were able to go forward. I didn't realise my mother was in the queue behind us at this stage, although she wasn't able to escape by this route and had to find another way out.

Those of us now in the sewer, including myself, started crawling forward until we all suddenly stopped. There was panic as the minutes slowly passed, particularly among some of the boys who started shouting. We knew the Germans were listening at various points, waiting to pour burning petrol down the manholes and many of these boys were crying out they didn't want to be killed in place like this. We told them to stay calm and be silent and it was a difficult moment for all of us. Now there was silence but we still didn't know what was going on. Finally, word came back from those at the front: each of us needed to push the person ahead at the next manhole. Someone had died at this spot on a previous journey, their body swelling and almost blocking the passage as a result. The extra push was needed to force the corpse aside as the next person passed through.

We'd started crawling through the sewers at about 8pm and, instead of taking three hours, we finally arrived in central Warsaw at roughly 12pm the next day. We were ordered to loop a rope under our arms and those manning the entrance pulled us up and out. I thought I could climb out but they insisted on me using the rope. It was strange because all of us fainted on exiting the sewer and they laid us out in a line until we recovered. It must have been the sudden contact with the fresh air that did this. Near to us was a public bathhouse and, although there was no flowing water, someone told us it had water barrels in which we could wash. I went into a barrel and the water was warm and I promptly fell asleep. I hadn't realised I was running a temperature because I'd scratched my forehead and arm, with material from the sewers obviously affecting me. My group departed and, on being shown new quarters, had suddenly realised I was missing and was last seen at the bath house. Anyway, they found me and called a doctor over to help. He gave me some medicine and plasters and I soon recovered.

My group wasn't involved in the fighting; our job was to find food, either by queuing for bread or finding anything that might help – even wine, beer and barley from a brewery. Supplies had become essential by this point and I learnt about the Allied airdrops, although most cannisters fell into enemy hands. The Germans were repeatedly bombing us and constantly using artillery and we wondered where the Red Army was. Today, we know they'd been halted and were waiting for us to be destroyed.

Each unit commander told their people it was over at the time of the surrender and the Germans were taking us as prisoners of war. 'However, you can stay in Warsaw but it will be risky because we don't know what will happen next,' they said. My sister and I decided to go as prisoners. At least we knew what the Germans were like having lived under their occupation for five years. For some reason, I was terribly frightened of the Red Army and my intuition told me not to stay because of this. We walked from Warsaw to Ożarów and I was with my sister all the time, going through four different camps until we reached Oberlangen.

The Germans were fairly well behaved and I never saw any serious problems during this period. However, the camp conditions we encountered were terrible, particularly at Oberlangen. We arrived in groups: the first in December 1944 and the third, which I was part of, in January 1945. There were no windows and some of the barracks were simply falling apart, while it was also bitterly cold. After the war, we discovered the camp had been closed before our arrival at the insistence of the Red Cross, which had condemned the barracks and conditions as unfit for human beings.

In fact, we destroyed one of the barrack blocks and used its wood for our fires. The Germans took the girl responsible for coming up with this idea and punished her by making her stand in the cold by the camp gate. We started throwing her shawls and blankets and the Germans didn't respond because we threatened to report them to the Red Cross. It was a rather dangerous thing to say because we weren't really in contact with the Red Cross, although the guards knew Germany was losing the war and the fighting would soon be over. They were probably thinking about what might happen when the Allies arrived and we knew this too, so we gave them rather a tough time of it.

We realised the Allies were very close by 12 April 1945 but had no idea the Polish 1st Armoured Division was in the area. We were obviously excited when the liberation unit was spotted. 'Are you English? Are you French? Are you Americans?' people shouted. You can imagine how mad with joy we were on discovering they were Poles. It really was unforgettable. However, things soon calmed down and we were supplied with new uniforms, improved rations and lots of blankets – everything we needed really. Then they transferred us to better barracks at Niederlangen and we were visited by various dignitaries, including Maczek and Anders.

My sister and I were told to report to the general office not long afterwards. We were informed our mother was at the Bergen-Belsen concentration camp, although she was in a poor condition after contracting typhus. There was a girl present who told us she'd been looking after her. She was also from the Underground movement but had been arrested much earlier and had been working in Bergen-Belsen's hospital. She'd promised my mother to look for us and had come to Niederlangen, visiting the camp office and giving our names. We were provided with transport and granted permission to transfer our mother.

News had already reached Bergen-Belsen that the mother's two girls had been found and were coming to collect her and this caused some excitement. There was a huge thunderstorm the day we arrived and we were directed to a former German depot, where many survivors were being housed because the conditions there were better. However, my mother had been transferred to another block because the rain had been seeping into this depot. We were told to wait by her original bed and they'd bring her to us. My mother didn't know what was going on after they said 'two doctors' were waiting at her original bedside. 'I don't want to go anywhere!' she exclaimed. They'd recently taken some of the liberated prisoners to Sweden for better care and she thought this was happening to her. She didn't want to go, saying she wanted to find her daughters.

They eventually convinced her to return after a lot of persuasion and there were crowds of people by now and she thought she was dreaming. Then we saw each other and she didn't believe it was true at first:

> 'Mummy, it's me and we've come to take you to our camp,' I said.
>
> 'Where's Ewa?' she asked, still not sounding very sure.

I pointed to my sister who was stuck behind someone because it was so crowded and it was such an unforgettable moment. We took my mother to our camp the next day, using a three-ton lorry because there were no ambulances available. The journey was lengthy because my mother was getting sick again – she really was very weak – and we stopped at an American hospital, a place where she could fully recover.

My next decision was to attend a Polish school established in Italy for younger people, one organised by General Anders. But how could we bring our mother with us? There was some hesitation at first and then it was decided she could go as a needlework teacher for sewing and knitting instruction. Our first stop was at the former prisoner of war camp at Murnau, with a lorry supposed to take us into Italy from there. Our group commander realised there would be no position for her after taking us to this school and she promptly convinced some of the remaining Polish officers at Murnau they could organise another school there and then. She managed to recruit some professional teachers from among them and it meant we spent about nine months in Murnau.

We became concerned as time went by because communist agents from Poland started turning up, trying to 'repatriate' Poles. We didn't want to hear what they had to say; we just wanted to reach Italy and join the school there for further education. Some liaison officers were at Murnau and one of them had married a girl we knew, so we asked him to help. 'Can't you go and see General Anders?' we asked. 'Explain to him we don't want to go to Poland and want to join the school in Italy instead.' This was done and General Anders sent over three lorries to transport our group. However, we didn't want the commander who'd arranged the Murnau 'school' to discover our plans and ruin them. So, we attended evening roll call and pretended to head to our rooms for sleep. Then we grabbed our stuff, snuck onto the lorries and took off. Previously, some boys had begged us to travel with our group and we took them as well. My mother remained in Murnau for a bit and later told us what happened; the commander was furious the following morning and accused my mother of lying about us etc. Anyway, we reached Italy and that's where my war came to an end.

Sadly, we never discovered what had happened to my father. He'd met my mother at a processing camp before she was sent to Bergen-Belsen. He was with a colleague and we later received a letter from this fellow, telling us some extra details. Apparently, my father was forwarded to a quarry near Leipzig, which was bad news because we knew the Germans treated prisoners in these places with appalling brutality. Unfortunately, there are no surviving records about him being held in Germany and we also know the area was liberated by the Red Army. If something happened to him at their hands… well, those details would have never been recorded. I've tried everything over the years to find out more but with no success.

ALICJA SIECIECHOWICZ

My grandfather was stripped of his property after the 1863 Uprising and deported to Siberia. He eventually settled in Ukraine and started a family there, with my father attending a polytechnic to study engineering in Kiev, which is where he met my mother. He was a good horseman and became a member of an aristocrat's escort in Ukraine, joining a Congress Poland unit during the First World War. My mother was visited by some Bolsheviks later in the war and they threatened to kill her if my father ever returned, so she packed a wagon and managed to escape into Poland. Sadly, my parents' first child died on the way but my mother eventually reached Lodz and was reunited with my father. He was serving in the newly-formed Polish Army by then.

My father became an engineer and was eventually based in Warsaw, working in a factory producing aircraft parts. My brother went to stay with him in summer 1939, while my sister was already in Warsaw, studying at university and living with one of our aunts. I stayed with my mother in Lodz and attended a private school. We had a good life and one that's hard to understand today. For example, a servant accompanied me to and from school. We owned a radio but I don't recall hearing about the build-up to war, although I clearly remember when the fighting started. We were in school and the class all stood up and sang a patriotic song; we were excited and thought the Germans were going to be beaten. An old history teacher was taking the class. 'Girls, you don't know what you're wishing for,' she said and I remember that warning very well.

My mother soon told me we needed to pack a suitcase and flee because the Germans were nearing Lodz. In fact, we could see enemy aircraft flying overhead and it was very frightening.[1] My mother and I walked out of the city, fleeing with an avalanche of people and eventually stopping for the night at a farm. The farmer put us into a cellar and returned the next morning. 'The Germans are here and you need to come out,' he said. We were told to return to Lodz and it was a total disaster out on the road: wrecked vehicles and people with wounds etc. It was terrible.

Three main groups of people lived in Lodz before the war. South of the city was where the owners and managers of the textile factories lived, plus their extended families, and most of these people had established themselves in the city during the Austro-Hungarian era. North Lodz was home to a large Jewish community, including a lot of Orthodox Jews, while Catholics and others mainly lived in the central areas. However, things were often very mixed and the differences between people weren't really thought about too much. For example, my sister attended a school that was half Catholic and half Jewish, while my school included Catholics, Jews and some girls of Austrian descent who were Protestants. The school reopened after the September campaign but the Germans excluded the Jewish girls.

My school was then closed at Christmas, along with all the other schools in the city. This was soon followed by an ultimatum: we either attended German-run schools or signed up for work. I hoped to continue my education but wanted nothing to do with the Germans. Somehow, my mother had my recorded date of birth changed and I officially became younger than I really was, which meant I wouldn't be taken away for work. However, it also meant there was no school for me to attend.

The Germans had evicted us from our home by Easter 1940 and ordered us to work at a factory. The conditions were appalling and I told my mother I'd die if we carried on working there. I decided to escape one night, crawling under some wire and racing to an aunt's home. She gave me food to take to my mother and I threw this to her over the factory fence for three or four days in a row. Then she didn't show up one day and a woman approached me from behind the wire, saying my mother had been released from the factory and been told to leave for Warsaw.

I returned to my aunt and said I needed to go at once. She gave me money for a ticket to Warsaw and the journey went fine until I reached Pruszków, where the Germans stopped the train and ordered everyone off. They were checking papers before allowing people to continue onwards because we were travelling from Warthegau[2] into the General Government. I sat there worrying until I spotted a guy cutting back some nearby trees and I asked him to get me away unnoticed. He didn't want to help at first but I had a ring from my mother and a little money on me and I offered him this. He then hid me under some branches on his wagon and took me to a place where I could safely reach another station and continue my journey from there.

I discovered some ladies running soup kitchens at Warsaw's central station and they were trying to help people thrown out of territories annexed by the Germans. One of them asked me if I knew anyone in the city and I remembered the address of my other aunt, the one who my sister lived with. Somehow, this lady got in touch with her and I was soon reunited with my mother and sister. I was now told about my father's fate. He'd been called up during the September 1939 campaign and escaped from the Germans after his unit was taken prisoner. I'm not sure of the exact details but they managed to capture and kill him. He'd been with my brother who they detained and deported into Germany for hard labour. My brother would eventually spend three years in captivity before escaping, although he was caught afterwards and sent to a concentration camp.

My mother, sister and I were soon renting a single room. My mother spoke five languages, embroidered well, sung very nicely and had been brought up as a lady – and none of this gave her the skills needed to earn a living. I also needed to continue my schooling, so my sister and I came to an agreement: she'd pay for the room and support our mother, while I'd attend lessons. However, I had to look after myself and help pay for food and that was important because the rationing was tough and the coupons never amounted to much. So, I did things like embroidery and painting little pictures on small vases, trying to earn extra money for things like bread.

Fortunately, I found a place at a sewing school that taught regular subjects in secret. Lessons took place once a week in different homes, including mine, with four or five us learning a particular topic. It was risky and you'd probably end up in Pawiak prison if you got caught. We didn't attend the theatre, cinema or dances because the Germans were present there and it was considered unpatriotic. However, people sometimes hosted small recitals in their homes but you'd usually stay overnight afterwards because of the curfew.

I was walking down a street one day and bumped into an instructor I knew. She'd helped run a course at my school in Lodz designed to prepare us for war, including things like civil defence or what to do during a gas attack. She was forming an Underground unit and asked if I was interested in joining. I readily agreed as my family was very patriotic and had fought in the various uprisings of the past, so I knew my mother would support this decision. My training was focussed on explosives, learning things like joining the necessary wires together and the requirements for various charges etc. I'd head out of Warsaw maybe once a month to practise my skills and this involved one or two live tests with a group of others. We always travelled separately and used different train stations. I had no idea about who the other people were – I didn't know their names, addresses or anything else about them.

There were several other tasks as well. For example, there were Underground printing presses in Warsaw and one of them produced large newssheets, the articles primarily sourced from radio transmissions via Britain. These were delivered to a group of around eight people, myself included, and we'd cut and prepare them as complete newspapers. I didn't really have time to read the contents but all of us were interested in the Polish forces abroad.

I finished my schooling in 1943 and was asked by the Underground to work at a local post office, where a German was in charge. He had a stamp for documents stating the bearer worked for the post office and was allowed out beyond the curfew and this could be shown to any German security patrol. I was friendly with his secretary who was also Polish and we'd go into this fellow's office whenever he went for lunch. We'd gather the necessary paperwork, find this particular stamp and hurriedly create a whole load of these special documents. I'd then take them to my commander – Irena Bredel 'Alina' – for use by the Underground.

I knew about the Warsaw Ghetto Uprising in spring 1943 because it happened near to where I lived. Previously, there'd been an effort to help Jewish children escape the ghetto by using the sewers and I'd helped carry a toddler with a guide assisting. The children involved were taken to a safe place and then transferred to an orphanage, where they'd be hidden. I still remember this child and the poor thing was in shock; the eyes seemed to get bigger and bigger and there was no response as we tried to help. Another time I used the sewers was to retrieve parts for a type of grenade launcher. However, we didn't use these runs too much before the Warsaw Uprising because you needed guides who really knew what they were doing. It could be fatal if you got lost down there on your own.

An AK colleague of mine was arrested by the Germans towards the end of 1943 and Irena rushed over and said we needed to move everything – the Gammon bombs and explosives etc.[3] – because the person detained knew where we kept our stuff. 'She probably won't last longer than a few hours,' Irena said. I immediately knew what she meant; they'd torture our girl until she cracked and revealed everything she knew. We raced to where our explosives were hidden and then started running all over Warsaw, trying to find Underground contacts who could help us stash them.

They eventually worked out who had informed on our girl: it was a Volksdeutsche person and the higher-ups decided he needed removing.[4] He often walked near my street and I was asked if the execution team could use my apartment. 'Of course,' I replied. They came just after I'd left for the office to ensure I had an alibi and Irena was the one who killed him. The team went to my apartment and hid their pistols after it was done and retrieved them when everything went quiet again.

What really affected us were the constant round-ups and executions in the streets, particularly of young men. They'd often take people to a little piazza in front of the Warsaw Barbican, lining them up against a wall and shooting them. Those poor guys would shout 'niech żyje Polska!' or 'long live Poland!' just before the firing started. Well, my anger and fury towards the Germans grew and grew because of this. Sometimes, you'd also spot Gestapo people prowling around; they preferred wearing black clothes and were utterly ruthless. They once grabbed a friend of ours and threw him into the back of a van. He had some clandestine paperwork on him, so he tore these documents up and ate them to avoid implicating himself or anyone else.

My sister didn't have a position within the Underground State; she just didn't have the nerve for it and we only recruited those who felt confident of doing the tasks asked of them. However, she worked at an ambulance depot, taking calls for whenever there was an emergency. Ambulances were 'borrowed' by the Underground because they were good for getting around without too much suspicion, although the Germans soon realised this and they'd take out a part for engine ignition when an ambulance wasn't needed. My sister knew where they hid these parts and she'd let us know when the Underground could use and return an ambulance without it being missed.

We knew the Germans were in trouble by spring 1944 and we were waiting for our moment to attack. You can't imagine how much hatred there was for them at this stage and what life was like under the Occupation; it can change you, almost down to your soul. The Germans demanded 100,000 Poles help build defensive structures for Warsaw in July and we knew they'd start taking people if they didn't get 'volunteers'. I think this was a factor in calling for an uprising. Meanwhile, I got a note from my commander saying a secret meeting had been arranged and I needed to 'take a toothbrush', which was our code for an uprising. In the event, I joined the action on 2 August and those first days were simply amazing because it was such a relief to feel free. Finally, I have a gun and a grenade – that's what I thought.

My group was based near the Main Post Office in Plac Napoleona[5] and we'd soon established an operations room. Some guys came in with a box not long afterwards and asked us about its contents, which they thought might be explosives. They were in a hurry because an enemy tank was causing problems at the Main Post Office and it needed to be stopped. We knew exactly what was in the box: Gammon bombs. We quickly prepped them and four of us went with the boys, reaching the plaza where the tank was. The best place to get a tank is on its corner and the guys managed this, getting their Gammon bombs right on target and causing it to explode. Sadly, Irena Bredel rushed a little bit over to the left and the Germans shot her down just beforehand.

Our unit now came under the command of Stefan Berent[6] and we were sent wherever people needed us most. Tasks included laying mines in corridors or using explosives to blow holes in the walls between buildings. These holes were very useful for the defending units as they could fall back or escape without having to expose themselves by going outside. There was another time when we helped blast out a trench on a particular street; it was being covered by enemy snipers and our guys needed cover to pass through without being targeted. The guys also found unexploded munitions and often took out the powder and they'd bring this to us. We'd use it to make grenades, with about four or five us doing this task on and off.

We'd look for other jobs if there was ever a lull in the fighting. This might be something simple like taking food to people or helping the elderly who'd been found disoriented and wandering the streets. We also assisted the burial parties, especially in the Uprising's second month. On other occasions, we'd focus on getting something to eat and I remember a brewery was captured and four of us went to get some barley. However, those in charge gave us stuff scooped out of the vats and we ate this instead. I was hungry, of course, but I don't remember needing that much food. Certainly, I didn't get up in the mornings and think 'where can I get breakfast' or anything like that.

Another incident I recall took place at a barricade. It was being guarded by some of our guys and they'd spotted a carbine under a vehicle. I was passing by and warned them not to go for it, telling them it could be booby trapped or placed there as sniper's bait. Well, one of them didn't listen to me and he was later wounded in the arm by a sniper's bullet. He was lucky not to have been killed. There was also a time when I was on the way to a job and spotted a group of people gathered in the street and a woman started begging me for help. 'My son went into that building to develop photographs,' she said, pointing to a building that had received a hit from a 'Big Bertha' shell.[7] The place was almost destroyed but there was just enough room to crawl down its side. However, nobody in the crowd was small enough to squeeze through. 'You're small, can you try?' the mother asked. 'Please go through and see if there's anything left of him.' The building was at a crazy angle and it seemed impossible for anyone to have survived but I crawled towards the end to make sure. Suddenly, people in the crowd shouted for me to return; they thought Big Bertha was about to fire again and I hurried back out. They weren't wrong because another shell suddenly landed nearby and destroyed a building.

There were some aerial supply drops but most of the cannisters fell into German hands, although I saw one brought in and it contained explosives and small arms. Later, we discovered the aircraft making these drops had been stopped from landing in Soviet-controlled territory and it meant they had dangerous return journeys. At the time, we thought the West didn't understand what was going on. The Russians sent some of Berling's troops over the River Vistula but right under the German guns and they got badly shot up. However, I wasn't near the areas involved and I didn't see any of this first hand.

Meanwhile, I'd taken a bullet clean through my leg. Two of the people with me wanted to take my trousers off to check the wound but I tried to stop them, thinking it wasn't appropriate – even though I'd just been shot and blood was seeping out! One of them used a pair of scissors and cut the trouser leg off. They patched me up and we returned to our unit and I was taken to a hospital from there. I was placed next to a guy who'd lost an arm and we were in the first level of the cellars when a bomb struck and everyone became very scared. A doctor shouted we needn't worry because they'd take us to a lower level but the guy next to me was concerned:

'They're going to leave us behind,' he said.

'Don't worry,' I replied. 'I had a bullet go through my leg but it didn't hit any bone – it only went through the muscles. You don't have an arm but your legs still work. We can help each other.'

So, he and I got up and helped each other down the stairs.

I didn't want to believe things were going badly as September progressed but we all knew it deep down. Nonetheless, the thought of defeat went unspoken. We were sleeping on floors and really trying to help the wounded around us in those final days and also eating anything that was available, including cat, dog and horse meat. There was an occasion when I went up some stairs to a place where I could see our immediate surroundings and it was a terrible sight. Then a commanding officer found me and told me not to look. 'Think only about the wounded,' he said and he was absolutely right and I reminded myself I couldn't start feeling self-pity.

The end finally came at the start of October and the civilians were taken out first. My mother had initially been in the Old Town and joined some Capuchin monks and left with them. She ended up in a German concentration camp. My sister had helped some hospital personnel during the Uprising and went with them, while my unit was one of the last to leave. We threw our weapons down in front of the Germans but most of this stuff was junk because the best equipment had been buried in the ruins for future use. Anyway, I remember a German inspecting the stuff we were leaving behind. 'Look at these weapons,' he said with disbelief. 'They did a good job.' Incidentally, most of those hidden caches were found by the communists after Warsaw's liberation and it's said they also discovered a lot of hidden film and photographic footage that they promptly destroyed.

My leg was healing but it was a tough ten-mile walk (16km) from Warsaw to Pruszków. I could see a lot of damage as I left the city but did I appreciate its full extent? Probably not. We also saw German units burning and destroying buildings and later discovered Hitler had ordered Warsaw's complete destruction. They put us into a paint factory at Pruszków and a rather funny thing happened there; the guys made room for us and we noticed some of the old paint splashed on the floor had transferred to their clothes, including reds, blues and greens and they all looked very odd because of it.

The Germans were soon loading people onto trains at Pruszków and sending us into captivity. It was roughly 50 people per cattle wagon and they gave us some bread and pieces of sausage just before departure. My journey took the whole day and we stopped near Lamsdorf. Unfortunately, part of the train was derailed and we walked to the prisoner of war camp, Stalag VIII-B. One of our friends couldn't move her legs and it was later discovered she'd caught polio. Myself and another person assisted, holding her up as her feet dragged along the ground and a German guard came over. He screamed at us for falling behind the others. I could speak a little German and replied with some choice words and he hit me, breaking some of my teeth.

I started running a fever after two days because the broken teeth started to decay. The Germans were very afraid of typhus, so they immediately transferred me with several others to another camp with a hospital. I kept telling the woman in charge I wasn't a typhus case and the problem was my teeth. She told the Germans and they sent along a dentist and he pulled them out. My temperature soon fell and they eventually said I was being transferred again. There were about 14 of us and we were unloaded at one point during the journey. I can't tell you where, other than it was a German town that had a central plaza. They had us standing there in freezing weather from morning until evening, with people watching us from the windows. Finally, they took us by train to another station, where we were suddenly unloaded because of an air raid. They put us back onboard and we stopped in Berlin, where they took us out again because of another raid.

We reached Oberlangen either just before or just after Christmas and I was put into Barrack 11, which was the last one. People who'd reached Oberlangen before us had things like blankets, pillows and sweaters but all I had were the clothes I'd been wearing during the Uprising: trousers and a summer top. Somebody gave me a sweater a little later, while I also had a German greatcoat. I'd been given this by my commander after a guy cut it to my size. We'd hidden some of our bomb-making instructions and manuals in its lining, which is why I never parted from it during my captivity.

The bunks at Oberlangen had three levels but earlier arrivals had taken slats from the ones they thought weren't being used. It meant we had gaps in our bunks and we complained to one of our commanders. Those who'd taken the slats refused to hand them back, so she gave us some old Red Cross boxes and we used the cardboard as a makeshift solution. Concerning rations, we each received a cup of black soup in the morning. In fact, it was more like water that had the occasional green leaf floating in it. This was all we got until evening, when we received another mug of soup and some pieces of bread. I must have been so used to the hunger that I didn't really feel it. The Germans mainly left us to ourselves, although they made us dig up peat for heating and then took most of it.

We had no idea what was happening in the wider world at Oberlangen but we eventually heard gunfire and knew the Allies were getting nearer. My block experienced a different version of the camp's liberation because we discovered Polish troops were in the area on 11 April, the day before we were all freed. It happened like this: Barrack 11 was near a guard tower and the camp fence and a jeep suddenly pulled up. We were watching it through cracks in the planking but couldn't tell who the vehicle belonged to. It stopped in front of the tower and a guy started shouting for the guard to come down, adding in some Polish swear words. Excited to hear our language, we hurriedly broke the barrack door's lock and ran up to the fence. We now saw there were two people in the jeep – a driver and the one who'd been shouting. This fellow turned to us: 'Girls, I promise we'll come back but we have to go now because it's just us.' The tower guard came running down with his carbine and he looked worried; he also looked ancient, like someone in their 90s! The Germans had already removed the younger camp guards and left those who wouldn't have been any use for fighting.

Anyway, it was very exciting and they came back as promised the next morning and brought a tank with them this time. I remember flags going up and the troops talking with us, while a doctor with them said he'd get us some extra rations.[8] Sensibly, he only had evaporated milk and biscuits delivered because he knew our stomachs wouldn't be able to take much more. Even then, some of us were sick afterwards. Our clothes were in a poor condition and they sent over some army uniforms, although the trousers I received were far too long and I used string to keep the legs up. They also implemented a disinfection process by standing us up against a barrack wall and spraying us with DDT,[9] which got rid of the bugs but maybe wasn't so good for our health!

It was wonderful to be free and we were soon thinking about the future. I applied to join Maczek's 1st Armoured Division but they were full, so I went to see my commander and asked how I could get a transfer to the Polish II Corps. They were setting up a kitchen and she promised to help if I volunteered to run it over the short term. I agreed and my commander kept her word, coming over one day and saying I'd been given a place on the next transport to Italy. I was allowed to take someone else, so I requested my brother join me. He'd been in a concentration camp near Hamburg and a Polish officer had brought him over to me. It was awful; his skin looked wrong and I think it was from kidney damage as the Germans always hit people on the kidneys, knowing this hurt much more. He had been 18 and full of life the last time I saw him and now he looked like a broken old man. Fortunately, a place was found for him with the 1st Armoured Division and I ended up taking a friend to the Polish II Corps, plus someone else who'd asked to come along.

We were taken to Murnau and told to wait for permission to cross into Italy. However, the three of us didn't want to just sit around, so we started out into the mountains and promptly got lost. Luckily, we came across some American soldiers who returned us to Murnau and, rather ironically, the next transport to Italy was given clearance soon afterwards. There was a choice of jobs on reaching the Polish II Corps and I was accepted into a cartographic unit. The war was over but there was still a lot of German equipment and vehicles lying around Italy and we'd study aerial photographs and report back if we spotted anything that looked out of place. They'd then send a unit out to investigate. There were about 25 of us doing this, while five other girls we knew were running a kitchen.

I was eventually demobilised and started a new life in London by studying at the Polish University. I also met my husband there; he was studying architecture and I was studying economics. He was in uniform and I was in uniform because neither of us had the money to buy civilian clothes and our studies took place from 1946-1948. It was during this period that I finally contacted my sister and mother who'd returned to Poland. My husband and I promised not to talk about what had happened in front of our children until they were in their 20s because we didn't want them to feel the pain of what we'd been through. I eventually returned to Warsaw in 1968 by travelling on a British passport and I finally saw my family, including my mother for what would be the last time. Obviously, a lot had changed in Warsaw but there was still plenty of damage visible from the war. They were also building lots of apartments – those terribly austere blocks you still sometimes see.

I think the Warsaw Uprising should be seen as part of Poland's long historical fight for freedom. There was the 1794 uprising by Tadeusz Kościuszko and then there were uprisings of 1830 and 1863. One of my grandfathers was killed in 1863 and, as I've said, the other was deported into Siberia. The Russians, Germans and Austrians took our lands and fighting against them was a repeated part of Polish history. People who aren't Polish don't fully understand this and its deeper meaning. For example, I remember pictures hanging in our apartment when I was growing up and each one had a patriotic verse underneath. I can still remember one of those verses and, in English, it went something like this: 'Murderers can chain my hands but they cannot chain my soul.'

MIECZYSŁAW STACHIEWICZ

My time in the military started when I was 14 and I attended a cadet school, which was rather like a secondary school with military training. I spent five years there and then joined the Polish armed forces as part of the 1937/38 intake, training as a military pilot through a programme that was difficult to get into because so many young men wanted to enrol. I then took an architectural course at Warsaw after I qualified with the PAF and was placed in the reserves. I attended a technical university and had completed the 1938/39 academic year when my life was interrupted by the war, which broke out on 1 September 1939.

I'd already been called up before the invasion started and my unit was stationed in north Poland, where I was in the reserve pool. We were ordered to evacuate on 4 September, with command putting us on a cattle train heading towards Warsaw. Unfortunately, the panzer columns had already cut our railway line, which meant we had to finish the journey on foot – a 40-mile trek (65km) that took about a day and a night to complete. We were then sent east to find another unit to which we'd been attached. Six cars picked us up but only my car reached its destination. I remained in the reserves and spent several days waiting around until we were ordered to head southeast, towards Romania. On reaching the border, we were informed the Russians had also invaded and there was now a general order for all Polish personnel to cross into Romania if they could make it. We managed this and I was subsequently interned in a camp near the River Danube.

International law had required the Romanians detain us because they were still neutral and we were military personnel from a country at war.

However, all of us wanted to reach France and join the Polish armed forces being built up there and the Germans knew this. They pressured Romania to keep us under close watch, which meant we were stuck. Still, the rules could be bent for the right amount of money and the Polish government soon organised clandestine 'runs' to get men out. I joined a group taken to Bucharest, where a local police chief put us in touch with Polish authorities based in the city. We stayed in the Romanian capital for about two weeks until receiving civilian papers and travel documents and I was later told everything had been paid for with cash up front.

There was quite a group of us by the time we left Romania at the start of January 1940. We travelled through Yugoslavia and down into Greece, stopping in Athens and even managing to visit sights like the Acropolis. A Polish ship called *Warszawa*[1] took us from Greece to Marseilles and our first destination in France was a camp near Toulouse. The conditions were poor because the barracks were unheated and the winter of 1939/40 was extremely cold. The camp wasn't clean either, with lots of mud that was sometimes ankle deep. Thankfully, this lasted just a couple of months and I was forwarded to the main PAF centre in Lyon, although this proved to be a big disappointment as the pilots lived in a huge exhibition hall, sitting around all day doing nothing. There was no hope and we had no idea why our skills weren't being used.[2] Our commanding officer couldn't answer our questions about what was happening or whether we'd be called for active service any time soon. Somewhat strangely, those in authority labelled my pals and myself 'rebels', simply because we were keen to do our jobs and fight the enemy.

The Germans attacked France in May 1940 and we were evacuated by train to a Mediterranean port before the enemy reached Lyon. A British ship was meant to have picked us up but nothing was there to greet us, so we took another train and arrived at an old fishing port in the Bay of Biscay and boarded a British liner that sailed for Liverpool. We were soon stationed in two camps near Blackpool and I was later transferred into the town as it had been designated a centre for the PAF. I was posted to a flight school in June 1941 and started my practical training all over again, flying Tiger Moths and Oxfords until I was ready for an Operational Training Unit. This was where the crews were formed and where we became familiar with Wellington bombers, our main aircraft.

The Wellington was a superb machine and the first thing I noticed about it was how its wings moved, almost as if it was flapping like some kind of bird. My crew and I were ready to be transferred to a Polish bomber squadron by the end of April 1942, of which there were four at this stage in the war: numbers 300, 301, 304 and 305. They assigned us to 301 Squadron, which was stationed at RAF Hemswell and located about 12 miles (20km) north of Lincoln. We soon got into the swing of things but I never liked the part where we dropped leaflets during missions. We'd be over the target and one of my crew would have to cut the string on each pack before opening the trap through which these things were dropped. It was time consuming and, quite frankly, we all had more important things to do when flying over enemy territory.

In response, I came up with what we all thought was a rather brilliant plan: I'd pre-cut the packs and leave them by the trap, ready to be thrown out in one go. Unfortunately, the wind proved so strong that the loose leaflets were blown around the aircraft immediately after the trap was opened. It created a paper snowstorm that covered everything and it might have been funny had the situation not been so dangerous. Later – and after giving it some thought – we concluded it would have been better to throw the leaflets down as uncut packets. That way there might have been a chance of killing an enemy or two!

We also dropped sea mines, usually flying to the German North Sea coast during the summer, when the nights were short and offered less operational time over enemy territory. The mouths of submarine ports were frequent targets and these 'gardening' missions were much simpler. The real difficulties came when flying over urban areas, which had a much higher level of enemy flak and night fighter cover. We also knew the Germans had radar and sound locators and were busy working out our aiming points. They'd guide their night fighters onto us, although I changed my course roughly every 30 seconds to make it harder for them to monitor us. Defensively, we were hampered by the blind spot on our aircraft's underbelly, which was a weakness the enemy exploited. In fact, there were times when our men only realised a night fighter had got them when the bullets started hitting their aircraft. Thankfully, we were never attacked in this manner.

One of my earliest operations was at the start of June 1942 and it was one of the scariest. The target was Essen in the centre of the

Ruhr Valley, the heartland of Germany's heavy industry. The Ruhr was ironically named 'Happy Valley' because of its heavy defences and the high rate of casualties taken when attacking targets in this region. Our aircraft was in the lead that night but we experienced some trouble soon after passing the British coast as our Wellington was not pulling very strongly. Anyway, we discovered everything was switched off and quiet over Essen.[3] Then the bomb aimer, having prepared us for the run-in, suddenly announced we'd passed over the target and I told the crew we'd have to go around again.

It was still quiet on the re-approach and we'd just dropped our bombs when a blue searchlight beam shot up and locked onto us. Other beams followed its example and we were tracked by at least 30 searchlights in a matter of seconds, with the flak rising to meet us.[4] One of my crewmates acted as a second pilot. 'Don't get blinded!' I shouted. 'Concentrate on the instruments and direct me!' He issued instructions to me and, changing course all the time, I tried to shake off the searchlights and the flak. They stayed on us for ten to 12 minutes until we left the defence zone and flew into the safety of darkness. Our aircraft had taken a lot of damage but thankfully nothing important had been destroyed and we counted at least 40 holes in the fuselage after landing.

Of the four crews who joined the squadron at the same time, including ours, only two were left by the end of June. The third crew was lost after returning from Emden. They were in trouble after a night fighter attack and it looked like they wouldn't make it home, although they managed to ditch into the North Sea. I noted the rough location of where they'd gone in and I rushed to the squadron commander on landing and got permission to fly back out to search for them. We flew squares, by which I mean you flew to a set point, turned 90 degrees and flew some more before turning another 90 degrees. You also increased the size of the area searched while doing this. Anyway, I suddenly spotted an orange dot floating on the ocean from the corner of my eye. We flew over to confirm it was a dingy and then flew up to 2,000ft to signal base the missing crew had been found and a rescue effort should be sent. There was a possibility the Germans had heard our signal because we weren't too far from the coast of Occupied Europe. Still, we continued flying over the dingy because I was afraid the rescuers wouldn't find it and we watched over the downed crew until they were hauled in. Happy with our success, we returned to base and organised a party. However, our celebrations were cut short when we were informed the men we'd helped rescue weren't from our squadron; they were Australians and they never wrote us a letter of thanks, let alone sent us a bottle of wine.[5]

I had my first crash in July. One of our engines stalled shortly after taking off and I had to turn back. The radio then packed up and the aircraft's lights went out and – with no ground communication and flying in total darkness – we prepared ourselves for a bail-out. However, I suddenly spotted a flare path for an aerodrome and I decided to land there and then. The lights on the ground were suddenly switched off as we were coming in on the approach at about 300ft. I had just one engine running and the undercarriage and flaps were already down and it would have been impossible to fly any further. I hazarded a landing and we arrived like a falling pancake and, luckily, nobody was injured except for a few bruises. Two weeks later, I was officially informed the crash landing was my fault and I shouldn't have attempted it but there was nothing else I could have done.

Our squadron had suffered badly by the end of July 1942, losing 11 crews in a working establishment of 12 crews.[6] We also lost two commanding officers in a week, one killed straight after the other. It was very difficult to maintain our numbers at this rate of attrition because the PAF was so short of manpower but we kept on and August involved lots of bombing and 'gardening'. On one occasion, both my engines started overheating shortly after take-off and I was afraid they'd catch fire, so I decided to turn back. It would have been best to ditch our bombs at sea, making our subsequent landing safer, but the distance to the ocean was simply too great. I found it hard to get the aircraft down on approach and there was hardly any runway left by the time I got us firmly on the ground. There was a bomb magazine at the airfield's end and it suddenly looked like a fully bombed-up aircraft was going to collide with it! Thankfully, I managed to turn rapidly on the one engine still running and the force of this collapsed the undercarriage and we ploughed to a halt. Nobody said a thing this time and there was no internal investigation.

They sent a doctor along the next morning and he gave us permission for a week's leave. We turned him down, so they ordered us to take a couple of days off. Then it was discovered that, technically-speaking, the crew had been flying without approval. For one reason or another, we'd all failed to have a proper medical since our arrival in Britain and those in charge promptly suspended us, forcing us to wait until called for an inspection by the medical authorities in London. We weren't allowed to go near our aircraft during this period and they labelled us 'non-flying personnel'. We were eventually examined and the medical officer gave everyone the all clear. He also offered me certification for a four-week holiday and I couldn't believe it; we were in the middle of a war and they were trying to give me a month off! I managed to haggle this down to two weeks and then had to find somewhere to take this unexpected break. There was a place in Perthshire where Polish airmen could rest up, a small castle set on a rocky outcrop and it was like walking into a completely different world. I returned to the squadron after this holiday and was re-joined by my crew who'd also been granted leave. We then got back to the business of war.

They told us we'd be transferred for an operation out of Tangmere, near Portsmouth, towards the end of our tour in November. The full briefing was to happen there and our aircraft was bombed up and we had just enough fuel to make this quick journey. They refuelled our aircraft after we landed and installed some auxiliary fuel tanks. Meanwhile, we were informed the target was Turin, Italy. This was shortly before the Allied landings in Sicily and the Italians were rather shaky by this stage of the war.[7] I think the bombing of Turin, which is an industrial area, was an effort to persuade them that the writing was on the wall. Anyway, Tangmere had a nice long concrete runway and I got off the ground at maximum speed. I soon noticed my starboard wing started to move up and down and had stopped responding to the controls. I got the problem resolved after several seconds and took the aircraft a bit higher but the wing started to play up again and I decided it was impossible to continue. Flying at about a 1,000ft and near the coast, I decided to ditch our bombs in the ocean and return to base. There was a funny thing I noticed when we did this: the incendiaries started to burn underwater, creating a fire beneath the sea. I then headed back to base, called mayday and landed.

Naturally, I was asked what had happened and said there was something wrong with the controls and the wing. The investigating officer discovered a flap covering the filling point for one of the spare tanks hadn't been properly secured. It was opening and closing in flight, changing the Wellington's profile and tilting the aircraft and it was quite a dangerous situation. Well, that was my 28th or 29th mission and they fixed up the aircraft and we returned to Hemswell the next morning. One of our colleagues met us on arrival:

> 'Your flying has finished,' he told me. 'You've completed a tour and they are posting you on.'
>
> I was confused and asked where I was being sent.
>
> 'Oh, don't you know? You're off to university.'

I was simply amazed at this response as I'd not even considered going to university, let alone asked anyone to apply for me. I soon discovered a Polish architecture department had just been opened at Liverpool University.[8] Someone, somewhere, had looked at my records and noted I'd studied architecture in Warsaw and it seemed the Polish government wanted a living architect rather than another dead airman. So off I went.

University life was almost a complete shock because the tension and pain of losing friends had gone. We all knew the loss ratio was running at three-in-every-four crews and that was reflected in our case; we were the last crew of four that had arrived at the same time. Fortunately, an architect I knew from my days in Poland attended the course with me. He'd also served with the bombers and proved to be good friend and a great moral support. I never got back to the 'frontline' after this. I met my wife during my time at university and she was also studying at the architectural school. We got married on 13 April 1944, during the Easter break. There was a long waiting list for civil marriages but no one was adventurous to try the 13th.

Almost all Poles were angry at the loss of our country to Stalin at the end of the war. Our fighter pilots had fought bravely during the Battle of Britain, making a name for us, while those of us in the bombers had also fought hard for a free Poland and an Allied victory. I remember a British Minister of Aviation sent an open letter to Sikorski giving thanks and praise for the Polish bomber crews. We were everyone's friends at the time and people would come up to us and pat us on the backs, thanking us for all we were doing. But we were being called fascists to our faces by summer 1944 and I was often called a fascist when I appeared in my Polish uniform. Everyone loved the Russians by then.

I obtained my Polish architecture degree from Liverpool University shortly after the war's end. Strangely – or not so strangely given the circumstances – but I'd never been on a British construction site because nobody was building during the conflict. I now had to learn the practical side of things but, fortunately, the country was focussed on rebuilding and architects and engineers were in great demand, which meant I could begin my civil career almost straight away.

My family back in Poland had suffered greatly during the war. My father had died of tuberculosis in 1934 but we had always gotten by. The Germans decided to 'Germanise' the area of Warsaw my family lived in and the Gestapo set up their headquarters nearby at 25 Szucha Avenue, which is where they interrogated and tortured people, including my cousin who they murdered. My family was soon forced to leave their home and they were given just two hours to gather up whatever possessions they could to take with them. My brother was eventually sent to a concentration camp and, being a talented artist, he painted portraits of camp guards and survived because of this. My mother endured the Occupation and Warsaw Uprising in 1944. I had to take British citizenship after the war to visit my family in Poland. My wife and I have dual nationality and we made our home in London.

DANUTA SZLACHETKO

I was born in Warsaw in 1929 and lived on Nowy Świat. My mother was a housewife, although she received an inheritance from her father and purchased a house and some land in Laski, a village not far from the city. Back then, it was a popular spot for holiday homes and today it's a special place where blind people live.[1] My parents had three daughters, me included, but one of us died when she was very young, while my sister, Henryka, was a couple of years older than me. My parents didn't have a happy marriage and they eventually separated but they never got divorced. I know my father was in the Polish Army but I don't know much about his career. All I heard about him after the Warsaw Uprising was that he'd been wounded and ended up in a hospital in Wola,[2] which was heavily bombed and almost destroyed. Nothing remained of him afterwards, while Wola was also where the Germans and their eastern units massacred many thousands of people.

My sister and I attended school in Warsaw before the war and our home was a happy one. I don't remember there being much talk about war until just beforehand and I recall Warsaw's mayor coming on the radio during the siege of September 1939, telling us we needed to fight for Poland and the city. I also remember enemy aircraft bombing us and the Germans eventually arriving, with lots of rubble around us. We just stood and watched and it was a tragedy.

My mother decided it was best for us to leave the city and head to Laski. There was a fruit orchard on our land and areas where potatoes had been planted. My mother had gone there just before the war and placed a lot of fruit in jars and buried these under the earth and, while we discovered trenches had been dug on our land, these jars lay undisturbed. Unfortunately, the Germans had plundered most of our home's contents before moving on and we received help from our neighbours by way of sheets and bedding etc.

My sister and I attended a school in the countryside for about a year, walking about three miles each way because there was no transport. Unfortunately, Laski didn't have any secondary schools, so we returned to Warsaw to receive an education beyond the elementary level. There was still a great deal of damage from the September 1939 siege, particularly when it came to the upper floors of buildings, although the ground and middle floors were usually fine and you could still rent them. My mother was a very capable person and we were soon making a life for ourselves in the city, although it was a dangerous time as the Germans liked to seize young people off the streets and send them to work in the Third Reich. You'd sometimes see their lorries arrive – the German soldiers jumping out and grabbing people – and you never knew when or where this would happen.

My sister and I attended a middle school and then a kind of grammar school run by nuns. The traditional subjects had to be dropped and we learnt practical subjects, things like making hats or sewing, plus there were German language classes. The enemy wanted Polish children to become their workers and I remember our German teacher was a horrible person who was also very strict. Rather ironically, it meant we learnt the language quickly and this proved helpful for me just after the Warsaw Uprising, when I was a prisoner of war.

The Germans eventually closed this school but my mother had a back-up plan; she knew a priest who taught at a school focussed on hat making and he helped secure me a place. However, I couldn't join the first year because the numbers were already fixed, so they sent along one of their best students to tutor me and prepare me for the second year. This girl later helped me join the Underground movement in 1943. The school secretly taught regular subjects but the Germans often made spot checks. We posted lookouts as a precaution and they'd warn us if inspectors were approaching and we'd quickly hide all of our books and get out the hats on which we pretended to work.

My mother earnt money on the black market to keep our family going and help pay for schooling. She'd head outside Warsaw to buy food from certain farms and then sell this produce to shops in the city. It was a dangerous thing to do, especially as the Germans often questioned passengers at stations or while on the trains. She took me with her once and it was scary. We got up early in the morning and took a train into the countryside, where we visited farms and made purchases. We returned that evening and ended up walking through the city after the curfew, hiding whenever we saw someone in the distance. I found it frightening but my mother did this all the time. We delivered our food to the shops the next day and I got scared again.

I joined the Underground movement when I was 14 and didn't tell anyone about the details, although my mother found out soon afterwards. Our building had suffered damage to the top floor but it was still possible to go up there and find some useful places to hide things. I was with the Scouts and they asked me to stash clandestine books and pamphlets in this upstairs section and I agreed, with several Scouts helping me put this stuff up there.

There were only two families in our building, my family and a couple with three smaller children. The father had been appointed to look after the property by the landlord and he noticed all the coming and going and went upstairs to see what we'd been up to. He soon discovered the boxes. 'Your daughter must belong to some movement,' he told my mother. 'Well, I don't want the things she's hidden in this building. I have a family with children and I don't want us to get into trouble.' He demanded I remove everything, otherwise he'd go to the German authorities and inform on us. My mother was upset and I found her crying when I returned home. 'What are you doing, my child?' she asked. I told her and then removed everything from upstairs, although she knew I wouldn't stop being part of the Underground and maybe she realised I was doing something meaningful because she never really tried to stop me.

I carried on my training with the Underground in the months that followed and much of this was done in the countryside. On other occasions, we'd distribute clandestine papers or put posters up designed to raise people's morale. Getting this stuff often involved leaving the city and returning by train or tram. Concerning the trams, their drivers kept an eye out for us and would shout a warning if they saw a German patrol up ahead. We'd then make a sudden and unscheduled exit, with plenty of people in the street willing to help us as well. Nonetheless, you couldn't be complacent and it was dangerous work. Incidentally, putting posters up involved two people: one to keep watch and the other to do the pasting etc. It seems quite scary in hindsight but we were young and didn't really feel a sense of danger.

We had some knowledge of the outside world during this time, particularly news from Britain, but we didn't know the full details of events like D-Day. We also knew the Russians were succeeding on the Eastern Front and getting nearer all the time. We certainly knew Polish units were still fighting elsewhere and we hoped our parachutist brigade would reach us after the Warsaw Uprising started. There were some supply drops but they weren't very successful because most of the containers were lost to the enemy. Some of them smashed on the ground if they were dropped too low, the parachute not having properly deployed. Still, it was difficult and dangerous for aircraft flying over the city and it must have been impossible for the pilots to get everything right on their approach.

My mother wanted us to all leave for Laski on 1 August 1944 – the start of the Uprising – but I refused because I wanted to help fight the Germans. My mother and sister left, while I tried and failed to reach my unit's rendezvous point. I spent the first night of the Uprising with a friend who was also in the AK and we left the next morning and I remember running through Plac Napoleona, with a plane overhead shooting. German troops were still trying to defend the Main Post Office and there was a house on the other side that had been reduced to rubble. I could see a naked woman standing there, her clothes ripped off by a blast. She was covered bruises and her hair was a wild mess and I'm pretty sure she was badly wounded. Unfortunately, I couldn't stop because I had to reach the other side and join my unit. In the meantime, my mother decided to return from Laski; she wanted to get me out of the city and my sister and aunt decided to join her.

I returned to our home in Warsaw to check on things after a few days of fighting. However, this wasn't easy because there were three badly-damaged properties near to where we lived on Nowy Świat. They had big gardens that had become a sort of no-man's land and I had to race pass them to reach my building. Well, I managed to make it through okay and I met my aunt, which surprised me. I asked her what was happening and she told me the details. On reaching Warsaw, my mother and sister visited some friends who lived nearby, thinking I was either with them or they knew of my whereabouts. They had to run past those three ruined houses there and back. On returning – and close to our home – an enemy aircraft came swooping over, firing its guns. My mother was struck in both legs and fell to the ground mortally wounded, while my sister's arm was cut off. She kept running and had just reached a window of our building when she was killed by a bullet straight to the heart. My aunt saw all of it… That evening, when it was quiet, she went outside and managed to dig a hole, placing sheets over their bodies and burying them in a temporary grave. She had their remains dug up and transferred to a cemetery after the war and I had the name of my father added to the gravestone because I wanted him remembered as well.

I stayed with my aunt that night and, after falling asleep, I was woken by the sound of a door opening and someone walking on the steps in our apartment. I thought it might be my mother's spirit. My aunt told me she'd had a dream about my mother the next morning. Apparently, my mother had asked to take me away. 'I said no,' my aunt explained. 'I said you'd stay with me and I'd look after you.' It was an experience I will always remember, although I also felt like the earth might swallow me up at any moment. I felt like it was the end…

I decided to return to my unit, which was helping deliver post and now using the Main Post Office as an important sorting area. I was involved in this until around mid-August, when I joined a seven-person courier unit. It was a dangerous job because we'd race along the streets behind barricades. Our unit was staying in a house when enemy bombs suddenly fell on it, collapsing the building. I lost conscious and can't remember being hauled out of the rubble or coming around. Indeed, there's quite a gap missing from my memory but I know only five of us made it out alive. A very good friend and I often ran messages together and there was the occasion I heard a shot and turned around to see she'd dropped dead. I went to check on her but there was nothing I could do and, again, I thought the world was starting to fall apart…

It took a while but we slowly realised the Russians were doing nothing to help us. The Old Town was collapsing by now and they were evacuating people into the centre of Warsaw via the sewers. Food was also getting scarce and they were already butchering the horses. Then it was the dogs and cats and we had to eat them, otherwise we'd have been starved into surrendering and that's what happened by October – there was so little left that it became a question of survival. Concerning our surrender, we walked along in fours or sixes and threw whatever weapons we had onto the ground in front of German soldiers. They stood there and watched us but they didn't laugh and, in a way, I think they had some respect for us.

The first day after our surrender involved walking to Ożarów and some people on the way tried throwing fruit to us but the guards soon stopped them. We slept on concrete floors at Ożarów and were then put onto cattle trains that took us into the Third Reich, where we were held as prisoners of war. It was standing room only and a lengthy journey. The Germans took us to a place to try and clean us, especially our hair that was dirty from dust and lice. They had bowls filled with disinfectant and we had to put our heads over them.

We were soon divided into groups and around 300 women, myself included, were taken to Bremerhaven and ordered to march to a camp at Sandbostel.[3] It had prisoners from various nations, including Poles who'd been detained there since 1939, and they handed over some of their Red Cross supplies to us, which was of great assistance. There were also French and Italian prisoners and some of them also tried to help. In fact, the French had quite a lot of autonomy in Sandbostel and a few of them left the camp to assist those of us struggling to complete the march.

We were given two barracks: one for the officers and their orderlies and another for the other ranks. The officers were eventually sent to an Oflag and they put some Russian prisoners of war into their former barracks. These men were fenced off, with only a small space for them to walk outside and they were treated little better than animals. However, some of them broke through the fencing and came into our barracks at Christmas time, which none of us liked. In fact, our leading women told the other Poles and they informed the Germans. Guards came running over and took the Russian prisoners of war back and gave them a severe punishment. We'd been at Sandbostel for about two months when they took us to Oberlangen not long after Christmas. The journey involved walking from Sandbostel back to Bremerhaven and being put into cattle wagons again. We could see the city had been badly bombed and Allied aircraft came over that evening, with the Germans fleeing for safety and leaving us on the train. Nothing hit us that night, thank God.

There were roughly 13 barracks for Polish women at Oberlangen and the Germans took us outside to work, which they shouldn't have done under the terms of our being held prisoner of war. But maybe we were the lucky ones; some of my friends were sent to other places and forced to work on factory lines and were treated very poorly. We collected wood in the forests but some of the girls made it into the surrounding fields and dug up potatoes or carrots, which wasn't allowed. The Germans sometimes spotted people trying to smuggle these vegetables into the camp and they'd confiscate whatever had been taken. I only ever did this once. Some people can cope with the stress of a situation like this but I was unable to withstand the pressure anymore. Overall, the German guards behaved reasonably towards us, although there was one Feldwebel whose behaviour was atrocious.

The reason for taking the vegetables was simple: we weren't getting enough food. The camp's bread was heavy and contained water to bulk it up, while the soup had some greens – usually a few garden peas – and that was about it. I remember some girls arrived at Oberlangen after being forced to work at a factory. They had some dried bread with them and one of the girls in this group spotted me crying.

'What's wrong?' she asked.

'I'm just so hungry,' I said.

She shared some of her dried bread with me and that's how we became life-long friends. I can say this with certainty: I know what real hunger means.

We heard explosions in the distance as spring 1945 arrived. The frontline was getting closer and then, one day, the sound of fighting started dying away. We knew something unusual was happening because some of our guards started leaving, although others remained, including the commandant and that horrid Feldwebel. A liberation unit was spotted approaching on 12 April and it included a tank and some jeeps. We stood by the fence, excited and shouting in English and French. None of us realised they were Poles at first. We were so surprised and elated to discover who they were and I think they were surprised and elated too.

The German commandant was taken into captivity and that appalling feldwebel was taken outside and shot. Let's just say he'd done a lot of bad things. We were transferred to another nearby camp that was in a much better condition and we were happy from that time onwards. All of this was done with the Polish 1st Armoured Division's help and they tried to find formal jobs for some of us. The Polish II Corps also assisted. Declaring us civilians would have made our lives harder but being in the Polish Army gave us an opportunity to attend Polish-run schools and complete our education. I initially attended a school that was supported by the 1st Armoured Division and, funnily enough, my old Latin teacher was there. She'd joined the AK and had also been taken as a prisoner of war to Oberlangen. We were eventually transferred to the Polish II Corps and my future husband, Jan, was part of this transport. Our first major stop was at Murnau in Bavaria.

The British didn't want General Anders to take us because it meant we'd start drawing on their supplies. But he'd discovered a loophole, whereby relatives of service personnel were accepted under British rules, so he had many of his soldiers put our names down as their 'sisters' or 'mothers' to get us through. Nonetheless, the British still weren't keen on the increase in food that our arrival represented, so Anders' men accepted a small cut in rations for us to be attached to the Polish II Corps.

I married my husband a little later and we were eventually transferred to Britain. There were Polish schools there as well and I attended my final school near Cheltenham. Jan and I then moved to London to seek work and I ended up making clothes. Our first journey to Poland occurred in 1966 and the second was in 1974, when Jan was ill with cancer. It was very emotional, although it was also difficult because the communists expected constant updates on our movements. We went to see Jan's family in Kielce and drove to Warsaw, where I met my aunt and uncle. Jan died in 1975 and I've been back to Poland a few times since, particularly after the communist regime fell, and it was beautiful to commemorate the Warsaw Uprising properly.

APPENDICES

As mentioned in the introduction, the purpose of the appendices is to assist the reader by briefly exploring some of the key events and battles highlighted by the interviewees. Those familiar with Polish history will have already encountered many of the topics presented below but some might be unaware of the finer points. Others will be approaching this information for the first time.

1: The Curzon Line was named after British Foreign Secretary Lord George Curzon following the First World War, although he had little to do with its creation as it was delineated by the Supreme War Council's Commission on Polish Affairs towards the end of 1919. It was rendered moot in the aftermath of Poland's victory against the Bolsheviks in 1920, with the country's eastern borders fixed via the Treaty of Riga signed on 18 March 1921. Leaping forward to 23 August 1939, Germany and the USSR agreed a secret division of Poland as part of the Molotov-Ribbentrop Pact. The boundary would run further west of the Curzon Line and was the Soviet Union's price for not intervening in any upcoming war. However, German forces had advanced beyond this line by the time the USSR joined the attack on Poland early on 17 September and border renegotiations were initiated in the aftermath. These culminated in the German-Soviet Friendship and Frontier Agreement signed on 28 September.

In return for taking less Polish territory, Stalin sought an updated boundary that roughly mirrored the Curzon Line, although a large chunk of territory around Bialystok and some areas in southeast Poland would still be taken into the USSR. He also wanted the USSR's sphere of influence to covertly extend into Lithuania, in addition to Estonia and Latvia as secretly agreed via the Molotov-Ribbentrop Pact. Hitler accepted these proposals, while Lithuania – ignorant of what had been arranged between the two dictatorships – signed a treaty with the USSR on 10 October. Wilno and its hinterland was ceded to Lithuania by the Soviet Union in return for Red Army basing rights.

Germany had seized just under 50% of Poland, although this territory included 20.2 million people[1] and the bulk of its industrial base. Swathes of northern and western Poland were immediately annexed into the Third Reich, while Poland's central core – Warsaw included – was turned into the General Government, with Krakow designated its capital. Reichsminister Hans Frank was appointed its Governor General. The population under Soviet occupation stood at 11.9 million, of whom 4.7 million were Polish speakers.[2] The Soviets then hurriedly divided eastern Poland into two, taking the northern part of their spoils into the Byelorussian Soviet Socialist Republic (SSR) and the southern part into the Ukrainian SSR. Further territorial changes occurred after the German invasion of the USSR in June 1941, with most of eastern Poland divided between the General Government; Reichskommissariat Ostland; Reichskommissariat Ukraine; and District Bialystok. Some smaller slices of land were also taken into the annexed territories.

Imposing a new Curzon Line became a Soviet war aim, with Stalin demanding this during the Tehran conference in November 1943. Roosevelt excused himself from discussing the topic but, privately, accepted the Soviet position concerning Poland and informed Stalin of this. Churchill also acquiesced and, while dining with Stalin at a banquet on the evening of 28 November, used some matchsticks to illustrate Poland being 'marched' westward. Lwów's status briefly became a sticking point as Eden had asked for the majority Polish-speaking city to remain in Poland, only for Churchill to fold in the face of Soviet protestations.

The USSR announced the Curzon Line would inform Poland's eastern border on 11 January 1944 and Churchill confirmed this in the House of Commons on 22 February. He also noted Poland would be compensated with German territory. Strongly objecting to these developments, the Polish government hoped the Western Allies would still argue for a revised border in Poland's favour at a more opportune time and expectations were raised on 7 June, when Roosevelt met Polish Prime Minister Stanisław Mikołajczyk. 'I will see to it that Poland does not come out of the war injured,' the President said.[3] The truth was fully revealed to Mikołajczyk at a meeting between himself, Churchill and Stalin in Moscow in October. Mikołajczyk had been the Polish Prime Minister since Sikorski's death in July 1943 and he resigned on 24 November 1944. The Yalta Conference from 4-11 February 1945 confirmed the Curzon Line for Poland with territorial compensation to the west and north at Germany's expense. Churchill and Roosevelt also requested Poland retain Lwów, plus some parts of the Galician oilfields, but Stalin categorically refused.

An agreement to recognise a new provisional government for Poland was reached as well, although it was agreed the Soviet-backed Polish Workers' Party and its proxies would hold key ministries and have the power to veto non-communist involvement.[4] The provisional government would form and receive international recognition once Germany was defeated and a nationwide election would take place soon afterwards. However, no election date was specified and no special envoys from the Western Allies would be allowed to monitor the process. The decisions taken at Yalta were a devastating blow for Poles fighting for a free and democratic country and the Polish government issued vigorous protests as a result. To their lasting credit, the Poles' battlefield performance was not adversely affected.

The British government struggled to resolve the status of Poles who refused to return to communist-dominated Poland after VE Day. Most knew exactly what Stalinism entailed but some went back, particularly those with families in urgent need of assistance. Unfortunately, the returnees soon rued their decision as they fell under suspicion of the communist-controlled security agencies and faced the threat of arbitrary arrest. Many were sentenced to hard labour and some were never heard from again. Meanwhile, Churchill had expressed hopes the remaining Poles would be granted resettlement rights in Britain and this was put into effect by Clement Attlee's subsequent Labour government. However, some Britons – particularly supporters of the USSR – were opposed to this and parroted Soviet-inspired anti-Polish propaganda.

Poles stationed in Britain had already reported being harassed, physically assaulted and called 'fascist' in public during the war's final years, while suicides had also been recorded. Adding insult to injury, several trade unions cried foul when the Polish Resettlement Corps was announced in May 1946.[5] This was the organisation designed to prepare Polish veterans, their families and refugees for life in Britain. Limited work opportunities in Britian and a desire to leave Europe behind spurred some Poles to emigrate onto Australia, Canada, the USA and several other countries. Fortunately, the pressures on the Poles in Britain soon receded and they helped establish today's vibrant British-Polish community.

2: All those living in eastern Poland were stripped of their Polish citizenship and made Soviet citizens in November 1939. The Soviets then launched an ethnic cleansing campaign of Poles that lasted from February 1940 until Operation Barbarossa in June 1941. This involved four mass deportations, with most forced to work on collectives or other state-owned enterprises in the USSR. They were following 200,000-250,000 Polish prisoners of war thrown into labour camps after the September 1939 campaign.[6] Separately, thousands of other Polish citizens were arrested and sentenced to the gulags for multiple reasons, including those caught trying to escape into neutral countries. In addition, around 150,000 Polish citizens were conscripted into the Red Army,[7] while thousands of others were press-ganged into Soviet labour battalions.

The first mass deportation started on 10 February 1940 and included between 200,000 and 220,000 people,[8] with most deportees given just several minutes to grab whatever possessions they thought necessary. They were then shoved onto trains comprising cattle wagons with almost no facilities, other than a hole in the floor for waste and – for some – cast-iron stoves with a little fuel. The deportees were primarily taken to the north European part of Russia, where the winter conditions led to horrific mortality rates. The second deportation started on 13 April 1940 and involved around 320,000 people, with most taken to Kazakhstan. The third deportation started in late June and witnessed roughly 240,000 Polish citizens scattered across northern Russia and deep into Siberia.

The fourth and final deportation occurred in June 1941 and involved 300,000 people who primarily came from the Wilno region and other locations in northeast Poland. Of the deported Polish citizens, historians Tuszynski and Denda estimated Catholics and others represented 52% of the total; Jews 30%; and Belarusians and Ukrainians 18%.[9] However, the precise number of Polish citizens forcibly taken into the USSR has been impossible to compute and historians have cited between 1 million and 2 million people. Mortality rates were eye-watering, with thousands upon thousands of Poles killed by exposure, starvation, overwork, disease and murder.

3: The Sikorski-Maisky Agreement was signed in London on 31 July and was followed by an 'amnesty' on 12 August 1941. All Poles were to be released and Polish citizenship reintroduced for those who had lost it because of prior Soviet policy. The Polish-Soviet Military Agreement was signed two days later and Poland given permission to raise a 30,000-strong army in the USSR to be commanded by General Władysław Anders.[10] He had been captured towards the end of the September 1939 campaign and detained in Moscow's Butyrka prison and the Lubyanka, the NKVD's headquarters. Batches of Polish prisoners of war were freed from captivity and allowed to enlist, although many were not told of the agreements. The situation was similar for Polish civilians.

Poles who reached the initial muster points at Buzuluk, Tatishchevo and Totskoye were usually half-starved and sick, although this was not a surprise because of the overall conditions. What was unusual – and a source of deep suspicion – was the low number of officers presenting themselves. Polish Prime Minister and Commander-in-Chief Władysław Sikorski met Stalin in Moscow on 3 December 1941, with the Soviet dictator feigning ignorance when asked about these missing men. In fact, Stalin had secretly confirmed the execution of 25,700 Poles in March 1940,[11] including officers, higher-ranking NCOs, Polish Border Corps personnel and landowners. They were executed from April-May 1940.

Stalin agreed the Poles could increase their army to 96,000 soldiers, including up to 25,000 soldiers, sailors and airmen who would be allowed to exit the USSR to help fill the ranks of Polish units fighting elsewhere.[12] Permission was also granted for Anders to move his formations to Central Asia as the region was nearer Persia, a key supply route for British materiel earmarked for the Poles. Anders' units were transferred to several new locations from January-February 1942, including Guzar, Kermine, Jalal-Abad, Lugovoye, Pamir and Yangiyul.

The Soviets then muddied the waters by requesting a Polish division join the battleline. The Poles baulked at this, insisting their army in the USSR would only deploy and fight as one entity. Meanwhile, the British had made little secret of their desire to have Polish forces transferred from the USSR to help protect their Middle Eastern interests and approaches to Stalin were made to this effect. On 6 March, the Soviets suddenly announced the rations provided to the Poles would be slashed to just 26,000 people per day effective 20 March.[13] Anders met Stalin on 18 March and renegotiated rations for 44,000 people per day and an evacuation of up to 30,000 Polish soldiers to join the British in Persia.

The transfer was conducted in nightmarish conditions as freighters and old transport vessels took the Poles across the Caspian Sea from Krasnovodsk to Pahlavi in Persia. Departures lasted from 24 March to 3 April, with 30,799 soldiers and 12,455 civilians making the journey.[14] British units sent to Pahlavi to assist the new arrivals were shocked by their poor health and the suffering they had obviously experienced at Soviet hands. Many Poles were gravely ill and mortality rates were correspondingly high. Fortunately, the conditions soon improved as medical teams and support units worked tirelessly to nurse the sick back to good health.

Sikorski wanted Anders' remaining forces in the USSR to play a role on the Eastern Front as originally intended but Soviet attitudes were hardening and Anders was concerned they would move against those under his command. In addition, the British were still keen to incorporate the remaining Poles into their Middle Eastern order of battle and a second evacuation was eventually agreed. The same vessels as before transferred the Poles to Pahlavi via Krasnovodsk from 5-25 August, while overland departures took place between August and early September. Again, many of the new arrivals were ill but hospital and support staff in Pahlavi were now better prepared to cope, while civilians were soon forwarded to refugee camps established in Peria, India, East Africa and South Africa. A total of 114,462 Poles were evacuated from the USSR, including 70,292 soldiers and 6,898 cadets.[15]

Thousands of Polish soldiers in the Middle East were siphoned off to serve in Britain and elsewhere, including those accepted by the PAF and the Polish Navy, while the Independent Carpathian Rifle Brigade that had fought at Tobruk in 1941 became the cadre unit upon which the 3rd Carpathian Rifle Division was formed. In total, Anders had around 40,000 men and women to shape into the Polish II Corps, with its units eventually transported from Egypt to Italy from December 1943 to April 1944. The formation comprised the 2nd Warsaw Armoured Brigade, the 3rd Carpathian Rifle Division and the 5th Kresowa Infantry Division at the campaign's start. There were also numerous logistical and medical units in support, while the Corps' heavy guns were pooled into an artillery group.

The Poles were initially deployed along the River Sangro towards the eastern end of the Gustav Line, which stretched across the Italian Peninsula. The focus then shifted westward as the Allies continued their efforts to force open the main road to Rome. However, the terrain favoured the defenders and enemy positions around Cassino town and the hills behind it were especially strong. The large abbey atop Monte Cassino was where the Benedictine Order had been founded in the 6th Century and the Germans declared it neutral ground. The Allies suspected a ruse and had bombed the abbey in mid-February 1944, with the ruins occupied by elite paratroopers of the 1st Fallschirmjäger Division.

The Polish II Corps would strike at the enemy's defensive positions immediately beyond Monte Cassino as part of the front-wide Operation Diadem in May 1944. The attack started with a massive artillery barrage at 11pm on 11 May, followed by infantry assaults early on 12 May. Only limited progress was made by the Poles and they reported heavy losses. The second attack started on 17 May and high casualties were suffered again, although the rate of advance improved and the Poles had captured enough ground to make the abbey's defence untenable. In addition, the Allies made solid progress elsewhere and the enemy was forced to retreat in several other key sectors. The Poles sent a reconnaissance unit from 12th Podolian Uhlans to scout the abbey early on 18 May and, apart from some wounded Germans, they found the ruins largely deserted. The Polish flag and the Union Jack were raised at around 10am, with the famous bugle call of St. Mary's in Krakow played two hours later.

The Poles had achieved a notable victory but fierce fighting continued in the immediate aftermath, with Polish units responsible for clearing Piedimonte San Germano and its environs from 20-25 May.

Replacements were found by transferring rear-line personnel and recruiting Poles who had been forcibly conscripted into the Wehrmacht and had either been captured or deserted and then volunteered for service. The Polish II Corps now returned to Adriatic side of Italy, capturing the strategic port of Ancona on 18 July after heavy fighting. It then fought its way through the Apennines, with the Allies reaching the Gothic Line by late August 1944. This was the Germans' last major defensive feature before the Po Valley and resistance stiffened accordingly. Unfortunately, the overall advance ground to a halt as winter arrived and Anders' forces found themselves stuck in the hills south of Forli. The Allied offensive resumed in spring 1945, with the Poles liberating Imola on 15 April and entering Bologna on 21 April. The fighting came to an end in the Italian theatre on 2 May and total losses for the Polish II Corps stood at 2,197 soldiers killed in action, 8,737 wounded and 264 listed as missing.[16]

4: German units first neared Warsaw on 7 September 1939, launching attacks that were thwarted from 8-9 September. Vital breathing room for the capital was won after the Polish Army started the Battle of Bzura on 9 September. This forced the enemy to peel away formations to contain and then crush the Poles' most effective counter-attack of the campaign. Warsaw was encircled by mid-September, with German formations launching full-scale assaults from 23 September onwards. The attack on 25 September was particularly bloody and included an aerial bombardment involving around 240 Junkers Ju87s, 100 Do17s and 30 Ju52s transports. Most German aircraft made three or four sorties that day, dropping a total of around 500 tons of bombs and 72 tons of incendiaries and phosphorous bombs.[17]

Garrison commander General Juliusz Rómmel and his senior subordinates decided Warsaw had suffered long enough as further resistance would only bring more death and destruction and a ceasefire was requested on 26 September. The fighting ended the following day and the capitulation took place on 28 September. Wehrmacht units and enemy security forces formally entered Warsaw on 1 October and a German victory parade was held in the city on 5 October, with Hitler taking the salute. Meanwhile, Poland's government had reached Romania on the night of 17/18 September and been detained under neutrality laws. However, a new Polish government coalesced in France, with Władysław Raczkiewicz – a former Marshal of the Senate – becoming President. He appointed Władysław Sikorski Prime Minister and then Commander-in-Chief.

General Franciszek Kleeberg's Independent Operational Group Polesie was Poland's last major formation to surrender, negotiating terms on 5 October and marching into captivity on the following day. The Germans reported a total of 10,600 killed in action during the campaign, with just over 5,029 missing and 30,332 wounded.[18] This was later revised to 15,450 dead.[19] The Red Army reported just 737 killed in action and 1,862 wounded,[20] numbers that were suspiciously low. Against Germany, the Poles lost 66,300 killed, 133,700 wounded and 420,000 taken prisoner.[21] Against the USSR, they suffered up to several thousand killed in action and wounded, plus 200,000-250,000 Polish soldiers taken prisoner.

5: Red Army formations were nearing Warsaw's eastern hinterland by late July 1944 and an uprising was launched at 5pm on 1 August on the order of AK Commander-in-Chief Tadeusz Komorowski 'Bór'. The Poles were determined to liberate their capital just before the Soviets arrived, hoping to underscore the Underground State's authority and, through this, the sovereignty of the Polish government based in London. AK numbers stood at around 30,000 soldiers in Warsaw and 10,000 soldiers in areas outside the city,[22] although they were chronically short of weaponry. The AK was also supported by several smaller clandestine organisations and thousands of enthusiastic civilian volunteers.

Notable victories were achieved in the first few days as the Poles liberated zones in the city centre and inner suburbs, although several critical elements remained in German hands, including Warsaw's airfields and bridges across the River Vistula. Enemy reinforcements were also swift to arrive, with the bulk of these formations under SS control and commanded by Obergruppenführer Erich von dem Bach-Zelewski. Their numbers stood at around 40,000 soldiers by 20 August, supported by an array of artillery, armour and various Luftwaffe units.[23] With Hitler's approval, Reichsführer-SS Heinrich Himmler insisted on no mercy for the Poles and the subsequent levels of depravity were shocking even by the Nazis' own subterranean standards. This included the mass murder of around 40,000 civilians in 48 hours by Gruppenführer Heinz Reinefarth's Kampfgruppe after it advanced into the Wola and Ochota districts from 5 August.[24] His ad-hoc formation included units from the Azerbaijani Legion; the RONA Brigade;[25] and the notorious Dirlewanger Brigade. However, the massacres only strengthened the defenders' resolve and Bach-Zelewski quietly dropped the policy of no mercy as a result.

The Poles made excellent use of the urban terrain and inflicted heavy casualties on the enemy and the Germans were soon backing their assaults with indiscriminate air strikes and artillery bombardments. They also relied on flamethrowers, high explosives, assault guns and Goliath remote-controlled demolition vehicles. The noose now started tightening and the defence of key areas slowly became untenable. For example, control of the Old Town was relinquished by the AK on 2 September, with the surviving units evacuated to Central Warsaw by using the sewer system. The Germans attempted to thwart this movement by dropping grenades through manholes or pouring down petrol and then setting it alight. Around 4,500 AK soldiers escaped but 2,500 wounded had to remain, along with 35,000 civilians. The Germans murdered an estimated 7,000 Poles after seizing the Old Town, with the survivors evicted and forwarded to concentration camps.[26]

Efforts were made to supply the Warsaw Uprising by using British, Polish and South African aircraft flying from southern Italy. However, the USSR refused landing rights in Ukraine, forcing the aircrews to make dangerous return journeys and lives were lost as a result. The Americans also wanted to launch a major supply drop but Stalin dragged his feet until finally granting landing rights on 9 September. However, Poltava airbase in Ukraine was only made available in mid-September and the mission finally took place on 18 September. High winds meant just 20% of the cannisters reached the AK, with the rest falling into enemy hands.[27] The Soviets undertook supply drops from 13 September onwards but the weapons delivered were frequently obsolete and the rations usually fouled. The containers were also released at low level without parachutes, their contents often rendered useless on impact.

There was one last tangible hope for the defenders by mid-September. The Red Army had finally cleared Warsaw's eastern Praga district and subsequent efforts to cross the River Vistula by the Soviet-sponsored 1st Polish Army resulted in the capture of some small bridgeheads. However, none of these hard-won successes were followed up and the footholds had been overrun by 23 September. In the meantime, German reinforcements continued arriving and AK-held positions were further reduced. The defenders' ammunition, food and medical supplies were now almost exhausted and Komorowski sought terms, requesting AK soldiers be treated as formal prisoners of war. Bach-Zelewski consented and the surrender agreement was signed on 2 October.

The Germans reported 16,000 killed and 9,000 wounded,[28] plus 310 tanks, armoured cars and self-propelled guns lost.[29] They also recorded 11,668 AK soldiers taken prisoner of war from 3-5 October, the days in which the city was emptied.[30] Around 15,000 Poles were estimated killed in action and 200,000 civilians either killed or murdered.[31] Between 350,000 and 550,000 people were marched to Durchgangslager 121 in Pruszków after the Uprising, with 60,000 people deported to concentration camps and 90,000 people forwarded to work in the Third Reich. The rest were sent to the parts of Poland still occupied by the Germans.[32] Others were taken to different processing areas and suffered the same fate. Meanwhile, Hitler had ordered the obliteration of Warsaw, with looting and demolition teams sent into the city to plunder and destroy whatever remained. A few inhabitants managed to hide amid the ruins and the ghost city was finally liberated by the Red Army and the Polish People's Army on 17 January 1945.

6: Auschwitz had become a sprawling complex by 1943 and its constituent parts comprised Auschwitz I, Auschwitz II-Birkenau, Auschwitz III-Monowitz and numerous sub- and branch camps. As its name suggests, Auschwitz I was the parent camp. It was created by utilising former Polish Army barracks and was operational by summer 1940 and its main entrance came to be adorned with a metal sign comprising the cynical lie 'Arbeit macht frei' or 'work makes you free'.

Prisoners at Auschwitz wore course clothes with vertical stripes and a downward-facing triangle, the colour of which was based on German prisoner categorisation. For example, political prisoners had red triangles and criminals green. Poles had the letter 'P' superimposed on their triangle or printed next to the label that displayed their prison number, while Jews had an inverted yellow triangle added to create a dual-coloured Star of David.[33] A prisoner's number was also tattooed onto the skin after October 1941, although some categories of prisoner were exempted from this. The day started with an early-morning rollcall, followed by work parties forming up for hard labour in gravel pits; forestry and lumber; road repair; and agriculture etc.

Kapos were prisoners given privileges for keeping those around them in order, with the prisoners frequently beaten, tortured or executed by the guards for the slightest infractions. The first gassings at Auschwitz I occurred in August and September 1941 in Block 11, the victims comprising Soviet prisoners of war and camp hospital patients. Afterwards, the mortuary next to the crematorium was converted into a gas chamber and used until July 1943. Auschwitz I comprised 18,418 prisoners at the start of 1944, including 8,649 Poles and 3,830 Jews of all nationalities.[34]

Construction of Auschwitz II-Birkenau started in October 1941, with the first gassings taking place there in March 1942. Arrivals faced a rapid selection process after hellish train journeys and around 10% were taken away for hard labour.[35] Others were removed for different purposes, including horrifying medical experiments, while the rest were marched away for 'disinfection' and 'showers' – euphemisms for being gassed. Sonderkommando prisoner units were responsible for disposing the bodies after first removing glasses, hair and gold teeth, while the victims' luggage was taken away to be plundered. Jews made up the overwhelming majority of those killed at Auschwitz II-Birkenau but other groups were killed there too, including non-Jewish Poles. The final mass murders included around 70,000 Polish Jews taken from the Lodz Ghetto between August and September 1944.[36]

Located several miles to the east, Auschwitz III-Monowitz's raison d'être was to provide workers for the IG Farben plant, which became operational in autumn 1942. It primarily produced a synthetic rubber called buna that was desperately needed by the German war machine and an estimated 35,000 people laboured there in total, of whom 25,000 lost their lives.[37] Further afield were the branch camps that provided prisoners for a variety of workshops, plants, factories and coal mines.

The latter were especially dangerous for those with no experience of working underground and the average life expectancy for many sent down the mines was estimated at just one month.[38]

German efforts to destroy evidence at Auschwitz started in the second half of 1944 and several Sonderkommando units were 'evacuated', a euphemism for being murdered. Realising they were doomed, Sonderkommando at Crematoria IV launched an uprising and set the building's roof on fire on 7 October 1944. Resistance spread to other sections of Auschwitz II-Birkenau but the guards were swift to respond and hundreds of prisoners were gunned down, with no escapes reported. The gas chambers and crematoria were demolished from November 1944 onwards in a poor attempt to hide their monstrous purpose. Around 1.1 million people, possibly more, had been murdered at Auschwitz by the time the Red Army liberated the camp complex on 27 January 1945. Of that total, around 960,000 were Jews, including 300,000 Polish Jews, and 70,000-75,000 non-Jewish Poles.[39]

7: The Fall of France from May-June 1940 was a disaster for Poland. The Polish 1st and 2nd divisions were deployed in northeast France, which meant most soldiers from these formations were either captured or forced to cross into neutral Switzerland. Fortunately, thousands of Poles from other units were evacuated or used their own initiative to escape and the Polish Army in Britain stood at 4,475 officers and 12,730 other ranks effective 26 July 1940.[40] It took time but the Polish 1st Armoured Division – the Polish I Corps' vanguard formation – formally came into existence on 26 February 1942, led by Stanisław Maczek.

The division's numbers were expanded by transferring soldiers evacuated out of the USSR via the Middle East during 1942, with the formation comprising 885 officers and 15,210 other ranks just before deploying to Normandy.[41] Its 10th Armoured Cavalry Brigade included the 1st Armoured Regiment, 2nd Armoured Regiment, 24th Lancers and 10th Dragoons. Its 3rd Rifle Brigade comprised the 1st Highland Battalion, 8th Infantry Battalion, 9th Infantry Battalion and a separate heavy machine gun section. The 10th Mounted Rifle Regiment also fielded tanks and was designed for reconnaissance in force, while vital artillery, medical, engineering and transport units were available as well.

The division was transported across the English Channel from late July into early August and added to the Canadian II Corps' order of battle. The Poles were soon in the thick of action, taking part in Operation Totalize launched on 8 August 1944. Unfortunately, the division faced well-prepared positions held by the 12th SS Panzer Division 'Hitlerjugend' and the initial attack was called off after more than 40 tanks were knocked out.[42] Maczek's formation was then re-positioned after a few days of fighting and took part in Operation Tractable launched on 14 August. The Canadian II Corps sought to link-up with American formations hooking their way around the Germans to the south, hoping to complete the encirclement of the German Seventh Army and Panzer Group West.

Hitler belatedly ordered a front-wide retreat on 16 August and the race was on to cut the enemy's escape routes. Maczek was ordered to seize Chambois and its environs and he created three battlegroups in response: two battlegroups to tackle the village and one to seize Mont-Ormel, a ridge located a few miles northeast of Chambois that included Hill 262 North. This feature resembled the outline of a medieval mace on the map and was nicknamed Maczuga, or Mace, as a result. The advance started late on 18 August but one of the battlegroups aiming for Chambois became lost and was mistakenly directed by a French farmer to Les Champeaux instead. On being informed of the error, Maczek ordered the battlegroup to relocate to the Mace, which it did after disengaging from Les Champeaux on the morning of 19 August. The other battlegroup aiming for Chambois had reached its target, clearing the village and surrounding area by the afternoon of 19 August and linking up with US forces in the process.

German counter-attacks came thick and fast across 20 August, including assaults on the Mace by 2nd SS Panzer Division 'Das Reich' and the German 3rd Parachute Division. Chambois and its immediate environs was attacked by an assortment of German units trying to escape. In between fighting the enemy, the Poles also called in air strikes and artillery barrages and enemy casualties were heavy. However, many German units bypassed the danger or ditched their vehicles and escaped cross-country. Enemy assaults resumed early on 21 August as the Poles were nearing the end of their reserves of ammunition. Fortunately, the Polish positions held firm and the Canadian Grenadier Guards reached the Mace at around 1pm, bringing ammunition, supplies and medical assistance. They relieved the Poles and the Falaise Pocket was considered closed a few hours later. The division had won a notable victory and, by the end of the Normandy campaign, had captured a general, 136 officers and 5,115 other ranks, while also knocking out 55 panzers, 44 guns, 38 armoured vehicles and numerous other vehicles and horse-drawn carriages. By contrast, 325 Poles were killed in action, 1,002 wounded and 114 listed as missing.[43]

After a spell recuperating, the Polish 1st Armoured Division joined the British and Commonwealth forces advancing through northern France and into Belgium from late August onwards, liberating some important locations along the way. The Poles eventually reached the Netherlands, south of the Scheldt, where they recorded several more successes before swinging northeast into Belgium again. The division then pushed back into the Netherlands and liberated the city of Breda in late October, doing so with minimal civilian casualties or damage to infrastructure. Breda later granted the division the freedom of the city in thanks. Maczek's soldiers reached Moerdijk village on 8 November as the front settled along the River Maas, although they were involved in several local actions afterwards, including the capture of Kapelsche Veer in January 1945.

The Allies' offensive resumed in Northwest Europe in spring 1945, with the Poles advancing along a corridor that initially straddled the Netherlands and Germany. The prisoner of war camp at Oberlangen was liberated by an ad-hoc reconnaissance unit on 12 April 1945, freeing female AK prisoners of war in the process. The Poles then fought their way into northwest Germany and reached the environs of Wilhelmshaven and its strategic port by 4 May – the same day the Germans agreed regional surrender terms with Field Marshal Montgomery. A front-wide ceasefire came into effect on 5 May, with the 1st Polish Armoured Division and a small Royal Navy contingent taking Wilhelmshaven's surrender. The Poles assumed complete control of the city the next day and later reported the capture of two admirals, one general, 1,900 officers, 32,000 other ranks, three cruisers, one command ship, 18 submarines and 205 smaller warships and support vessels.[44]

ENDNOTES

Introduction

1. Topol, Olga (editor), *Forgotten Force, A Journey of Memory* (Józef Piłsudski Institute of Research in Modern History London, 2020) p.25

Stanisław Adam

1. Modern Poland's independence was achieved on 11 November 1918. It had been partitioned between Austria/Austro-Hungary, Prussia/Germany and Russia since the late 18th Century.
2. Kyiv.
3. Lviv.
4. German formations took several of Lwów's outlying suburbs and villages before the arrival of the Red Army in the vicinity on 19 September. The Polish garrison surrendered to the Soviets on 22 September.
5. Not quite the case in late September 1939, although the Curzon Line certainly had a baleful influence on Poland. See appendix 1.
6. The Soviet Union conducted four major deportations of Polish citizens from February 1940 to June 1941. See appendix 2.
7. Adam's father was a policeman and would have been identified as a threat by the NKVD. He was probably executed in the Katyn massacres.
8. Embi.

9. The Sikorski-Maisky Agreement normalised diplomatic relations between Poland and the USSR and was signed in London on 31 July 1941. It was the first step towards the eventual creation of what became the Polish II Corps. See appendix 3.
10. Türkmenbaşy.
11. Adam was understandably mistaken here. The 'Greek unit' was from the Cyprus Regiment, which mainly comprised Greek Cypriots and some Turkish and Armenian Cypriots.
12. 14th Wilenski Rifle Battalion, which was part of the 5th Wilno Infantry Brigade.
13. A position known as a sangar.
14. The 5th Kresowa Division's 18th Lwówski Rifle Battalion officially liberated Predappio on 27 October 1944.
15. The ceasefire in Italy came into effect on 2 May 1945.

Stanisław Berkieta

1. The Cegielski works at Rzeszów came on stream in 1937. It produced locomotives, engines and materiel, including the Bofors 37mm anti-tank gun and the 40mm anti-aircraft gun under licence.
2. Probably to avoid paying the associated licencing fees.
3. Using the approximate mid-to-late 1930s historic exchange of 5 zloty to the US dollar, Berkieta was given around $4,000 dollars. This equates to a real price of about $85,000 at the time of writing.
4. Primarily Ukrainian ultranationalists who intimidated and attacked Poles in the immediate wake of the USSR's invasion.
5. Kovel.
6. Warsaw endured a gruelling siege in September 1939. See appendix 4.
7. A renewed Polish Army was raised in France after the September 1939 campaign, with most of its rank and file conscripted from France's sizable Franco-Polish community. However, it also included the majority of those who had escaped Poland via the neutral nations.
8. Berkieta and Srodowski intended to head due south of Przemyśl and cross into the former Czechoslovakian province of Ruthenia that had recently been annexed by Hungary.

9. Starobelsk had held almost 3,900 Polish officers. They were removed in batches in April-May 1940 and murdered at the NKVD's local headquarters in Kharkov/Kharkiv, with their bodies buried in nearby wooded parkland. Their remains were discovered in May 1990.
10. Thousands of the ethnic Poles living in the USSR had been deported to Kotlas and the surrounding region during the 1930s.
11. Stanisław Kot, Poland's ambassador to the USSR. Berkieta's journey to Uzbekistan occurred in September 1941, which was well before the relocation of Anders' forces to Central Asia and it seems likely his transport had always been earmarked for fieldwork. Telling those affected Kot had ratified the decision ensured their compliance and attempted to sow seeds of hatred towards the Polish government.
12. Correctly guessing the Soviets would target them after being captured, some Polish officers removed their insignia and took their chances with the other ranks, trying to remain undetected.
13. Qarshi.
14. Taraz.
15. Yangiyo'l.
16. Anzali.
17. The Poles took over from the British 78th Division.
18. A German handheld anti-tank weapon based on the US Bazooka, albeit larger and with a greater range.

Aleksander Bogdan

1. The Red Army officially occupied Grajewo on 21 September 1939.
2. Many Polish Jews welcomed the arrival of the Red Army because they feared the dangers of life under German occupation. However, a small number willingly collaborated with the Soviets as did some of their non-Jewish compatriots.
3. The Germans and Soviets co-operated in deporting Poles or hunting down those wanted by their respective security services.
4. Yekaterinburg.

Jan Brodzki

1. Sokół was founded in 1867 and promoted gymnastics and Polish patriotism.
2. Fear had turned to panic in Warsaw after all service-aged men not yet in uniform were told to evacuate east by the Polish government. The roads out of Warsaw became packed until the order was rescinded on the night of 7/8 September.
3. Formally Brest-Litovsk, it included an important fortress complex that guarded a crossing over the River Bug. It was also where the Bolsheviks agreed terms with the Central Powers on 3 March 1918. Today, it is the Belarusian border city of Brest.
4. Brodski is almost certainly describing Grochówka, a classic canteen dish.
5. Garwolin is also about 40 miles (65km) southeast of Warsaw.
6. Pawiak prison was much feared and primarily used by the Germans to process Polish prisoners, sending them onto concentration camps or places of execution.
7. Skilled operators and specialist equipment were required and many of those involved were Cichociemni, the Silent and Unseen. These were elite agents trained in Britain and dropped into Poland from 1941 onwards.
8. Perhaps the best-known actor to collaborate was Karol 'Igo' Sym. He was appointed the head of Warsaw's Polish Theatre and several other positions before being executed by ZWZ for collaboration on 7 March 1941. Hostages were shot and Polish actors and directors arrested in retaliation.
9. The Warsaw Ghetto Uprising lasted from April-May 1943. Facing desperate and determined resistance from Jewish fighters, the Germans systematically destroyed this closed part of Warsaw block by block. Surviving Jews were either shot or marched to the Umschlagplatz railhead, with most then taken straight to the Treblinka death camp.
10. The Warsaw Uprising was a defining moment for Poland during the war. See appendix 5.
11. Brodski was pretending to have belonged to the Polish Independent Carpathian Brigade.

Barbara Buczek

1. The Jews of Skawina and several surrounding villages had been forced into a ghetto, increasing the town's Jewish population to around 2,000 people. The ghetto was liquidated from 29-30 August 1942, with around 180 Jews murdered in the market town. The fittest men were sent to concentration camps and worked to death, while the others were killed at the Belzec death camp.
2. The Germans were forced out of Skawina by 23 January 1945.
3. The Polish 1st Armoured Division and various support units were based in and around the environs of Haren, western Germany. The town had temporarily been renamed Lwów and then Maczków in honour of General Maczek.

Antoni Budzynski

1. The 5th Wilno Infantry Brigade.
2. Tanzania.

Jerzy Cynk

1. A limited French offensive was launched against the Saarland. It was wound down by French Commander-in-Chief General Maurice Gamelin after 12 September 1939.
2. Several Polish formations avoided destruction or capture and reached Warsaw as the Battle of Bzura entered its final phases.
3. The irregular bombing raids of Warsaw by the USSR have indeed been largely forgotten. This included two major attacks in August and September 1942.
4. Auschwitz had become an enormous and horrifying complex of slave labour and mass murder by 1943. See appendix 6.
5. Wladislaw Dering. His role has been the subject of much debate.
6. Nierychlo helped establish the orchestra at Auschwitz I but he was removed in 1942 and Adam Kopyciński took over.
7. The 2-SS Bauzug, later redesignated 7-SS Eisenbahnbaubrigade.

8. Munich fell to the Americans on 30 April 1945.
9. Yugoslav communist forces loyal to Josip Tito entered Trieste on 1 May, while the battle-hardened 2nd New Division arrived on 2 May.
10. Poland's clandestine efforts to track the V1 and V2 programmes provided critical intelligence. This included V2 components and schematics supplied to Britain via Operation Most III on 25 July 1944.

Antoni Fedorowicz

1. Ternopil.
2. Fedorowicz was referring to the crossing effort early on 24 September. The boats were canvas-sided and had to be paddled across.
3. Baltussen knew first aid and helped care for the Polish wounded. She also tirelessly lobbied the Dutch government to formally recognise the IPB's role after the war.
4. Sosabowski was scapegoated by his British peers following the Arnhem campaign, particularly by Field Marshal Bernard Montgomery and General Frederick Browning.

Zbigniew Gondek

1. German forces entered Przemyśl on 15 September 1939, including Einsatzgruppe and Sicherheitspolizei personnel, and massacred between 500 and 600 Polish Jews.
2. The River San informed the German-Soviet partition, with Przemyśl divided in two. Gondek lived on the eastern side.
3. Gondek's father was probably one of those murdered in the Katyn massacres.
4. This devious 'debt' trap was often used by managers across the USSR.
5. Point 593 was a key feature on Snakeshead Ridge, northwest of the monastery.
6. Piedimonte San Germano.
7. The Virtuti Militari was established in 1792. It has various classes, with strict criteria for acts of personal bravery. First-time recipients are awarded the Silver Cross, while the Golden Cross is only awarded to those who already hold the Silver.

8. Gondek was indeed lucky to receive penicillin as mass production only really started after 1945. Meanwhile, maggot therapy to stop wounds festering has been used since ancient times.

Eugenia Jarkiewicz-Werynski

1. The murder programme of those with disabilities or serious psychiatric issues was established via the Reich Chancellery and called Aktion T4.
2. Although badly outnumbered, the Poles put up fierce resistance in northeast Poland. The fighting at Wilno took place from 18-19 September; Grodno lasted from 20-22 September; and the Battle of Kodziowce – a Polish defensive victory – occurred from 23-24 September. The Red Army took Augustów on 25 September.
3. The Augustów Round-up almost certainly resulted in a Katyn-like massacre and the bodies of the missing have never been found. Historians have estimated around 2,000 people were killed by the Soviets.
4. The NKVD murdered around 30 prisoners held in a block next to their headquarters in Augustów's Water Administration building on 22 June 1941.
5. Stutthof concentration camp was located roughly 20 miles (32km) east of Danzig.
6. Storing root vegetables in this manner was common before the widespread availability of fridges and freezers.
7. Ravensbrück was Nazis' largest camp complex for women and noted for the brutality of its female guards, SS-Helferin, many of whom were trained at the camp before being sent to other locations. This included Irma Grese, the infamous 'Hyena of Auschwitz'.
8. Heinkel produced the He111 bomber and, later in the war, the He177 bomber. The mention of 'small bombers' suggests the He219, a night fighter that entered production from mid-1943 onwards.
9. Allied bombers were almost certainly aiming for the factory but there was no such thing as precision bombing during the Second World War.

Grażyna Kopeć

1. Pipera, Francizka and Świebokiej, Teresy, *Auschwitz, Nazistowski Obóz Śmierci* (Państwowe Muzeum Oświęcim-Brzezinka, 1993) p.216
2. Doctor Zieliński was on the Board of the Polish Red Cross. He also helped establish a hospital for mothers with babies and toddlers in the immediate aftermath Auschwitz's liberation.
3. The 'Eastern Strip' or 'Eastern Zone' lay within Regierungsbezirk Kattowitz. Germanisation was temporarily placed on hold in the Eastern Strip.
4. Ethnic Germans were recorded on the Deutsche Volksliste. However, it also included many unwilling participants as those placed on the list were liable for conscription to serve the Third Reich, including Poles living in annexed territory.
5. First floor for British English speakers.
6. Kopeć was referring to *The Red Plague*, or *Czerwona Zaraza*, by Józef Szczepański. He was killed in action on 10 September 1944 during the Warsaw Uprising.
7. Formally Swinemünde.
8. Heilbad Heiligenstadt, which was located roughly 18 miles (28km) from the British Zone.
9. French Equatorial Africa included the French Congo. It was an important waypoint for a major Allied aircraft transfer programme.

Zbigniew Kowalski

1. Zaliszczyky.
2. Possibly dating this incident to the French armistice on 22 June 1940 or the days immediately afterwards. Vichy France was formally created on 10 July.
3. For those who really want to know, urine in a situation like this has no efficacy. See: Schimelpfenig, Tod, *Is Urine Sterile? And Other Questions About Using Pee in First Aid* (National Outdoor Living School, 1 May 2015)
4. Sant Ferran Castle, which was also used as a concentration camp.

5. Possibly Miranda de Ebro camp, where most Poles caught crossing the border were detained. Its conditions were grim.
6. See appendix 7 for a brief history of the Polish 1st Armoured Division.
7. Operation Totalize start date.
8. Operation Tractable start date.

Zbigniew Mieczkowski

1. Mieczkowski had been transferred to the 10th Armoured Brigade commanded by Stanisław Maczek. It acquitted itself well during the Fall of France and many of its personnel were successfully evacuated to Britain. Those in support roles or still in training did not see combat.
2. Operation Cobra and its aftermath.
3. Lieutenant-Colonel Stanislaw Koszutski's battlegroup.
4. The Kübelwagen performed a similar role to a jeep.
5. Almost certainly Auster aircraft flown as an air observation post.
6. Taking Kapelsche Veer had been a miserable slog for Polish, British and then Canadian units in January 1945.
7. Grudziński accepted Wilhelmshaven's surrender on 5 May 1945, with the Poles taking control on 6 May.

Marcelino Ostrowski

1. The Imperial Russian partition of Poland. It was widely known as Congress Poland after the Congress of Vienna 1814-1815 delineated parts of Europe – Poland included – following Napoleon's downfall.
2. Brazil declared war on Germany on 22 August 1942.
3. The final version of 301 Squadron served with RAF Transport Command.
4. Ostrowski was also awarded the Polonia Restituta in 2012.
5. Enemy pilots still needed great skill to strike British bombers from underneath. Across 1943, the Germans started installing a purpose-built firing system into their night fighters nicknamed Schräge Musik, or Slanted/Strange Jazz. It comprised reversed guns angled

to fire upwards and backwards, with the targeting made possible by a special Revi gun site.

6. Gardening missions involved dropping sea mines to hinder German naval efforts, particularly U-boat activity.
7. An early type of chaff called 'Window' that was introduced in 1943.
8. British recognition of the Polish government – based in London since summer 1940 – was withdrawn in July 1945 in favour of the communist-dominated Provisional Government of National Unity. The latter was formed on 28 June 1945 per the agreements made at Yalta.
9. Polish Women's Auxiliary Air Force (PLSK) was formed in April 1943 and came under the WAAF umbrella.

Elizabeth Piekarski

1. Wilno/Vilnius and its hinterland was ceded to Lithuania by the Soviets in October 1939. In return, the Red Army was awarded basing rights.
2. Wojtek the bear was with 22nd Artillery Supply Company and he liked to wrestle, chew cigarettes and drink beer. He was formally enlisted in the Polish Army to circumvent British restrictions on the transportation of pets or mascots into Italy and ended the war as a corporal. He spent his retirement in Edinburgh Zoo.
3. *Czerwone maki na Monte Cassino*. It was written and composed by Alfred Schütz, a member of the Polish Soldiers' Theatre.

Alicja Sieciechowicz

1. Lodz was captured by the Germans on 8 September 1939.
2. A German-created region comprising territory annexed from Poland and taken into the Third Reich.
3. The British No.82 Grenade was more commonly known after its inventor's name R.S. Gammon. It held a plastic explosive, the amount of which was varied depending on the user's requirements.

4. The target was a Polish turncoat called Mieczysław Darmaszek. Sieciechowicz was probably not told his particulars for reasons of operational security. His denouncement of Bredel's team member, Jadwiga Kuberska, led to her death and the execution of several others. Darmaszek was sentenced to death by an Underground court, with Bredel – assisted by Elżbieta Ostrowska – carrying out the sentence on 15 March 1944.
5. Plac Powstańców Warszawy or Warsaw Uprising Square.
6. Lieutenant Stefan Berent 'Steb'. He was with the Military Printing Works Security Squad during the Warsaw Uprising and based in the City North Centre sector.
7. 'Big Bertha' was the Polish nickname for the Karl-Gerät super-heavy mortar. Three were eventually deployed to assault Warsaw.
8. Lieutenant Doctor Władysław Kulesza.
9. DDT is a hazardous insecticide now banned by most countries.

Mieczysław Stachiewicz

1. *Warszawa* was from the Polish merchant fleet. It was lost to a U-Boat attack in December 1941, roughly 40 miles (65km) east of Tobruk.
2. The PAF in France was severely constrained by the small number of aircraft made available to it. Just 86 machines were in Polish service at the start of May 1940.
3. The absence of defensive fire was to be expected if Stachiewicz was in the lead and the bombers had caught the enemy off guard. It is worth recalling Bomber Command's system of pathfinders and flare guidance – albeit just around the corner – were still not present in early summer 1942.
4. The blue beam was not a master searchlight as many crews believed. It was a colouring effect from being directly coned and the angle at which the light entered the cockpit. German searchlights worked in teams and, if an aircraft was coned, several would track it for the nearest anti-aircraft batteries. Nonetheless, for Stachiewicz and his crew, the glare and sense of danger must have made it feel like every searchlight for miles around had been directed solely onto them.

5. In 2007, a friend of the Jozef Pilsudski Institute of London informed the Australian embassy about Stachiewicz's role in the rescue of the Australian crew. Surprising one and all on his 90th birthday celebration, a high-ranking RAAF officer arrived in full dress uniform with a bottle of wine – the one Stachiewicz had waited so long to receive – and a message of thanks on behalf of the Australian people.
6. Stachiewicz did not mean only one crew was left. A squadron's roster of flying personnel was always larger than its working establishment as crews needed to be replaced because of operational losses or, more mundanely, because some of its crews were on leave; had reported persons sick; were rotated out after completing a tour; or had been grounded for other reasons. Nonetheless, the figure quoted still makes for grim reading.
7. Stachiewicz was wrong and right here as the Sicily landings, codenamed Operation Husky, occurred in July 1943. However, missions against Italy increased during 1942 as Bomber Command hoped to weaken Italian resolve.
8. The Polish School of Architecture at Liverpool University was established to train architects to assist Poland's rebuilding efforts after the war. The school was formally inaugurated by Sikorski in November 1942.

Danuta Szlachetko

1. Laski village is located northwest of Warsaw, not far from the Kampinos forest.
2. A district in west Warsaw.
3. The journey from Bremerhaven to Stalag X-B (Sandbostel) is about 28 miles (45km). It takes little imagination to realise how gruelling this march would have been for exhausted and half-starved prisoners of war.

Appendices

1. Noakes, J., and Pridham, G., *Nazism 1919-1945, Vol.3, Foreign Policy, War and Racial Extermination* (University of Exeter Press, 2001), p.315

2. Idem.
3. Press photograph's reverse details (author's collection) and Davies, Norman, *Rising '44, 'The Battle for Warsaw'* (Pan Books 2004) pp.66-67
4. Britain and the USA still had high hopes for Mikołajczyk and, with their backing, he joined the provisional government as a Deputy Prime Minister in summer 1945. However, the communists intimidated, arrested and executed their enemies and also rigged the first post-war election in 1947. Mikołajczyk fled Poland in the aftermath and resettled in the USA. He died in 1966.
5. Zamoyski, Adam, *The Forgotten Few, The Polish Air Force in World War II* (Pen & Sword, 2011) p.203-207
6. The number Polish prisoners of war in Soviet hands varies depending on the source. For example, Józef Garliński recorded 200,000 Polish prisoners of war in *Poland in the Second World War* (Macmillan Press, 1987), p.25, while Tomasz Piesakowski cited 250,000 in *The Fate of Poles in the USSR 1939-1989* (Gryf Publications, 1990) p.39
7. Piesakowski, Tomasz, op. cit., p.49 and Snyder, Timothy, *Bloodlands: Europe between Hitler and Stalin* (Vintage Books, 2011), p.128. Those conscripted into the Red Army faced anti-Polish prejudice and, while many were transferred to Soviet-sponsored Polish forces after April 1943, thousands were already dead or badly wounded.
8. All deportation figures are taken from Garliński, Józef op. cit., pp.36-37; Piesakowski, Tomasz, op. cit., pp.50-51; and Tuszynski, Marek and Denda, Dale F., *Soviet War Crimes Against Poland During the Second World War and its Aftermath: A Review of the Factual Record and Outstanding Questions* (The Polish Review, 1999) p.197
9. Tuszynski, Marek and Denda, Dale F., op. cit., p.198
10. Davies, Norman, *Trail of Hope, The Anders Army an Odyssey Across Three Continents* (Osprey Publishing, 2015) p.59
11. Margry, Karel, *The Katyn Massacre* (After the Battle, No.92, 1996) p.31
12. Bałuk, Stefan, *Poles on the Fronts of World War II* (Ars Print Production, 1995) p.257
13. Piesakowski, Tomasz, op. cit., p.122

14. Ibid, p.123
15. Ibid, p.131
16. Bałuk, Stefan, op. cit., p.401
17. Margry, Karel, *The Siege of Warsaw 1939* (Battle of Britain International, *After the Battle*, No.158, 2012) p.17
18. Cawthorne, Nigel, *Army of Steel* (Arcturus Publishing, 2020) p.17
19. Zetterling, Niklas, *Blitzkrieg from the Ground Up* (Casemate, 2017) p.78
20. Garliński, Józef, op. cit., p.25
21. Hempel, Andrew, op. cit., p.23
22. Garliński, Józef, op. cit., p.282
23. Idem.
24. Rabiet, Lionel (editor), *La Libération de la Pologne, La Seconde Guerre Mondiale 1939-1945*, No.25 (Le Figaro, 2009) p.30
25. The Russian People's Liberation Army, or Russkaya Osvoboditelnaya Narodnaya Armiya (RONA). Also known as the Kaminski Brigade after its turncoat commander Bronislav Kaminski.
26. Forczyk, Robert, *Warsaw 1944: Poland's bid for freedom* (Osprey Publishing, 2009) p.69
27. Olson, Lynne, and Cloud, Stanley, *A Question of Honor, the Kosciuszko Squadron forgotten heroes of World War II* (Alfred A. Knopf, 2003) p.346
28. Forczyk, Robert, op. cit., p.89
29. Hempel, Andrew, *Poland in World War II* (Hippocrene Books, 2000) p.100
30. Davies, Norman, *Rising '44, 'The Battle for* Warsaw', p.437
31. Forczyk, Robert, op. cit., p.89. Stefan Bałuk recorded 18,000 insurgents killed and 25,000 wounded, plus 180,000 civilians killed in *Poles on the Fronts of World War II* (Ars Print Production, 1995), p.369
32. Rabiet, Lionel (editor), *La Libération de la Pologne*, p.30
33. Lachendro, Jacek (editor), *German Places of Extermination in Poland* (Parma Press, 2009) pp.12-13
34. Walker, Jonathan, *Poland Alone: Britain, SOE and the Collapse of Polish Resistance, 1944* (Spellmount, 2010) p.119
35. Davidowicz, Lucy S., *The War Against the Jews, 1933-1945* (Bantam Books, 1986) p.148

36. Steinbacher, Sybille, *Auschwitz, a History* (Harper Perennial, 2005) p.109
37. Ibid, p.51
38. Noakes, J., and Pridham, G., op. cit., p.596
39. Steinbacher, Sybille, op. cit., pp.133-134
40. Filipow, Krzysztof and Wawer, Zbigniew, *Passerby, Tell Poland* (Arkady, 1991) p.30
41. Ibid., p.126
42. Jarzembowski, Janusz and Bradley, David T., *Armoured Hussars, Vol.2* (Helion & Co., 2015) p.61
43. Stella-Sawicki, Markek, Garliński, Jarek, and Mucha, Stefan (editors), *First to Fight* (MSS Consulting, 2009) p.120
44. Filipow, Krzysztof and Wawer, Zbigniew, op. cit. p.143

BIBLIOGRAPHY

In addition to the works listed below, newspapers from the era and various files held at the UK's National Archives were also consulted.

Books

Ascherson, Neal, *The Struggles for Poland* (The Bath Press, 1987)
Bałuk, Stefan, *Poles on the Fronts of World War II* (Ars Print Production, 1995)
Bethell, Nicholas, *The War Hitler Won, The Fall of Poland, September 1939* (Holt, Rinehart and Winston, 1973)
Buckingham, William, *Arnhem 1944* (Tempus, 2004)
Cussans, Thomas, *The Holocaust, Origins, History and Aftermath c.1920-1945* (Welbeck, 2020)
Davidowicz, Lucy S., *The War Against the Jews, 1933-1945* (Bantam Books, 1986)
Davies, Norman,
Heart of Europe, the Past in Poland's Present (Oxford University Press, 2001)
Rising '44, 'The Battle for Warsaw' (Pan Books 2004)
Trail of Hope, The Anders Army an Odyssey Across Three Continents (Osprey Publishing, 2015)
Dean, Martin and Hecker, Mel, *The United States Holocaust Memorial Museum Encyclopaedia of Camps and Ghettos, 1933-1945, Volume II* (Indiana University Press, 2012)

Ellis, John, *Cassino, The Hollow Victory* (Aurum Press, 2003)
Erickson, John, *The Road to Berlin, Stalin's War with Germany Volume 2* (Weidenfeld and Nicolson London, 1983)
Filipow, Krzysztof and Wawer, Zbigniew, *Passerby, Tell Poland* (Arkady, 1991)
Forczyk, Robert, *Warsaw 1944: Poland's bid for freedom* (Osprey Publishing, 2009)
Garliński, Józef, *Poland in the Second World War* (Macmillan Press, 1987)
Hempel, Andrew, *Poland in World War II* (Hippocrene Books, 2000)
Hoffman, Eva, *Shtetl, The History of a Small Town and an Extinguished World* (Secker & Warburg, 1998)
Jarzembowski, Janusz, *Armoured Hussars, Vol.1* (Helion & Co., 2014)
Jarzembowski, Janusz and Bradley, David T., *Armoured Hussars, Vol.2* (Helion & Co., 2015)
Kelly, Matthew, *Finding Poland, from Tavistock to Hruzdowa and Back Again* (Vintage Books, 2010)
Kleczkowski, Stefan, *Poland's First 100,000* (Fisher, Knight & Co. 1944)
Koskodan, Kenneth K., *No Greater Ally, the Untold Story of Poland's Forces in World War II* (Osprey Publishing, 2009)
Lachendro, Jacek (editor), *German Places of Extermination in Poland* (Parma Press, 2009)
Lukas, Richard C., *Forgotten Holocaust, the Poles under German Occupation 1939-1944* (Hippocrene Books, 2010)
Mastny, Vojtech, *Russia's Road to the Cold War* (Columbia University Press, 1979)
Middlebrook, Martin, *Arnhem 1944, The Airborne Battle, 17-26 September* (Penguin Books, 1995)
Mieczkowski, Zbigniew (editor), *The Soldiers of General Maczek in World War II* (Matrix, 2004)
Mieczkowski, Zbigniew, *Horizons* (Adam, 2008)
Moorhouse, Roger, *The Devil's Alliance* (Vintage, 2016)
Neillands, Robin, *The Bomber War* (John Murray, 2004)
Noakes, J., and Pridham, G., *Nazism 1919-1945, Vol.3, Foreign Policy, War and Racal Extermination* (University of Exeter Press, 2001)
Olson, Lynne, and Cloud, Stanley, *A Question of Honor, the Kosciuszko Squadron forgotten heroes of World War II* (Alfred A. Knopf, 2003)

Paul, Allen, *Katyń, Stalin's Massacre and the Triumph of Truth* (Northern Illinois University Press, 2010)

Piekalkiewicz, Janusz, *Arnhem 1944* (Ian Allan, 1977)

Piesakowski, Tomasz, *The Fate of Poles in the USSR 1939-1989* (Gryf Publications, 1990)

Pipera, Francizka and Świebokiej, Teresy, *Auschwitz, Nazistowski Obóz Śmierci* (Państwowe Muzeum Oświęcim-Brzezinka, 1993)

Piotrowski, Tadeusz, *Poland's Holocaust, Ethnic Strife, Collaboration with Occupying Force and Genocide in the Second Republic, 1918-1947* (McFarland & Co., 1998)

Plokhy, S. M., *Yalta, The Price of Peace* (Penguin Books, 2010)

Rabiet, Lionel (editor)

La Seconde Guerre Mondiale Commence en Pologne, No.2 (Le Figaro, 2009)

La Libération de la Pologne, La Seconde Guerre Mondiale 1939-1945, No.25 (Le Figaro, 2009)

Rees, Laurence, *The Holocaust, a New History* (Public Affairs, 2017)

Snyder, Timothy, *Bloodlands: Europe between Hitler and Stalin* (Vintage Books, 2011)

Sosabowski, Stanislaw, *Freely I Served* (William Kimber, 1960)

Steinbacher, Sybille, *Auschwitz, a History* (Harper Perennial, 2005)

Stella-Sawicki, Markek, Garliński, Jarek, and Mucha, Stefan (editors), *First to Fight* (MSS Consulting, 2009)

Stachura, Peter D., *Poland 1918-1945, An Interpretive and Documentary History of the Second Republic* (Routledge, 2004)

Topol, Olga (editor), *Forgotten Force, A Journey of Memory* (Józef Piłsudski Institute of Research in Modern History London, 2020)

Walker, Jonathan, *Poland Alone: Britain, SOE and the Collapse of Polish Resistance, 1944* (Spellmount, 2010)

Watt, Richard M., *Bitter Glory, Poland and its Fate 1918-1939* (Hippocrene Books, 1998)

Williams, Martin, *From Warsaw to Rome, General Anders Exiled Polish Army in the Second World War* (Pen and Sword, 2017)

Williamson, David G.,

Poland Betrayed, the Nazi-Soviet invasions of 1939 (Stackpole Books, 2009)

The Polish Underground 1939-1947 (Pen & Sword, 2012)

Zaloga, Steven J.,
The Polish Army 1939-1945 (Osprey Publishing, 2002)
Poland 1939, The Birth of Blitzkrieg (Osprey Publishing, 2003)
Zamoyski, Adam,
The Forgotten Few, The Polish Air Force in World War II (Pen & Sword, 2011)
Poland, a History (Harper Press, 2009)

Periodicals and magazines

Buffetaut, Yves,
La Campagne de Pologne, Septembre 1939 (1) (Armes Militaria Magazine, No.37, Histoire & Collections, July 2000)
La Campagne de Pologne, Septembre 1939 (2) (Armes Militaria Magazine, No.40, Histoire & Collections, February 2001)
Margry, Karel,
The Katyn Massacre (After the Battle, No.92, 1996)
The Siege of Warsaw 1939 (After the Battle, No.158, 2012)
Orzell, Laurence, *Poland and Russia, July 1941-April 1943: The 'Impossible' Alliance* (The Polish Review, Vol.21, No.4, 1976)
Rossino, Alexander B., *Nazi Anti-Jewish Policy during the Polish Campaign: The Case of the Einsatzgruppe von Woyrsch*, German Studies Review, Vol. 24, No. 1, February 2001)
Siegelbaum, Lewis H., *Soviet Norm Determination in Theory and Practice, 1917-1941* (Soviet Studies, January 1984, Vol. 36, No. 1)
Schimelpfenig, Tod, *Is Urine Sterile? And Other Questions About Using Pee in First Aid* (National Outdoor Living School, 1 May 2015)
Tuszynski, Marek and Denda, Dale F., *Soviet War Crimes Against Poland During the Second World War and its Aftermath: A Review of the Factual Record and Outstanding Questions* (The Polish Review, 1999)

Online

Baker, Philip (curator), *Stalag VIIIB/344 Lamsdorf History* (The Online Memorial and Museum of Prisoners of War, retrieved 29 May 2021)

Carr, Gilly (project lead) *Stalag X-B/Sandbostel Concentration Camp* (Frank Falla Archive, retrieved 19 March 2023)

Centralne Muzeum Jeńców Wojennych, *Stalag VIII B (344) Lamsdorf* (Centralne Muzeum Jeńców Wojennych, retrieved 29 May 2021)

Königsberg, Wojciech, *Mieczysław Darmaszek – konfident zastrzelony przez kobiety* (Polska Zbrojna, retrieved 11 March 2023)

Memorial and Museum Auschwitz-Birkenau, *SS Bauzug* (Auschwitz-Birkenau State Museum, retrieved 30 May 2021)

Music and the Holocaust, *Auschwitz* (ORT, retrieved 28 February 2023)

Newsweek Polska, *Was Doctor Wladislaw Dering a hero or was he a criminal?* (Newsweek Polska, retrieved 7 May 2014)

Porta Polinica, *Stalag X B Sandbostel* (Documentation Centre for the Culture and History of Poles, retrieved 19 March 2023)

Sub Camps of Auschwitz, *2 SS Bauzug* (Tiergartenstrasse 4 Association, retrieved 28 February 2023)